P9-EMB-770

Empirical Methods for Evaluating Educational Interventions

This is a volume in the Academic Press
EDUCATIONAL PSYCHOLOGY SERIES

Critical comprehensive reviews of research knowledge, theories, principles, and practices.

Under the editorship of Gary D. Phye

Empirical Methods for Evaluating Educational Interventions

EDITED BY

Gary D. Phye
Department of Psychology
Iowa State University

Daniel H. Robinson
Department of Educational Psychology
University of Texas

Joel R. Levin
Department of Educational Psychology
The University of Arizona

San Diego London Boston New York Sydney Tokyo Toronto

Elsevier Academic Press
30 Corporate Drive, Suite 400, Burlington, MA 01803, USA
525 B Street, Suite 1900, San Diego, California 92101-4495, USA
84 Theobald's Road, London WC1X 8RR, UK

This book is printed on acid-free paper. ♾

Library of Congress Cataloging-in-Publication Data

Empirical methods for evaluating educational interventions / editors, Gary D. Phye, Daniel H. Robinson, Joel R. Levin.
p. cm. – (Educational psychology series)
Includes bibliographical references and index.
ISBN 0-12-554257-7 (alk. paper)
1. Educational evaluation–United States. 2. Education–Research–United States–Methodology. 3. Educational productivity–United States. 4. Educational psychology. I. Phye, Gary D. II. Robinson, Daniel H. III. Levin, Joel R. IV. Educational psychology series (Academic Press)

LB2822.75.E56 2005
370′.7′2—dc22 2004062760

British Library Cataloguing in Publication Data
A catalogue record for this book is available from the British Library

ISBN: 0-12-554257-7

For all information on all Elsevier Academic Press publications visit our Web site at www.books.elsevier.com

Printed in the United States of America

05 06 07 08 09 9 8 7 6 5 4 3 2 1

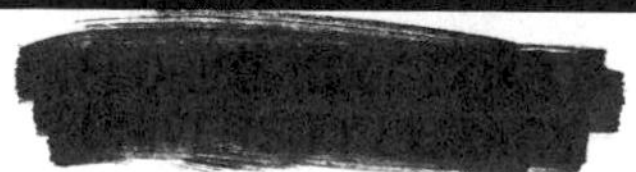

Contents

Basic Issues When Addressing Human Behavior: An Experimental Research Perspective

Producing Credible Applied Educational Research

Contributors

Numbers in parentheses indicate the page on which the author's contribution begins.

John T. Behrens (147), Assessment Development and Innovation, Cisco Systems, Inc., San Jose, California

Robert Boruch (177), Graduate School of Education, University of Pennsylvania, Philadelphia, Pennsylvania 19104

Harris M. Cooper (85), Duke University, Program in Education, Box 90739, Durham, North Carolina 27708-0739

Jerry D'Agostino (113), Department of Educational Psychology, The University of Arizona, Tucson, Arizona 85721

Steven Graham (235), University of Maryland, Department of Special Education, College Park, Maryland 20742

Diane F. Halpern (53), Department of Psychology, Claremont McKenna College, Claremont, California 91711

Karen H. Harris (235), University of Maryland, Department of Special Education, College Park, Maryland 20742

Joel R. Levin (3), Department of Educational Psychology, The University of Arizona, Tucson, Arizona 85721

Richard E. Mayer (67), Department of Psychology, University of California, Santa Barbara, California 93106

Angela M. O'Donnell (213), Department of Educational Psychology, Rutgers, The State University of New Jersey, New Brunswick, New Jersey 08901

Gary D. Phye (193), Department of Psychology, Iowa State University, Ames, Iowa 50011-3190

Valerie F. Reyna (29), Department of Psychology, University of Texas at Arlington, Arlington, Texas 76019-0528

Daniel H. Robinson (147), Department of Educational Psychology, University of Texas, Austin, Texas 78712

Jeffery C. Valentine (85), Duke University, Program in Education, Durham, North Carolina 27708-0739

Jennifer Zito (235), University of Maryland, Department of Special Education, College Park, Maryland 20742

Preface

Today, we are on the cusp of a reaffirmation that experimental research strategies provide the strongest evidence of change in student and teacher classroom behaviors. Fueling this move back to a more centralist position of what constitutes credible educational research is a combination of political realities and advancements in social science research methods. This reaffirmation is a worldwide phenomenon. As a part of this reaffirmation, the United States has transitioned through three distinct political phases during the last twenty years. Politically this transition started with *The Nation at Risk* phase, through the *Goals* 2000 phase, to the current *No Child Left Behind Act* of 2002.

The political realities of the *No Child Left Behind* (NCLB) *Act* have raised the benchmark for credible evidence when defining "scientifically-based practices," and when using data-driven decision-making during policy analysis and policy implementation. Interestingly, this legislation occurs at a time when educational psychologists, educational measurement experts, and educational researchers in general are engaging in a debate about future research efforts focusing on educational interventions for changing classroom learning and achievement. This appears to be one of those moments when a unique synergy of scientific and political views is on the ascendancy. From a political perspective, the quest involves an identification of educational practices that can be implemented in order to change (read improve) student learning and achievement in mathematics, reading, and science. With the NCLB Act identifying student learning and achievement as targeted outcome measures *caused* by *educational interventions*, the field of educational psychology is in a position to make critical contributions. While the empirical methods discussed and described in this volume are framed by mandates of the NCLB Act, the methods, procedures and issues described have worldwide application.

In a common sense way, the NCLB definition of credible data means empirical data that credibly defines cause, effect, and causal relationships. Historically, experimentation has been viewed as a credible process for producing such data. As we know it today, a minimalist definition of experimentation as a process involves some form of 1) observation, 2) manipulation of the environment, and 3) efforts to control extraneous influences that might limit or bias observations. What makes the NCLB legislation such a driving force for the educational research community is that these requirements hold for all types of educational research activities ranging from 1) laboratory studies, through 2) classroom research studies in the natural environment (field research), to 3) scaling up activities involving implementation of "best" practices identified in laboratory and field studies (Levin & O'Donnell, 1999).

It is the scaling up activities involving implementation that has interesting implications for researchers constructing research designs because this requires a working knowledge of an area commonly referred to as program/policy evaluation. In such cases, credible data from intervention studies is used to inform state and local policy analysis. In cases discussed in this volume, the policies reviewed and modified (when necessary) involve those dealing with learning, instruction, and curriculum within the context of individual and group differences of students. Thus, the unit of analysis extends from considering students, classrooms, school buildings, and school districts, to the generation of state department of education policies by state legislatures.

In a sense, NCLB legislation defines two primary dimensions of experimental research that should be acknowledged when considering educational interventions. The first dimension is the familiar "basic research–applied research" continuum that is predicated on experimental and quasi-experimental design logic (Campbell & Stanley, 1963; Cook & Campbell, 1979) with a differential emphasis on issues involving internal and external reliability. This dimension can also be portrayed as the Pasteur quadrant.

The second dimension, "scaling up" educational interventions, is more of a "unit of analysis" dimension that draws heavily on both measurement logic and statistical logic (Levin & O'Donnell, 1999; Mosteller & Boruch, 2002; Shadish, Cook, & Campbell, 2002). Consequently, the NCLB definition of educational science can be viewed as an expansion and integration of the traditional experimental and quasi-experimental views of educational research. These dimensions provide a focus consistent with the use of the term *empirical* as an adjective where the preferred meanings are 1.a. "Relying upon or gained from experiment or observation ⟨*empirical* techniques⟩ b. Capable of proof or verification by means of experiment or observation ⟨*empirical* knowledge⟩" (Webster's II New Riverside University Dictionary, 1984).

The storyline of this volume is divided into three sections. The first section consists of four chapters and focuses on framing educational research to meet today's realities. The first two chapters discuss educational intervention research within the experimentalist tradition and the political realities of NCLB. Joel Levin (Chapter 1) addresses issues encountered with randomized classroom trials when conducting classroom research. In a clever courtroom scenario titled *Randomized Classroom Trials on Trial*, he provides a sterling defense of the use of randomized classroom trials. Valerie Reyna (Chapter 2) provides a Washington, D.C. based view of the NCLB Act and its impact on educational research reflecting her experience working at the Institute for Educational Sciences.

The last two chapters in this section address issues that involve the dissemination and use of credible data by educational policy makers. Diane Halpern (Chapter 3) relates unexpected attitudes encountered when providing testimony to the U. S. House of Representatives Committee on Science. As current president of the American Psychological Association, she has been a strong advocate for the role of psychology and educational psychology in addressing issues currently confronting the educational establishment in the United States. Richard Mayer (Chapter 4) addresses the historical failure of educational research to impact educational practice. As a prominent researcher contributing to the literature on classroom learning/problem solving and a local school board member of several years standing, he provides a balanced view of six obstacles to educational reform.

Section two frames the current discussion of experimental methodology for educational intervention squarely within the context of human behavioral research. The three chapters in this section address issues including 1) the identification of quality research in education, 2) measurement issues of reliability and validity of learning outcome measures, and 3) the use of statistical analyses to disaggregate large-scale data collection efforts and to aggregate across published studies the effectiveness of educational interventions.

Jeff Valentine and Harris Cooper (Chapter 5) address the question "Can we measure the quality of causal research in education?" and conclude in the affirmative. This chapter provides an excellent theoretical foundation for better understanding the designation "what works" when applied to educational research findings. Jerry D'Agostino (Chapter 6) identifies the pitfalls frequently encountered when measuring learning outcomes. These reliability and validity issues are extremely important, not only for large stakes assessment upon which educational policy is based, but also for classroom research used to inform instruction. John Behrens and Dan Robinson (Chapter 7) provide an excellent review of micro and macro analysis techniques when interpreting and understanding experimental data. The micro analysis technique discussed (exploratory data analysis) provides a basis for obtaining a finer-grained analysis than that provided by standard sum-of-squares computations. The macro analysis technique (meta-analysis) can be successfully used to promote programmatic educational research. This means exploiting the power of meta-analysis for information integration and modeling.

The third and last section is devoted to issues encountered when application of basic experimental logic is introduced into the practical world of the school environment. The first two chapters of this section are devoted to internal and external validity issues encountered during the generalization and scaling-up of laboratory or classroom studies.

Robert Boruch (Chapter 8) provides an excellent view of the empirical basis for the development of educational policy. This view is one that is not frequently introduced to educational psychologists. This level of policy analysis involves developing educational policy for states, nations, and developing countries. However, the empirical basis for data collection parallels that used for studying the effectiveness of educational interventions at the classroom or school district level. Chapter 9 (Gary Phye) addresses experimental design considerations when dealing with the issue of aligning measures of academic learning during instruction and the assessment of end-of-the-year achievement. A second alignment issue is one of integrating data collection efforts that not only provide school districts with *accountability* data (adequate yearly progress) but also *impact* data identifying the educational intervention as the cause for improvement in student achievement. Both accountability and impact data are required by the NCLB Act.

The last two chapters are devoted to discussions of approaches to educational intervention research efforts focusing on classroom studies. Angela O'Donnell (Chapter 10) focuses on experimental research in classrooms and a discussion of *evidence-based research*. Angela considers both the gold standard of random assignment and experimental control and the design experiment. Steve Graham, Karen Harris and Jennifer Zito (Chapter 11) have produced an enlightening account of a research agenda that reflects a synergy of laboratory-like experiments and class-room based research. This approach reflects a systematic research program that emphasizes experimental methodology, replication with extension, and scaling-up efforts. The story line serves as an excellent model for young educational researchers seeking to develop a career based on developing, maintaining, and implementing classroom interventions that makes a positive difference in the classroom.

Gary D. Phye

References

Campbell, D. T., & Stanley, J. C. (1963). *Experimental and quasi-experimental designs for research.* Chicago: Rand-McNally.

Cook, T. D., & Campbell, D. T. (1979). *Quasi-experimentation: Design & analysis issues for field settings.* Boston: Houghton Mifflin.

Levin, J. R., & O'Donnell, A. M. (1999). What to do about educational research's credibility gaps? *Issues in Education: Contributions from Educational Psychology*, 5, 177-229.

Mosteller, F., & Boruch, R. (Eds.). (2002). *Evidence matters: Randomized trials in education research*. Washington, DC: Brookings Institution Press.

Shadish, W. R., Cook, T. D., & Campbell, D.T. (2002). *Experimental and quasi-experimental designs for generalized causal inference*. Boston: Houghton Mifflin.

PART I

Framing Educational Research Inquiry to Meet Today's Realities

CHAPTER

1

Randomized Classroom Trials on Trial

JOEL R. LEVIN

University of Arizona

[Scene: A somber courtroom]

Prosecutor: Please state your full name.

Plum: Reginald Quincy Plum, PhD.

Prosecutor: Thank you, Professor Plum. Now, if it pleases the court, would you tell us why you did it?

Plum: Yes, sir! All those bogus classroom "innovations" that are continually being foisted upon us innocent law-abiding taxpayers. First this instructional fad, then that technological boondoggle, with no scientifically credible research evidence supporting the worth of any of them. And sure enough, in every case, before long the lack of scientific evidence transforms itself into a lack of instructional efficacy. Somebody had to do something. So, sporting my best Peter Finch impersonation, I simply stood up and yelled as loud as I could: "I'm mad as hell and I can't take it any more!"

Prosecutor: And then?

Plum: So, I initially conducted an exhaustive search of the literature from which I painstakingly and systematically designed a promising classroom intervention for improving students' mathematics competence. This was followed up with a number of small-scale experimenter-administered laboratory investigations, each of which suggested that the components of the instructional package were quite effective in enhancing children's mathematics performance.

Prosecutor: And then? And then?

Plum: And then I did it: I conducted a randomized classroom trials study!

Empirical Methods for Evaluating Educational Interventions

Courtroom: [Audible courtroom gasps and exclamations, including "No!," "I don't believe it!," "How could he?," "Animal!," etc.]

Judge: Order, order!

Prosecutor: You . . . did . . . what?

Plum: I conducted a randomized classroom trials study on the effects of a highly touted innovative instructional technique on inner-city fifth-grade students' mathematics achievement.

Prosecutor: Why? What were you thinking? Were you acting alone? If not, who were your accomplices? Please answer these questions one at a time.

Plum: I was persuaded by recent writings about the importance of elevating the status of educational intervention research through the conduct of more scientifically credible studies, based on the randomized control trials model of medical research. I was convinced that a single scientifically rigorous evaluation of the novel mathematics instructional approach would speak more loudly than would all of the anecdotes and testimonies selectively provided by educators and politicians. I most certainly did not participate in this enterprise by myself. The research, funded by the National Institute for Credible Education Research (NICE Research) under the supervision of our program officer, Retired Colonel Hamilton Mustard, was conducted as part of a multisite effort in collaboration with several highly respected educational researchers: Rhonda Scarlett, MS; Jonathan Green, PhD; Deirdre White, EdD; and Priscilla Peacock, PhD. Given the impeccable reputations of these researchers and the scientific integrity of the research itself, I am deeply troubled by these allegations.

FLASHBACK TO LEVIN AND O'DONNELL (1999b)

In an article that was instrumental in shaping the focus and form of the present volume, Levin and O'Donnell (1999b; see also Levin, O'Donnell, & Kratochwill, 2003; and Levin, in press) provided an indictment of contemporary educational research, as it is typically practiced (by academic researchers) and promoted (by educators and policy makers). Among other things, Levin and O'Donnell claim the following:

- Compared with the research emanating from other disciplines, educational research has long been criticized for its low quality; even more embarrassingly, whatever "recognitions" educational research has received have been for its "awful reputation" (Kaestle, 1993).
- This pervasive negative attitude stems from educational research generally not being theory-driven, not based on "strong inference" (Platt, 1964) designs, and yielding trivial ("so what?") outcomes.
- Many educational "innovations" are adopted on the basis of anecdote, testimony, opinion, and haphazard observations rather than on the basis of scientifically credible and generalizable research-based evidence (see Chapter 4; McCardle & Chhabra, 2004; and Stanovich & Stanovich, 2003).
- Empirical investigations that may give the appearance of being systematic and rigorous typically are not: They typically suffer from a number of serious conceptual, methodologic, and data analysis flaws.

- Educational intervention research, in particular, would benefit greatly from incorporating the medical research model's "stage" approach, ranging from informal observations and hypothesis-generating research to methodologically rigorous "randomized classroom trials" studies (for a nice summary and application of this approach, see Chapter 11).
- Before any instructional interventions are formally endorsed for public consumption, they should be carefully scrutinized with respect to their evidence credibility and their "creditability" (i.e., their potential value to society; Levin, 1994) on the basis of some type of educational research vetting process, such as that applied by the What Works Clearinghouse (*www.w-w-c.org*) and the Campbell Collaboration (*www.campbellcollaboration.org*).

Levin and O'Donnell (1999b, p. 221) summarize the intent of their essay as follows:

> When it comes to recommending or prescribing educational, clinical, and social interventions based on "research," standards of evidence credibility must occupy a position of preeminence . . . A frightening state of affairs currently exists within the general domain of educational research and within its individual subdomains. It is time to convince the public, the press, and policy makers alike of the importance of credible evidence, delineating the characteristics critical to both its production and recognition.

[Back to the courtroom]

Prosecutor: Professor Plum, you claim that you were persuaded by others' arguments concerning the need for more scientifically credible research—specifically, randomized control trials adopted from the medical model—to evaluate classroom-based instructional interventions. What, specifically, bothered you about the way in which educational intervention research is typically designed and conducted, and its outcomes analyzed?

Plum: First, we must eliminate from this discussion the informal observations, surveys, and other unscientific *nonexperimental* approaches to assessing the worth of new instructional interventions. Based on the by-now familiar Levin—O'Donnell (1999b) stage model, such investigations must be regarded as strictly "preliminary" with respect to establishing causal connections between specific interventions and observed outcomes. Anecdotal, observational, and other nonexperimental approaches are becoming so commonplace that a vocal number of mental health researchers are arguing that you can't even trust your therapist anymore! As *New York Times* writer Erica Goode notes, and I quote, "Like medicine, these experts contend, psychology should have clinical practice guidelines, and psychotherapists should favor treatments that are backed by evidence from controlled clinical trials over treatment[s] whose effectiveness is supported by anecdotes and case histories only" (Goode, 2004, p. D6). Well, if you can't trust your therapist, who can you trust? Forgive me for digressing. And so what precisely does this have to do with classroom-intervention research? Setting aside all the nonexperimental studies, we find that in the so-called *experimental* classroom instructional-intervention research studies that have been conducted over the past 40 to 50 years, the modal approach has been to compare two or more methods of instruction (e.g., the standard method with a thought-to-be-improved approach) according to the following procedure or a similar variation thereof: One classroom of, say, 25 students is assigned (sometimes randomly, sometimes by convenience) to receive the new method of instruction and another classroom of 25 students is assigned to receive the standard method. The two different instructional methods are typically implemented by two different teachers in the two classes, but they might also be implemented by a single teacher using one method with one classroom and the other method with another classroom. In other cases, the researcher may have the luxury of having access to four to six different classrooms, in which case half (i.e., two or three) of the classrooms may be assigned to receive the new method of instruction and the other half to receive the standard approach. At the end of the intervention period, which might consist of several weeks or several months, one or more curriculum-based measures are administered and the average performance of students in the two instructional conditions is compared statistically.

Prosecutor: So, what's the problem with that, especially if a random process is used to determine which teacher/classroom receives which instructional method? Isn't that sort of randomization of treatments consistent with standard practice in the medical research randomized control trials model to which you refer? And, why isn't the prototypical educational intervention experiment that you just described consistent with the medical model? Would you kindly tell the court why such a seemingly accepted research process has bothered you to the extent that you thought it necessary to take matters into your own hands?

Plum: Contrary both to what you are implying and to what many conductors and consumers of educational research may believe, arguing that there is a procedural correspondence between medical research's randomized control trials and the prototypical educational intervention research study that I just summarized fails in several fundamental respects. For present purposes, the three most important failures relate to (a) the manner in which the randomization of treatments—for example, drugs in medical research versus instructional methods in educational research—are randomly assigned to recipients of those treatments—individual patients in medical research versus classrooms in educational research, and which are referred to as the study's experimental *units*; (b) the manner in which the treatments are administered/implemented; and (c) the statistical methods used to analyze the data associated with the outcome measures—for example, health- and achievement-related measures, respectively, for medical and educational research.

Prosecutor: I'm dying to hear the details. Please proceed, Professor Plum.

Plum: With pleasure, as will be appreciated from this prolonged but particularly persuasive three-pronged PowerPoint presentation . . .

THREE CLASSROOM-BASED INTERVENTION RESEARCH ARGUMENTS

In Professor Plum's testimony, he provides three essential classroom-based intervention research arguments that were previously explicated by Levin (1992). These arguments are reiterated here.

How Are Students Typically Assigned to Classroom-Based Instructional Interventions?

In the prototypical instructional intervention study, two different methods of instruction are compared after their implementation by two different teachers in two different classrooms. It should be obvious, even to the unseasoned researcher, that if the two classrooms in question were not randomly constituted (which is overwhelmingly the case in such research), any postinstructional outcome-measure differences between the two classrooms might plausibly be attributable (either partially or completely) to preinstructional student differences in aptitude or achievement (i.e., methods of instruction are confounded with initial student differences). Even for the rare situation in which classrooms are randomly constituted, interpretive problems persist if the two classrooms/teachers are not randomly assigned to the two different methods of instruction. Suppose, for example, that one teacher favors Method A and so is assigned that method, whereas another teacher prefers to use Method B and so is assigned that method. In that scenario, teachers (along with their associated classrooms) and methods of instruction become inextricably confounded. Any similar process by which methods of instruction are nonrandomly assigned to the two teachers produces a method—teacher confounding. In particular, if mean outcome differences result, are they attributable to the two different instructional methods (a researcher's preferred explanation) or to the two different teachers (a competing explanation)?[1] This situation is paralleled in the psychotherapy research literature by method-therapist confoundings (see, for example, Wampold, 2001).

In contrast, in the prototypical medical-research two-treatment study, (a) multiple individual patients are randomly assigned to receive the two treatments and (b) because of that random assignment, the two treatment groups are probabilistically equated with respect to preexisting differences among individuals. As such, treatments and preexisting differences among patients are *not* confounded (and neither are treatments and the treatment deliverers confounded), which enhances the likelihood that whatever observed outcome differences might materialize can be traced to the treatments themselves.

How Are Classroom-Based Instructional Interventions Typically Administered?

Random assignment of students to classrooms is not a critical characteristic of scientifically credible classroom-based instructional intervention studies. A problematic feature of the prototypical instructional intervention study, which must be dealt with, relates to the manner in which the instructional treatments are administered. If each teacher delivers instruction to students in the context of a typical classroom setting, then that en-masse

[1] An important realization is that even if the two teachers are randomly assigned to the two methods of instruction, there is still a 50% chance that teachers/classrooms (rather than instructional methods) are the source of any observed mean outcome differences. For an excellent introduction to general methodological concerns and confoundings in educational intervention research, see Chapter 5.

instructional delivery comprises a *single* treatment administration and must be regarded as the equivalent of administering the treatment to a single experimental "participant" (rather than, say, to the 25 individual students in the classroom). This is because of the *interdependence* that exists among a classroom's constituent members, as reflected by the following: (a) the obvious interactivity among the students and (b) general and specific factors associated with the instruction as delivered by the teacher. Each of these factors can be expected to exert common influences on all student recipients of that instruction, for as Page (1965, p. 1) persuasively argued two generations ago:

> [Such influences] could be any variable affecting the class as a whole: a particular teacher who depresses score[s], a particular student whose noxious attitudes are contagious, the particular timing of the class after lunch hour when students are sleepy, etc. The point is that this [type of interdependence] is not ordinarily detectable through the usual procedures of experimental research or reporting.

That is, apart from different teachers' unique styles, skills, and personalities (reflected in the arguments of the preceding section), there are countless other critical features that differ from one classroom to the next, including instructional settings (room location, heating, ventilation, sound proofing, attractiveness, and so forth) and logistics (e.g., the day of the week and the time of day when classes are held). Each of these is a potential influencer of within-classroom student performance and contributes to what Page (1965) has termed "lawnmower effects" in reference to his own vivid hypothetical example in which weekly recurring distracting noise from a power lawnmower just outside a particular classroom would obviously exert a common deleterious effect on students' attention to, and learning from, whatever instructional lesson is being presented at the time. To make this methodological concern completely transparent, Page (1965, p. 1) adds, "And this [lawnmower] disturbance, although no part of the treatment, is assigned to one treatment group [i.e., one classroom] and not to the other." In short, when one teacher administers instruction to one intact class, it is imperative that the administration be counted as a single *replication* of the instructional method. Incorporating more than one independent replication requires that other teachers deliver the same instructional method to students in other classrooms.

The unit interdependence/interactivity problem extends to situations in which *schools* are randomly assigned to receive different instructional methods but all classrooms within a particular school receive the same method. This was the case in a recent mathematics intervention study by Kramarski and Mevarech (2003), where three classrooms in one school received one method of instruction and three classrooms in another school received a different method. Indeed, as the authors themselves readily acknowledge, "We did not assign classrooms to different conditions within one school because our experience shows that teachers in the same school tend to share materials and talk to each other about their teaching activities" (p. 294).[2]

Does the same situation exist in the prototypical medical-research intervention study? Not if the intervention (e.g., drug treatments, medical procedures) is separately and independently administered to individual patients, either at different sites or without opportunities for interactions among study participants. Moreover, different medications (even if they are the "same" pill) likely differ in their specific chemical compositions in slightly different ways. As noted above, however, this is not the case when a single unit of instruction is delivered by a single teacher in a single classroom. The unique characteristics of the teacher and instructional lesson delivery are constant for all students (even if they are not perceived as being identical by all students). Add to this the usual drug treatment "double blind" requirements to counteract *subject and experimenter expectancy effects*—namely that patients should be unaware of the particular medication (active ingredient or placebo) they are receiving and that treatment administrators should be unaware of the particular medication they are administering, through the use of experimental drugs and placebos that are not discernible in their surface aspects (i.e., color, odor, taste, and so forth).

How Are the Data from Classroom-Based Instructional Intervention Studies Typically Analyzed?

The two major areas of concern regarding educational intervention research, which were outlined in the preceding discussion (namely, how students/classrooms are typically assigned to experimental conditions and how classroom-based treatments are administered), have direct implications for how the data from such studies are analyzed statistically. The major concern ("problem") here is that if interdependence among experimental observations/measures exists because of questionable unit-assignment and/or treatment-administration practices (as was just attributed to the prototypical classroom-based intervention study), commonly applied methods of statistical analysis are more than simply inappropriate—they are dangerously deceptive (see, for example, Barcikowski, 1981; Cornfield, 1978; Kenny & Judd, 1986; Levin & O'Donnell, 1999b, pp. 208–209; and for a very early recognition of the problem, Lindquist, 1940, pp. 567–568).

[2] Although beyond the topic of present concern, there are many research tactics for reducing within-classroom interactivity/interdependence during an instructional intervention. For example, different instructional materials can be delivered to students working on separate computers, to students reading their own books or other print media, or in other formats that overcome the problem of a single teacher simultaneously presenting a single lesson to a single intact class.

Consider the following examples, as applied to three different nonindependent intervention scenarios. For each of these scenarios, the specific claims made about a researcher's erroneous and misleading conclusions are based on the results of computer-based Monte Carlo (sampling) simulation studies.

Scenario 1: *Classroom-based intervention studies.* Scenario 1 consists of the prototypical classroom-based intervention that we have been discussing in this section, where one intact classroom is randomly assigned to receive one instructional method and another classroom receives a different method (or the standard method). Suppose that each classroom contains 30 students and that mean outcome differences between the two methods are assessed by the usual data analysis procedure in which individual students are incorrectly regarded as the independent units (namely, an independent samples *t* test applied to the 30 student outcomes associated with each instructional method). Barcikowski (1981, Table 1) has shown that with a modest degree of within-classroom interdependence operating (reflected by what is called an "intraclass correlation" value of 0.20 that arises from student interactivity, as well as general and specific classroom-related factors), a researcher would incorrectly claim that there are student mean outcome differences associated with the two different instructional methods far more often (i.e., 50% of the time) than he or she believes such an error is occurring (conventionally, 5% of the time). Equivalently, in more technical statistical hypothesis-testing parlance, even though one's *nominal* Type I error probability (γ) is thought to be 0.05, the empirical (or *actual*) Type I error probability turns out to be 0.50, a substantially higher value—specifically, 10 times greater than the "advertised" value. In starker policy terms, *even if the two instructional methods were equivalent with respect to student outcomes*, a researcher would incorrectly conclude that the two methods differed in their effectiveness half the time they were being compared. That is, only 50% of the time (rather than the hoped for 95%) would a researcher come to a correct decision about the two methods' equivalence. Speaking of "equivalence," under such conditions the statistical analysis would be equivalent to a researcher simply flipping a coin to determine whether one instructional method was better than the other! Is this any way to build a scientifically credible catalog of instructional methods that "work?"

Scenario 2: *Small-group intervention studies.* Scenario 2 consists of small-group intervention studies (for example, in group counseling or therapy contexts, or when different instructional treatments are administered in groups ranging from a few to a dozen participants, as is the case in many common "psychology experiments" with undergraduate participants). For the present illustration, suppose that treatments are administered to groups of six participants at a time, assuming a reasonable degree of within-group interdependence (as reflected by an intraclass correlation of 0.40)—which might be expected when the group's participants know each other and are allowed to work together or converse by asking questions, discussing issues, reacting to their peers, expressing their opinions, and so forth. For that particular combination of group size and degree of interdependence within groups, Levin and Serlin (1993, Table 2) found that a conventional analysis that ignores the within-group correlational structure inflates the nominal γ of 0.05 to 0.28, almost six times higher. Even in the simplest small-group case, where two-person dyads comprise the "groups," the actual Type I error probability of 0.10 turns out to be twice as large as it should be.

Such examples clearly illustrate Raudenbush's (1997, p. 174) recent reminder of Cornfield's (1978, p. 101) blunt depiction of the problem, "Randomization by cluster [here, classroom or group] accompanied by an analysis appropriate to randomization by individual is an exercise in self-deception." But, let us continue.

Scenario 3: *Single-case intervention studies*. A final example of within-unit nonindependence consists of what have come to be known as *single-case designs* (e.g., Kratochwill & Levin, 1992), where the experimental units (typically individual participants but also groups or classrooms) are measured repeatedly over time. In such designs, the just-mentioned Type I error probability inflation problem becomes even worse. The simplest single-case design (which will serve as Scenario 3) is known as the AB design, where A represents a baseline (or Method 1) phase and B an experimental (or Method 2) phase. Within each phase, a number of outcome measures are taken on the same unit (participant, group, or classroom). Even the relatively uninitiated reader should be able to discern that such measures are not independent of one another. Why? Because from an intuitive standpoint (and almost by definition), a distinguishing characteristic of temporally or serially connected measures produced by the same entity is that such measures are at least to some degree *related* (see, for example, Kratochwill et al., 1974). Yet, once again researchers commonly treat the measures *as though* they were independent and perform a conventional (although incorrect) statistical analysis of the data to determine whether the A and B phases produced equivalent mean outcomes (e.g., Gentile, Rodin, & Kline, 1972; Shine & Bower, 1971). Toothaker, Banz, Noble, Camp, & Davis (1983) have shown that when the measures from a single-case four-phase AB design (i.e., a design with two alternating A and B phases) are statistically treated as though they were independent, there are disastrous conclusion consequences regarding differences between mean A and B outcomes (when, in reality, the two means are equal; see also Lall, 2002). In the Monte Carlo sampling study of Toothaker et al. with 20 repeated measures associated with both of the overall A and B phase means and a "medium" degree of nonindependence among the within-phase measures (as reflected by an "autocorrelation" of 0.70 between adjacent observations), for a nominal Type I error probability of 0.05 the empirical Type I error probability associated with the commonly applied (although incorrect) statistical test was 0.61, 12 times more than it should have been. With 60 repeated measures per overall phase mean, the empirical Type I error probability became 0.74, a whopping 15 times more than it should have been (Toothaker et al., 1983; Tables 3 and 7). If this were a stock market futures index, an investor would be pleased; but because it is an erroneous inference index, a researcher should be embarrassed and ashamed!

[Back from the classroom to the courtroom]

Plum: So you see, sir, this is serious business with serious consequences. Therefore, I beg to differ with you regarding the methodological and procedural similarities between prototypical educational- and medical-research intervention studies. From a scientific standpoint, such similarities are more apparent than real. From a methodological standpoint, however, there is a clear remedy that can be prescribed in educational and other group-based intervention research investigations, prescriptions that are sure-fire antidotes for the dreaded interdependence problems to which I have devoted so much attention to during this trial. The remedy is a simple one indeed: Instead of selecting only two intact units (whether dyads, small groups, or classrooms) and randomly assigning one to each intervention condition, select multiple units and randomly assign those units to conditions.

Prosecutor: Professor Plum, you really seem to be on a mission here. Would you please tell us why you are so passionate about, deeply troubled by, and even obsessed with this so-called independence problem in classroom-based research?

Plum: Cautions about treating nonindependent outcome measures as though they were independent have been echoed by mathematical statisticians for more than 50 years. The particular educational intervention research problem of which we speak has been recognized for almost a century and interpretive limitations associated with statistical analyses that ignore the classroom, group, or single-case nonindependence issue have been preached by methodologists and statisticians every generation or so throughout the past 60 years.[3] Yet, with the dawning of the 21st century, here are educational researchers adopting an ostrich mentality and still applying the same flawed designs and associated analyses. What will it take to help these researchers realize that despite the hard work they are putting into their experimental investigations, they are nonetheless deceiving themselves in thinking that their studies (and, in particular, their conclusions and recommendations) are credible ones, while "pulling the wool over the eyes" of unsuspecting consumers? If I have to be dragged back into this courtroom 1,000 more times to testify on behalf of conducting scientifically credible educational intervention research, then so be it! Have I made my point?

Prosecutor: Yes, I believe you have. [Under his breath] Darn, I'll get those legal aides of mine for not doing their homework!!

[3] In chronological order, concerns about these particular methodological and statistical issues have been raised throughout the past century by, for example, Thorndike (1910, p. 7); Lindquist (1940); Cochran (1947); Scheffé (1959); Page (1965); Peckham, Glass, and Hopkins (1969); Kratochwill et al. (1974); Cornfield (1978); Barcikowski (1981); Toothaker et al. (1983); Levin (e.g., 1985, pp. 221–223; 1992); Levin and O'Donnell (1999b, pp. 208–209); and Silverman and Solmon (1998).

THE CASE FOR RANDOMIZED CLASSROOM TRIALS

Our preceding classroom-based intervention research arguments map directly onto analogous research contexts involving siblings in families, participants in a group-implemented training program, families within communities, or any other "cluster" sampling and randomization situation (see Chapter 8; Green, 1997; Raudenbush, 1997). So, the question becomes: What should one do statistically in such contexts? There is widespread agreement among methodologists and statisticians that the superordinate units of randomization (classrooms, teachers, schools, families, small groups, communities, and so forth) must be regarded as a random factor either in hierarchical analyses of variance (e.g., Serlin, Wampold, & Levin, 2003; Wampold & Serlin, 2000)—for which the treatment effect of major concern can be equivalently produced by an analysis based on the unit means (e.g., Levin, 1992; Levin & O'Donnell, 1999)—or in hierarchical linear model analyses (e.g., Raudenbush & Bryk, 2002). Hundreds of such unit-appropriate assignment, administration, and analysis examples exist in recent educational and other related randomized intervention trials contexts (see, for example, Chapter 8 and Boruch, 1974). For a modest sampling of these, see Beresford et al. (1997); COMMIT Research Group (1995); Conduct Problems Prevention Research Group (1999); Finn, Gerber, Achilles, & Boyd-Zaharias (2001); Mosteller & Boruch (2002); and Peterson, Mann, Kealey, & Marek (2000).

In a nutshell, and among many other carefully controlled factors, even being considered as a "scientifically credible" instructional intervention study requires that the experimental units (typically classrooms) be randomly assigned to intervention and nonintervention conditions, with the resulting data statistically analyzed at a units-appropriate level.

Ten Ideal Characteristics of Educational Intervention Research

As is clearly articulated by Valentine and Cooper (see Chapter 5), numerous criteria must be taken into consideration when assessing the quality/credibility of an intervention study's evidence. These criteria essentially reflect specified methodological, psychometric, and statistical standards. A checklist and flowchart for helping journal reviewers and readers evaluate the scientific credibility of research presented as "randomized control trials," originally devised by a committee known as CONSORT (Consolidated Standards of Reporting Trials), have been adopted by the medical research community (Moher, Schulz, & Altman, 2001) and more recently by *Health Psychology*, a publication of the American Psychological Association (APA)—see Stone (2003). Along with these research credibility standards, fundamental criteria for assessing the societal significance/creditability of research-based educational intervention programs are represented in Crane's (1998, Chapter 1) highly recommended edited volume. As Levin (in press) has recently pointed out, a variety of educational research collaborations, task forces, funding agencies, and funded products [e.g., APA Divisions 12 (Clinical Psychology) and 16 (School Psychology) Task Forces on Evidence-Based Interventions, Campbell Collaboration (see Chapter 8), Institute of Education Sciences (e.g., see Chapter 2; Coalition for Evidence-Based Policy, 2003), What Works Clearinghouse (see Chapter 5)] have begun to take such criteria seriously, by making them operational—and even imperative—in their respective endeavors. In what follows, I briefly submit my own personal "top 10" list of the ideal characteristics that educational intervention research should possess. Specifically, such research, ideally (according to my standards), should be as follows:

1. *Problem focused*. This gets at my notion of educational creditability (Levin, 1994). Ideal educational intervention research should address problems of societal importance, such as how to improve the teaching and learning of fundamental content and skills; how to reduce student dropouts, school violence, or teen pregnancy; how to enhance students' real-world and job-related adaptive behaviors; and so on. As Levin (2004) has noted, educational creditability also reflects Wolf's (1978) *social validity* construct, which in this context would refer to societal acceptance/approval of an intervention's outcomes. Of course, even though all (or even most) intervention research cannot and does not tackle such educationally meaty problems, this criterion nonetheless provides food for preliminary thought and subsequent action.

2. *Theoretically grounded*. The more that educational interventions are grounded in the theory or psychological processes underlying them, the more valuable they are. In the case of a cognitive-instructional intervention, for example, more important than leaping in and trying out a variety of techniques to determine which ones "work" is to develop promising techniques on the basis of theoretical or process analyses of the underlying cognitive components associated with the intervention. That is, generally more valuable than simply assessing whether a particular intervention *is* effective is to understand *why* it is effective, with "why" in this context defined as students' specific internal cognitive processes or behavioral components that are affected by the intervention.

3. *Data-based*. Yet, assessing whether a particular intervention is effective is critical in its own right, and—consistent with the theme of this volume—should be based on actual empirical data (evidence) rather than on opinions, anecdotes, or flights of fancy. Carefully and comprehensively conducted meta-analyses can also be relied on when assessing the scientific credibility (i.e., believability) of a given intervention's effectiveness,

especially when the meta-analysis scores high on the various "quality" standards outlined by Valentine and Cooper (see Chapter 5).

4. *Psychometrically sound.* D'Agostino (see Chapter 6) has persuasively argued throughout his chapter that the characteristics of a given study's operations (reflecting construct validity) and its measures (again reflecting construct validity, in addition to outcome reliability and validity) are critical determinants in assessing the potential value of an educational intervention study, including the generalizability of its findings (see also Shadish, Cook, & Campbell [2002], Chapter 3). As D'Agostino points out—and as is generally underappreciated by educational researchers—with inadequate measurement properties of both the latent constructs and manifest variables, not only does the statistical power of the data analyses decline, but the internal and external validity foundations of the study crumble as well. Underlying constructs that are well defined and measured enhance what Levin (2004) refers to as a study's contextual *accretability*, or the scope of an intervention's applicability.

5. *Representative.* Accretability is also enhanced if an intervention study's participants and implementation contexts are either randomly sampled from or otherwise representative of the respective populations to which outcome generalizations are desired (i.e., if external validity criteria are satisfied). Note that whereas this representative criterion says everything about generalizability prerequisites, it is silent concerning the methodological quality and associated credibility of the research outcomes as interpreted/promoted by the researcher. In that sense, then, just as scientifically credible research findings may not be generalizable without random sampling or representativeness, representative samples may produce generalizable findings even though the researcher's desired interpretations of intervention "causality" may not be justified (as a result of inadequate experimental control).

6. *Randomized.* One does not have to search very far to discover that graduate students and researchers alike often confuse (and misuse) the concepts of random sampling/selection (a primary *external validity* consideration), on the one hand, and random assignment or participant/unit randomization (a primary *internal validity* consideration), on the other—see Levin (2004). To echo a concern raised by both Cook and Campbell (1979, p. 84) and Shadish et al. (2002, pp. 97–98), the immediately preceding statement requires clarification of Campbell and Stanley's (1963, p. 5) assertion that internal validity is the *sine qua non* of experimental research. Yes, it is true that (a) without high internal validity, a study's causal claims (i.e., that the study's outcomes are exclusively attributable to the intervention) are suspect, and (b) randomization is an essential component of a study's internal validity. However, not all educational research is or should be "experimental" (i.e., investigating causal connections between interventions and outcomes). In that sense,

then, it might also be claimed that *external validity* is the *sine qua non* of other (nonexperimental) research genres—specifically, survey research and correlational/observational studies—in that (a) without high external validity, inferences about population characteristics and responses estimated from those in the study are suspect, and (b) random sampling is an essential component of a study's external validity. Having made that distinction, I hasten to emphasize that randomization in the form of random assignment of the independent experimental units to intervention conditions (as was discussed earlier) is an absolute necessity to assure initial equivalence of groups (within known statistical sampling error), thereby strengthening one's attribution of the intervention to the observed outcomes. Without unit randomization, such attribution claims are not scientifically credible and, therefore, lack an ideal characteristic of educational intervention research (see Chapter 8).

7. *Carefully implemented*. In addition to randomization, which ensures initial equivalence of the studied groups or conditions, a good intervention researcher is careful in conducting the experiment itself. By "careful," I mean that other variables (sometimes referred to as *extraneous* or *confounding* variables) apart from the intervention *per se*, which could plausibly (Campbell & Stanley, 1963) account for outcome effects, are scrupulously monitored and controlled.[4] Such variables encompass Campbell and Stanley's (1963) internal invalidity considerations (i.e., factors that are not directly associated with an intervention's efficacy), including a wide variety of participant and experimenter effects; differential attention, boredom, fatigue, or practice; contamination through information leakage; and pretest sensitization; among many others (for a comprehensive listing, see Shadish et al., 2002). Interventions that are not implemented either as designed or as scripted (i.e., with poor fidelity) also compromise a study's internal validity. Moreover, as has been recently cautioned by Levin and O'Donnell (1999) and Levin (2004), even though random assignment to conditions ensures initial group equivalence (see Characteristic 6), with selective participant attrition (or "mortality") throughout the intervention's duration, a study's group equivalence is destroyed and its internal validity weakened (often irreparably).

8. *Properly analyzed*. Appropriate statistical treatment of one's data and conclusions that justifiably follow from those analyses are part and parcel of what Cook and Campbell (1970) refer to as *statistical conclusion validity*. In Levin's (2004) conceptualization, statistical conclusion validity is an integral component of an intervention study's credibility. For data to be analyzed properly, a statistical test must be selected that is appropriate

[4] This characteristic also literally captures the E (for Eliminating all other competing explanations for an outcome) in Levin's (1997) and Derry, Levin, Osana, Jones, and Peterson's (2000) four critical components of CAREfully conducted educational intervention research.

with respect to the distributional characteristics and underlying assumptions needed for the valid application of the test. If those assumptions are not satisfied, the error probabilities associated with the test outcomes are not correct and so the inferences drawn from those outcomes are not valid. A poignant example of statistical conclusion invalidity and its disastrous consequences is represented by the earlier extended discussion of the interdependence problem created by a researcher randomizing and administering interventions to intact classrooms, and yet analyzing the data as though the students within those classrooms were independent entities. Researchers not taking into account the statistical power characteristics associated with their inferential tests is another oft-overlooked statistical conclusion validity issue, as are many others (e.g., Levin, 1985; Shadish et al., 2002, Chapter 2).

9. *Replicable.* Replicability here refers to both an intervention study's operations and its outcomes. If a given intervention study's operations are replicable, other researchers are able to apply those operations with sufficient veridicality to investigate research questions and constructs in a manner similar to how they were investigated in the initial study. With comparable operations thus applied, if the initial study's results are replicated in one or more independently conducted studies, then a researcher is able to offer conclusion generalizations about the intervention, beyond the original study to other (either similar or different) participant populations, contexts, intervention implementers, and procedural variations. Generalizations derived from replicating results in multiple studies contribute to the external validity of a body of research, as does the previously discussed random sampling within the context of a single study (see Characteristic 6). I note in passing that Thompson's (1996) "internal" replication notions (different analyses of a given set of data—through statistical "jackknifing" or "bootstrapping" techniques—that yield converging conclusions) are not regarded as a legitimate substitute for "external" replications (similar outcomes produced in independently conducted studies). Internal replications indicate simply whether a given study's findings are sufficiently "robust" to withstand data analyses of different types and with different underlying assumptions. Contrary to what Thompson implies, such robustness says little or nothing about one's ability to generalize the findings beyond the context of the single study (e.g., Levin, 1998, p. 47; Robinson & Levin, 1997, pp. 24–25).

10. *Transportable.* "Transportable" interventions contain components that make it feasible for practitioners (other than the original developer of the intervention) to implement the intervention *as intended* (see Characteristic 7) in their own settings. Cost-effective methods, well-constructed materials, and clearly described procedures (often in the form of instructional manuals) will help in that regard. Classroom interventions that "work" only when in the hands of the original developer or master teacher are interven-

tions that are not transportable to other consumers; therefore, they lack an essential aspect of external validity. Transportability also relates to the previously discussed methodological concern about the criticality of disentangling method and teacher effects, rather than confounding the two (e.g., Wampold, 2001; see also, Levin, 2004).

[Back to the courtroom]

Prosecutor: Pshaw, Professor Plum, "ideal" characteristics indeed they are! You're living in a world of fantasy, of wishing wells, witches' spells, and magic mushrooms that can make you grow taller. Sure, if cows could fly then conducting randomized classroom trials research might well be an attainable goal. But we're talking "real world" here, not dream world. Who in their right mind would have the courage to conduct a randomized trial out there amidst real students, teachers, and classrooms? Who with half a mind would even *consider* conducting one? It simply can't be done. The climate of classrooms is too "messy," too uncontrolled, and to use the language of what has come before, too interactive. Because of that, conducting well-controlled, scientifically valid, randomized trials in classrooms requires overcoming too many constraints and would require the utilization of too many economic and physical resources. In short, carefully controlled classroom-based research simply cannot be conducted because it is too "everything!" Wouldn't you agree, Professor Plum?

Plum: Yes. That is, I would agree that you are voicing the same objections to randomized classroom trials that are commonly heard from taxpayers, lawmakers, school boards, and even academic researchers in education and the related social sciences—most likely everyone except the medical research community. But, with all due respect, sir, your objections are simply not correct. Carefully controlled randomized trials studies can be conducted in real-life classroom settings, and have been many times over in this great country of ours. Reviewing the record of this trial [as well as other proceedings in the present volume] will attest to that. As for the popular objections to conducting randomized classroom trials studies, now is the time to quash certain unfounded accusations for one and all, once and for all. In my own personal closing arguments, I will target one commonly heard complaint: The limited resources that are generally available for implementing randomized classroom trials critically undermine both the practicability and precision of them . . .

[Professor Plum provides his closing arguments, which are summarized here]

STRATEGIES FOR COMBATING THE "LIMITED RESOURCES" CONCERN

Three decades ago, Boruch (1975) wrote a compelling piece in which he presented and countered commonly offered objections to conducting randomized control trials in the "real world" (including classrooms). Levin (1992) referred to Higbee's (1978) "pseudo-limitations" notion in providing a compressed set of arguments directed at classroom-based research. Most recently, Cook and Payne (2002) objected to nine common objections about randomized classroom trials research by offering a well-reasoned counterargument to each objection (see Chapter 8).

In addition to Cook and Payne's (2002) list of commonly heard complaints about randomized classroom trials studies, likely the most often heard focuses on the vast resources (including money, time, and the number of students, teachers, classrooms, and even researchers) that are required to conduct them (see, for example, Slavin, 1999, pp. 263 and 265). As the complaint goes, the requisite resources are generally far in excess of what most educational researchers could hope to amass in the absence of considerable extramural funding. Consequently, researchers elect to conduct more manageable, less ambitious, and typically, less carefully controlled classroom-based investigations as well. My response is that the scientific credibility of classroom-based research need not, and should not, be compromised just because optimal resources are not available (Levin, 1994). So, as a variant of Weiss' (2002) "What to do until the randomizer comes" theme, I offer some generally underused, yet experimentally sound, solutions to the problem, "What to do until the humongous pie-in-the-sky extramurally funded randomized-classroom-trials grant comes."

Fewer Classrooms

A popular "resource" criticism of randomized classroom trials research is that the number of students and teachers/classrooms required to produce adequate statistical power for detecting intervention effects of interest is excessive. For example, Slavin (1999, p. 265) presents a hypothetical situation that is characteristic of this concern:

> Imagine a study of a school-level intervention in which four experimental elementary schools are compared with four controls. If each school has 500 children, this is a study of 4,000 children, yet it is too small for the appropriate analysis!

Slavin's assertions were challenged by Levin and O'Donnell (1999a, p. 286), who actually "did the math." They found that assuming 20 students per classroom and a moderate degree of interdependence within each classroom (as reflected by an intraclass correlation of 0.20), 20 classrooms per condition (resulting in 800 students, rather than Slavin's stated 4,000) would be needed to achieve statistical power of almost 0.90 to detect a medium-sized intervention effect.

Similarly, an otherwise useful document targeted at educational research consumers cites two previous papers (including one by Slavin, 2003) to support the following claim:

> If schools, rather than individual students, are randomized, a minimum sample size of 50 to 60 schools or classrooms (25–30 in the intervention group and 25–30 in the control group) is needed to obtain [statistical significance for an intervention that is modestly effective] . . . If an intervention is highly effective, smaller sample sizes than this may be able to generate a finding of statistical significance (Coalition for Evidence-Based Policy, 2003, p. 8)

If true, such requisites would pose a considerable deterrent for classroom researchers, not just with respect to the excessive financial resources associated with a large-scale study, but also with respect to the vast number of teachers who must be contacted and enlisted during the recruitment process. Yet, such power and sample-size claims are misguided. For example, let us reconsider our Scenario 1 example. Suppose that one wishes to conduct a two-condition intervention study using classrooms as the proper experimental units (as is assumed in the above quote). With 30 students per classroom and a reasonable degree of within-classroom interdependence (again reflected by an intraclass correlation of 0.20), Barcikowski (1981, Table 1) shows that 30 classrooms (15 per condition) are required to detect a moderate ("modestly effective" in the above quote) intervention effect and only 15 classrooms (seven to eight per condition) are needed to detect a large effect ("highly effective" in the above quote). Although the number of classrooms required in these cases is not trivial, it is about half the number of what is prescribed in the Coalition for Evidence-Based Policy (2003) guidelines. So where did such "guidelines" come from, one wonders?

Examples of classroom-based intervention research that incorporates units-appropriate analyses abound in the educational research literature (see, for example, Foorman, Francis, Novy, & Liberman, 1991; Levin, Pressley, McCormick, Miller, & Shriberg, 1979, Exp. 6; Stevens, Slavin, & Farnish, 1991[5]; and Whitehurst et al., 1994). Such intervention studies have not just proven tractable and affordable to conduct, but they—even those with extremely small numbers of classrooms and students relative to what is specified in the preceding "guidelines"—have proven capable of yielding statistically nonchance intervention effects. In addition, if statistical power is an issue of concern, the incorporation of one or more outcome-related antecedent variables into the design and analysis should be considered. This can be achieved at both the group and individual levels through either blocked random assignment of units to conditions and/or analyses of covariance following random assignment to conditions (e.g., Levin, 1992; Levin & Serlin, 1993; Shadish et al., 2002, pp. 304–307). Such strategic design-and-analysis selections can serve to reduce error variance and, as a result, increase the likelihood of detecting true intervention effects.

Less Balance

The "limited resources" issue can be thought of in general and specific terms. The former refers to the money and time resources required to recruit

[5] Somewhat ironically, one of the authors of the study by Stevens et al. (Slavin) provided the "fighting words" (concerning the impracticality of conducting randomized classroom trials research) that were quoted earlier in this section.

and test *all participants* in the research project, whereas the latter refers to the additional resources required to produce and deliver the intervention to *participants in the intervention condition*. If (a) limited resources associated with implementing the intervention are the primary issue, and, as is generally the case, (b) the cost of implementing an instructional intervention is much greater than that of collecting outcome-measure data on an untreated control condition, then a straightforward (although underused) research-design strategy is available. That strategy is simply to assign fewer participants to the intervention condition than to the control condition (for related consideration of unequal resource allocation, see Raudenbush, 1997). For example, in response to Slavin's (2003) "too small" claim in the preceding section, Levin and O'Donnell (1999a) again "did the math." With the same specifications, they found that adequate statistical power (of 0.72) to detect a medium-sized intervention effect would result from halving the number of intervention classrooms (from 20 to 10), while keeping the number of control classrooms at 20, which in turn would reduce the total number of students required from 800 to 600 (see also Shadish et al., pp. 299–300).

Even when the degree of unit imbalance is extreme (including when the number of units receiving an intervention is very small), valid research studies can be conducted and intervention effects identified. One striking example of this approach is a study of an experimental mathematics program, the Wisconsin Emerging Scholars Program, at the University of Wisconsin-Madison (Millar, Alexander, Lewis, & Levin, 1995). In that program, promising mathematics students from underrepresented groups were assigned to special sections of an undergraduate calculus course.[6] One purpose of the study was to compare the end-of-semester achievement of the special-section students with that of students in all other sections of the calculus course. Such comparisons were made (on the basis of exact *randomization tests*) after statistically equating students on precollege general academic and mathematics ability measures. In one semester, 64 regular sections (containing 1,021 students) were compared with just two special sections (28 students) and a statistically significant performance advantage ($p = 0.02$) was associated with the latter. In a second-level calculus course the following semester, once again students in the two special sections (29 students) statistically outperformed those in 43 regular sections (657 students), $p < 0.001$, by a creditable margin (almost 0.8 of a grade point). As an even more extreme "imbalance" example, renowned educational researcher Herbert Walberg (April 17, 2004) reports being involved in a "schools as

[6] Participating students were not randomly assigned to sections and so this is not a randomized experiment from which causal conclusions can be made. The point to focus on here is the considerable imbalance between the number of control and intervention sections and students and, in particular, the very small number of sections and students assigned to the intervention condition.

units" national study in which the instructional outcomes of a handful of experimental schools are being compared with those of some 6,000 control schools!

The implications of the foregoing discussion are clear: Not all intervention research conditions need be created equal. In particular, whenever interventions are costly to implement, assigning fewer units to the intervention than to the control condition may be a wise design decision. Doing so can help make efficient use of resources without compromising the experimental integrity (specifically, the internal and statistical conclusion validities) of the study. In addition, with scarce resources it is easier for researchers to explain to would-be participants why there can be no guarantee that they will end up receiving the (presumed, although not proven, effective) intervention.

Eligibility Requirements

Alternatively, if resources are limited, access to an intervention can be reserved for candidates (e.g., students, classrooms) most "in need" of the intervention. In such situations, a two-step selection—assignment process should be invoked: (a) all candidates for inclusion in the study would first have to meet eligibility requirements (based on the specified "need" criteria); and (b) random assignment to intervention and control conditions would be restricted to only those qualifying candidates. For example, suppose that 22 classrooms are initially identified as potential candidates for an intervention and yet there are sufficient program resources for only seven classrooms. The original candidate pool would then be narrowed down (based on the "need" criteria) to 14 classrooms, with seven apiece randomly assigned to intervention and control conditions. When resources are adequate to accommodate all or most candidates but incorporating random assignment is necessary for scientific credibility purposes, additional justifications and approaches must be marshaled, as is next discussed (see also Shadish et al., 2002, Chapters 8 and 9).

Intervention Delays

Without question, researchers who conduct randomized classroom trials studies must confront a number of ethical issues associated with randomly (rather than systematically or subjectively) assigning participating students or classrooms to the study's experimental conditions (Shadish et al., 2002, Chapter 9). A predominant (and recurring) ethical issue is one of withholding a thought-to-be beneficial intervention from those participants who are thought to be most likely to benefit from it. In certain contexts, it is not so much a question of permitting all participants to receive the intervention but rather (because of ethical and concurrent resource concerns) permitting all participants to receive the intervention *at the same time*. Under conditions where intervention resources may be available at some time in the future (e.g., during an ensuing week, semester, or year), it might be desirable to adopt a *wait-list* control design. With such designs, it is initially explained that there are insufficient resources for all participants to receive the experimental intervention simultaneously. Through random assignment (which might be described as a "lottery process"), some participants will end up in the intervention condition and others in the nonintervention control condition. Importantly, however, after the formal portion of the study has been completed, all control participants (who so desire) will have access to the same intervention that was administered to participants in the experiment proper. This wait-list control strategy was recently adopted by McDonald, Kratochwill, Levin, and Youngbear Tibbits (1998) and often offers an enticement to potential participants to enlist in a "research study."

Alternative Designs

Finally, let us consider alternative design options that take into account resource and other constraints. If the costs associated with administering an intervention are not as much of a concern as are the costs associated with the number of units (e.g., the number of classrooms) incorporated, a variety of creative design alternatives are available. Sample alternatives include *crossover designs*, where classroom units are systematically switched from an intervention to a nonintervention condition, and vice versa, at different stages of the randomized trial (e.g., see Chapter 5; Levin et al., 1990, Exp. 1), and within-classroom *microexperiments*, which are possible when an instructional intervention can be implemented individually, independently, and simultaneously within classrooms in print, multimedia, or electronic formats (see Footnote 2). The most extreme alternative, yet scientifically credible, approach is manifested in certain single-case designs, where either one or a very small number of experimental units (classrooms or individual students) are repeatedly assessed in *time-series* fashion under different intervention conditions. Both within- and between-unit comparisons can be built into both the intervention design and its analysis. Specific single-case possibilities worth considering include (among others) *replicated simultaneous treatment*, *alternating treatment*, and *reversal designs* (e.g., Kratochwill & Levin, 1978), *multiple-baseline designs* (e.g., Koehler & Levin, 1998; Wampold & Worsham, 1986), and *replicated randomized* AB *designs* (e.g., Levin & Wampold's, 1999, simultaneous startpoint model; see also Lall & Levin, 2004), along with their corresponding unit-appropriate statistical analyses.

[Back to the courtroom]

Judge: Would the courtroom kindly come to order? Professor Plum, do you have any final words before I turn this case over to the jury? And, more important, how do you plead?

Plum: And so, ladies and gentlemen of the jury, in summary: If it were done when 'tis done, 'twere well it were done quickly. No, wait, I'm just a little confused; that was my 11th grade Macbeth recitation. Let me try again. I did what I did because, from my perspective, the time was right to conduct a randomized classroom trial on the instructional intervention, and it was the just, honorable, and scientifically credible thing to do. On that account, I plead innocent. Yet, if conducting randomized classroom trials research is deemed a crime in the eyes of the law, then I must proudly plead guilty, Your Honor!

[Court adjourns; jury assembles; time passes; court reconvenes]

Judge: Reginald Plum, please rise. [Plum rises.] Ladies and gentlemen of the jury, have you reached a verdict?

Jury foreman: We have, Your Honor. We, the jury, find the defendant . . . [pregnant pause] . . . *not guilty*.

[Hoops, hollers, wild applause, amid cries of "Reg-gie, Reg-gie!" Program Officer Retired Colonel Mustard, along with the jubilant research team of Scarlett, Green, White, and Peacock, assemble]

Scarlett: Reginald, oh Reginald, we're all so happy for you! Congratulations on your acquittal! But, why do you suppose this randomized classroom trial ever came to trial in the first place?

[Professor Plum, puffing on his pipe, in the courtroom]

Plum: Frankly, Miss Scarlett, I don't have a clue!

References

Barcikowski, R. S. (1981). Statistical power with group mean as the unit of analysis. *Journal of Educational Statistics*, 6, 267–285.

Beresford, S. A. A., Curry, S. J., Kristal, A. R., Lazovich, D., Feng, Z., & Wagner, E. H. (1997). A dietary intervention in primary care practice: the eating patterns study. *American Journal of Public Health*, 87, 610–616.

Boruch, R. F. (1974). Bibliography: illustrative randomized field experiments for program planning and evaluation. *Evaluation*, 2, 83–87.

Boruch, R. F. (1975). On common contentions about randomized field experiments. In R. F. Boruch & H. W. Riecken (Eds.), *Experimental testing of public policy* (pp. 107–145). Boulder: Westview Press.

Campbell, D. T., & Stanley, J. C. (1963). *Experimental and quasi-experimental designs for research*. Chicago: Rand McNally.

Coalition for Evidence-Based Policy (2003). *Identifying and implementing educational practices supported by rigorous evidence: a user friendly guide*. US Department of Education, Institute of Education Sciences, National Center for Education Evaluation and Regional Assistance, Washington, DC (available at *www.excelgov.org/evidence*).

Cochran, W. G. (1947). Some consequences when the assumptions for the analysis of variance are not satisfied. *Biometrics*, 3, 22–38.

COMMIT Research Group (1995). Community intervention trial for smoking cessation (COMMIT), 1: cohort results from a four-year community intervention. *American Journal of Public Health*, 85, 183–192.

Conduct Problems Prevention Research Group (1999). Initial impact of the Fast Track prevention trial for conduct problems, II: classroom effects. *Journal of Consulting and Clinical Psychology*, 67, 648–657.

Cook, T. D., & Campbell, D. T. (1979). *Quasi-experimentation: design and analysis issues for field settings*. Chicago: Rand McNally.

Cook, T. D., & Payne, M. R. (2002). Objecting to the objections to using random assignment in educational research. In F. Mosteller & R. Boruch (Eds.), *Evidence matters: randomized trials in education research* (pp. 150–178). Washington, DC: Brookings Institution Press.

Cornfield, J. (1978). Randomization by group: a formal analysis. *American Journal of Epidemiology*, 108, 100–102.

Crane, J. (1998). Building on success. In J. Crane (Ed.), *Social programs that work* (pp. 1–42). New York: Sage.

Derry, S., Levin, J. R., Osana, H. P., Jones, M. S., & Peterson, M. (2000). Fostering students' statistical and scientific thinking: lessons learned from an innovative college course. *American Educational Research Journal*, 37, 747–773.

Finn, J. D., Gerber, S. B., Achilles, C. M., & Boyd-Zaharias, J. (2001). The enduring effects of small classes. *Teachers College Record*, 103, 45–83.

Foorman, B. R., Francis, D. J., Novy, D. M., & Liberman, D. (1991). How letter-sound instruction mediates progress in first-grade reading and spelling. *Journal of Educational Psychology*, 83, 456–469.

Gentile, J. R., Roden, A. H., & Klein, R. D. (1972). An analysis of variance model for the intrasubject replication design. *Journal of Applied Behavior Analysis*, 5, 193–198.

Goode, E. (March 9, 2004). Defying psychiatric wisdom, these skeptics say "Prove it." *New York Times*, D1, D6.

Green, S. B. (1997). The eating patterns study: the importance of practical randomized trials in communities. *American Journal of Public Health*, 87, 541–543.

Higbee, K. L. (1978). Some pseudo-limitations of mnemonics. In M. M. Gruneberg, P. E. Morris, & R. N. Sykes (Eds.), *Practical Aspects of Memory* (pp. 147–154). New York: Academic Press.

Kaestle, C. F. (1993). The awful reputation of education research. *Educational Researcher*, 22(1), 23–31.

Kenny, D. A., & Judd, C. M. (1986). Consequences of violating the independence assumption in analysis of variance. *Psychological Bulletin*, 99, 422–431.

Koehler, M. J., & Levin, J. R. (1998). Regulated randomization: a potentially sharper analytical tool for the multiple-baseline design. *Psychological Methods*, 3, 206–217.

Kramarski, B., & Mevarech, Z. R. (2003). Enhancing mathematical reasoning in the classroom: the effects of cooperative learning and metacognitive training. *American Educational Research Journal*, 40, 281–310.

Kratochwill, T. R., Alden, K., Demuth, D., Dawson, D., Panicucci, C., Arntson, P., McMurray, N., Hempstead, J., & Levin, J. (1974). A further consideration in the application of an analysis-of-variance model for the intrasubject replication design. *Journal of Applied Behavior Analysis*, 7, 629–633.

Kratochwill, T. R., & Levin, J. R. (1978). What time-series designs may have to offer educational researchers. *Contemporary Educational Psychology*, 3, 273–329.

Kratochwill, T. R., & Levin, J. R., Eds. (1992). *Single-case research design and analysis: new developments for psychology and education*. Hillsdale, NJ: Erlbaum.

Lall, V. F. (2002). *An investigation of the statistical properties of four single-case randomization tests*. Unpublished doctoral dissertation, University of Wisconsin, Madison.

Lall, V. F., & Levin, J. R. (2004). An empirical investigation of the statistical properties of generalized single-case randomization tests. *Journal of School Psychology*, 42, 61–86.

Levin, J. R. (1985). Some methodological and statistical "bugs" in research on children's learning. In M. Pressley & C. J. Brainerd (Eds.), *Cognitive learning and memory in children* (pp. 205–233). New York: Springer-Verlag.

Levin, J. R. (1992). On research in classrooms. *Mid-Western Educational Researcher*, 5, 2–6, 16.

Levin, J. R. (1994). Crafting educational intervention research that's both credible and creditable. *Educational Psychology Review*, 6, 231–243.

Levin, J. R. (1997, March). *Statistics in research and in the real world*. Colloquium presentation, Department of Psychology, University of California, San Diego.

Levin, J. R. (1998). What if there were no more bickering about statistical significance tests? *Research in the Schools*, 5(2), 43–53.

Levin, J. R. (2004). Random thoughts on the (in)credibility of educational-psychological intervention research. *Educational Psychologist*, 39, 173–184.

Levin, J. R., & O'Donnell, A. M. (1999a). Educational research's credibility gaps, in closing. *Issues in Education: Contributions from Educational Psychology*, 5, 279–293.

Levin, J. R., & O'Donnell, A. M. (1999b). What to do about educational research's credibility gaps? *Issues in Education: Contributions from Educational Psychology*, 5, 177–229.

Levin, J. R., & Serlin, R. C. (1993, Apr.). *No way to treat a classroom: alternative units-appropriate statistical strategies*. Paper presented at the annual meeting of the American Educational Research Association, Atlanta.

Levin, J. R., & Wampold, B. E. (1999). Generalized single-case randomization tests: Flexible analyses for a variety of situations. *School Psychology Quarterly*, 14, 59–93.

Levin, J. R., Levin, M. E., Cotton, J. W., Bartholomew, S., Hasty, K., Hughes, C., & Townsend, E. A. (1990). What do college students learn from and about an innovative vocabulary-learning strategy? In S. A. Biggs, (Ed.), *Innovative learning strategies, ninth yearbook*, 1989–1990 (pp. 186–206). Pittsburgh, PA: College Reading Improvement Special Interest Group of the International Reading Association.

Levin, J. R., O'Donnell, A. M., & Kratochwill, T. R. (2003). Educational/psychological intervention research. In I. B. Weiner (Series Ed.), and W. M. Reynolds & G. E. Miller (Vol. Eds.), *Handbook of Psychology: Vol. 7—Educational Psychology* (pp. 557–581). New York: Wiley.

Levin, J. R., Pressley, M., McCormick, C. B., Miller, G. E., & Shriberg, L. K. (1979). Assessing the classroom potential of the keyword method. *Journal of Educational Psychology*, 71, 583–594.

Lindquist, E. F. (1940). Sampling in educational research. *Journal of Educational Psychology*, 31, 561–574.

McCardle, P., & Chhabra, V. (Eds.) (2004). *The voice of evidence in reading research*. Baltimore: Brookes.

McDonald, L., Kratochwill, T. R, Levin, J. R., & Youngbear Tibbits, H. (1998, Aug.) *Families and schools together: an experimental analysis of a parent-mediated intervention program for at-risk American Indian children*. Paper presented at the annual meeting of the American Psychological Association, San Francisco.

Millar, S. B., Alexander, B. B., Lewis, H. A., & Levin, J. R. (1995). *Final report on the Pilot Wisconsin Emerging Scholars Program*: 1993–94. University of Wisconsin-Madison.

Moher, M., Schulz, K. F., & Altman, D., for the CONSORT Group (2001). CONSORT statement: revised recommendations for improving the quality of reports of parallel group randomized trials. *Journal of the American Medical Association*, 285, 1987–1991. (available at *www.consort-statement.org/statement/revisedstatement.htm*)

Mosteller, F., & Boruch, R. (Eds.) (2002). *Evidence matters: randomized trials in education research*. Washington, DC: Brookings Institution Press.

Page, E. B. (1965, Feb.), *Recapturing the richness within the classroom*. Paper presented at the annual meeting of the American Research Association, Chicago.

Peckham, P. D., Glass, G. V., & Hopkins, K. D. (1969). The experimental unit in statistical analysis. *Journal of Special Education*, 3, 337–349.

Peterson, A. V., Jr., Mann, S. L., Kealey, K. A., & Marek, P. M. (2000). Experimental design and methods for school-based randomized trials: experience from the Hutchinson Smoking Prevention Project (HSPP). *Controlled Clinical Trials*, 21, 144–165.

Platt, J. R. (1964). Strong inference. *Science*, 146, 347–353.

Raudenbush, S. W. (1997). Statistical analysis and optimal design for cluster randomized trials. *Psychological Methods*, 2, 173–185.

Raudenbush, S. W., & Bryk, A. S. (2002). *Hierarchical linear models: applications and data analysis methods* (2nd ed.). Thousand Oaks, CA: Sage.

Robinson, D. H., & Levin, J. R. (1997). Reflections on statistical and substantive significance, with a slice of replication. *Educational Researcher*, 26, 21–26.

Scheffe, H. (1959) *The analysis of variance*. New York: Wiley and Sons.

Serlin, R. C., Wampold, B. E., & Levin, J. R. (2003). Should providers of treatment be regarded as a random factor? If it ain't broke, don't "fix" it: comment on Siemer and Joormann. *Psychological Methods*, 8, 524–534.

Shadish, W. R., Cook, T. D., & Campbell, D. T. (2002). *Experimental and quasi-experimental designs for generalized causal inference*. Boston: Houghton Mifflin.

Shermer, M. (1997). *Why people believe weird things: pseudoscience, superstition, and other confusions of our time*. New York: Freeman.

Shine, L. C., & Bower, S. M. (1971). A one-way analysis of variance for single-subject designs. *Educational and Psychological Measurement*, 31, 105–113.

Silverman, S., & Solmon, M. (1998). The unit of analysis in field research: issues and approaches to design and analysis. *Journal of Teaching in Physical Education*, 17, 270–284.

Slavin, R. E. (1999). Educational research in the 21st century: lessons from the 20th. *Issues in Education: Contributions from Educational Psychology*, 5, 261–266.

Slavin, R. E. (2003, Apr.). *Practical research designs for randomized evaluations of large-scale educational interventions: seven desiderata*. Paper presented at the annual meeting of the American Educational Research Association, Chicago.

Stanovich, P. J., & Stanovich, K. E. (2003). *Using research and reason in education: how teachers can use scientifically based research to make curricular and instructional decisions*. Portsmouth, NH: RMC Research Corp. (available at *www.nifl.gov/parntershipforreading*)

Stevens, R. J., Slavin, R. E., & Farnish, A. M. (1991). The effects of cooperative learning and direct instruction in reading comprehension strategies on main idea identification. *Journal of Educational Psychology*, 83, 8–16.

Stone, A. A. (2003). Editorial: modification to "instructions to authors". *Health Psychology*, 22, 331.

Thompson, B. (1996). AERA editorial policies regarding statistical significance testing: three suggested reforms. *Educational Researcher*, 25, 26–30.

Toothaker, L. E., Banz, M., Noble, C., Camp, J., & Davis, D. (1983). N = 1 designs: the failure of ANOVA-based tests. *Journal of Educational Statistics*, 8, 289–309.

Wampold, B. E. (2001). *The great psychotherapy debate: models, methods, and findings*. Mahwah, NJ: Erlbaum.

Wampold, B. E., & Serlin, R. C. (2000). The consequence of ignoring a nested factor on measures of effect size in analysis of variance. *Psychological Methods*, 5, 425–433.

Wampold, B. E., & Worsham, N. L. (1986). Randomization tests for multiple-baseline designs. *Behavioral Assessment*, 8, 135–143.

Weiss, C. H. (2002). What to do until the random assigner comes. In F. Mosteller & R. Boruch (Eds.), *Evidence matters: randomized trials in education research* (pp. 198–224). Washington, DC: Brookings Institution Press.

Whitehurst, G. J., Epstein, J. N., Angell, A. L., Payne, A. C., Crone, D. A., & Fischel, J. E. (1994). Outcomes of an emergent literacy intervention in Head Start. *Journal of Educational Psychology*, 86, 542–555.

Wolf, M. M. (1978). Social validity: the case of subjective measurement or how applied behavior analysis is finding its heart. *Journal of Applied Behavior Analysis*, 11, 203–214.

CHAPTER

2

The No Child Left Behind Act, Scientific Research and Federal Educational Policy: A View from Washington, DC

VALERIE F. REYNA
University of Texas at Arlington

Three days after taking office in January 2001 as the 43rd president of the United States, George W. Bush announced proposals for educational reform that he described as "the cornerstone of my administration." Both the *No Child Left Behind Act* and the *Education Sciences Reform Act* were subsequently signed into law. In this chapter, I discuss the implications of this historic legislation for educational research. In particular, I draw on my experience in Washington, D.C. with these initiatives as a senior advisor in the U.S. Department of Education and, more important, as a scientist who has published extensively on a variety of topics in learning and memory.

BACKGROUND

Despite the terrorist attacks on September 11, 2001 and a national economic downturn, the *No Child Left Behind Act* was signed into law on January 8, 2002

Empirical Methods for Evaluating Educational Interventions

with broad bipartisan congressional support. With less fanfare, the *Education Sciences Reform Act* was signed into law on November 5, 2002 to establish a new federal research agency, capping a 2-year effort to ensure that educational practices in the United States be based on sound scientific evidence. The phrase "scientifically based research" is mentioned more than 110 times in the *No Child Left Behind Act* and, naturally, is the raison d'ètre behind the establishment of the research agency, the Institute of Education Sciences, that supports the gathering of statistical, evaluation, and research data relevant to education. Although I cannot cover all of the intricacies of these pieces of legislation in this chapter (the full texts can be accessed via the Web at *http://www.ed.gov/legislation/*ESEA02/ and *http://www.ed.gov/legislation/*Ed*Sciences*Ref, respectively), I will review definitions of scientific research offered in the legislation, domains of educational practice that are now mandated to be based on scientific research, and the implications of these mandates for the nature of educational research and the training of educational professionals. The main conclusion that emerges from this analysis is that if this legislation is to be successful, fundamental changes must be made in the kind of educational research that is conducted and in how colleges and universities prepare prospective researchers, practitioners, policy makers, and other educational decision makers.

OVERVIEW OF SOME CONCERNS THAT MOTIVATED THE LEGISLATION

The concerns that I now discuss are documented in press releases from the U.S. Department of Education, public statements by officials of both the legislative and executive branches, and numerous internal and external communications. For example, Figures 2.1–2.4 display the dismally low levels of educational achievement as measured by the National Assessment of Educational Progress (and increasing expenditures) that antedated the *No Child Left Behind* legislation. In Figure 2.1, reading achievement among fourth graders (a meager 32% are proficient) is plotted against federal spending and shows little improvement despite increases in federal spending (Figure 2.2). Figures 2.3 and 2.4 provide snapshots of even lower achievement levels in mathematics and science among twelfth graders. Figure 2.5 categorizes achievement in mathematics and reading by ethnic group, revealing still lower performance among a heretofore "invisible" minority, Hispanics. Against this depressing backdrop of low achievement, the stage was set for legislation that promised a new approach.

Some of the philosophic assumptions that motivated the legislation include the beliefs that current levels of academic achievement are unacceptably low, low achievement threatens our national economic competitiveness, almost all children (save those with profound cognitive disabilities)

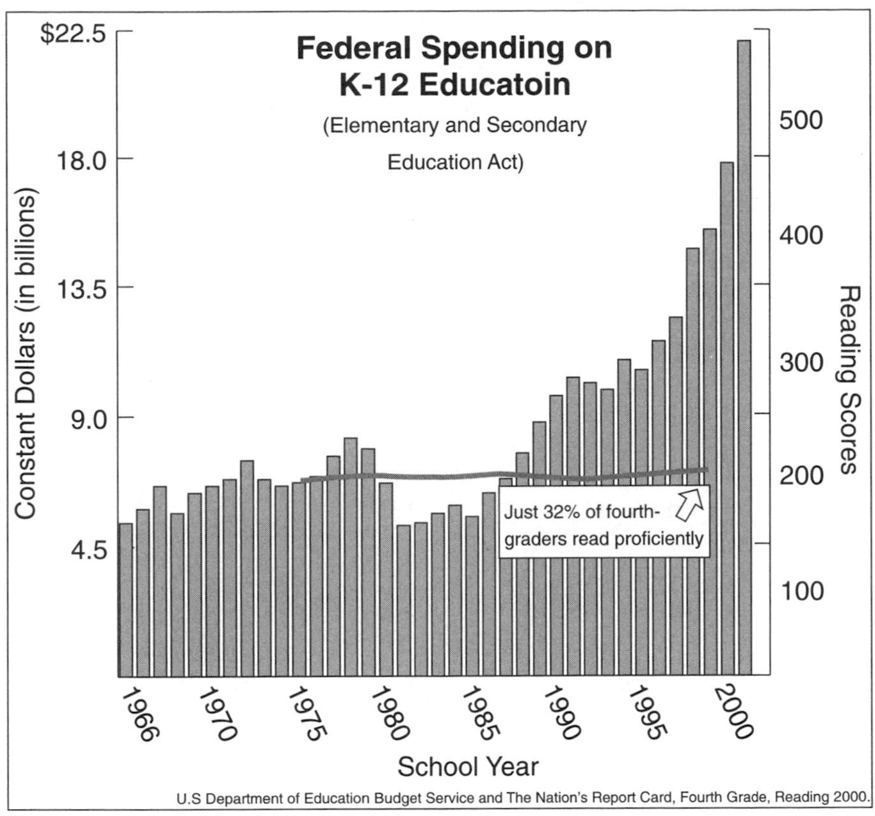

FIGURE 2.1

Federal spending on kindergarten through grade 12 education. (From U.S. Department of Education Budget Service and National Center for Education Statistics.)

can learn, and disparities in achievement across racial, ethnic, and socioeconomic groups are offensive to the American ethos of equal opportunity and are impractical in the light of changing demographics. The nation will increasingly depend on women and minorities to fill crucial roles in the economy, and the lower achievement of these groups (especially in science and technology) places the nation at risk. A corollary of the latter view is that disparities in educational outcomes across groups should not be papered over with summary statistics (Figure 2.5). The status quo of low achievement can be changed, it is argued, by basing educational practices on scientific research demonstrating effectiveness of those practices, assessing academic achievement reliably, and holding educators accountable for results.

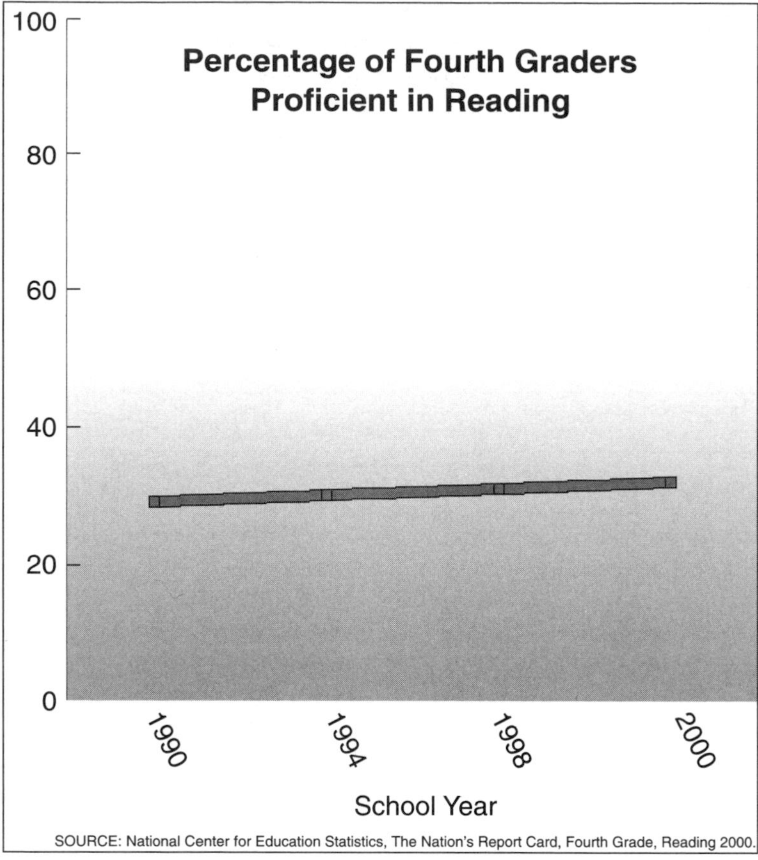

FIGURE 2.2

Percentage of fourth graders proficient in reading. (From National Center for Education Statistics.)

This thinking about accountability fits a triage model, which is implied in the title of the legislation *No Child Left Behind*, as contrasted with a metaphor of getting ahead or being first in the world in educational achievement. (The word *triage* in emergency medicine refers to the practice of prioritizing treatment so that patients who are most severely injured or ill, or whose situation is most critical, are stabilized first.) I should hasten to add that the legislation mentions and supports leading the world in education (e.g., providing financial incentives to encourage more students to take advanced placement courses), but the dominant metaphor involves shoring up achievement levels of the lowest achieving students to ensure a minimum acceptable level of reading and other basic skills. The logic is that resources are limited and should be assigned first to basic needs and second to anything else. Once basic verbal and quantitative skills have been mastered (as

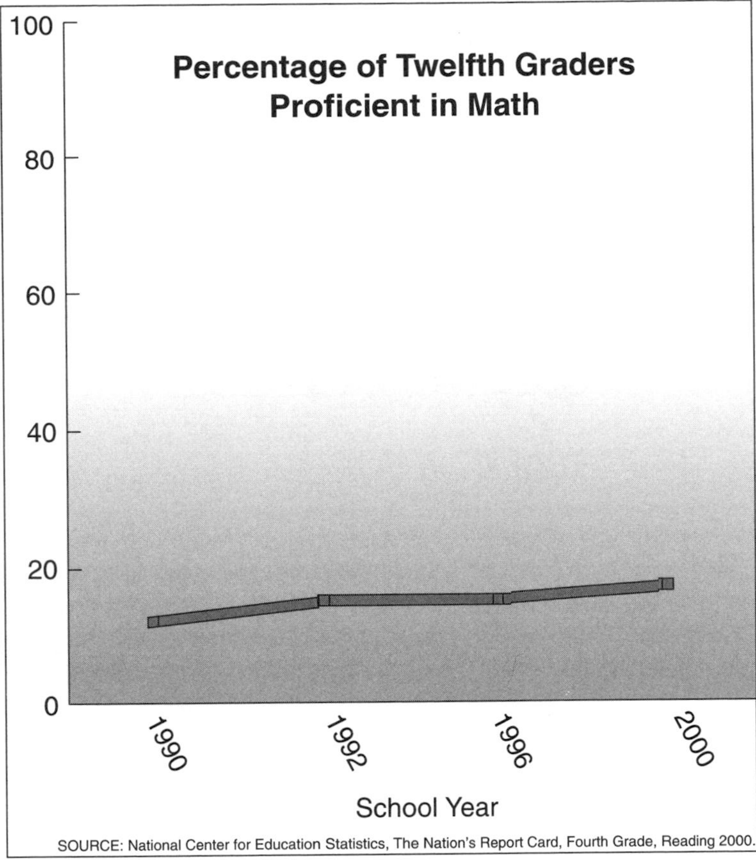

FIGURE 2.3

Percentage of twelfth graders proficient in mathematics. (From National Center for Education Statistics.)

well as content knowledge in domains such as history and science), students have the means to learn other material. Without basic skills, however, students are trapped, unable to read to learn as opposed to learn to read. A key assumption is that schools that excel well beyond minimum standards do not have to be concerned about assessments of basic skills; such advanced students should easily pass basic-skills tests. (The issues of which tests, how many tests, and their lengths should be separated from the core issue of accountability in principle.) Hence, concerns that high-achieving schools will abandon challenging curricula in order to "teach to the test" seem ill founded: Overpreparing for tests unnecessarily or administering invalid tests is not a consequence of what is in the legislation but are examples of poor implementation of sound principles. Therefore, supporters of the legislation maintain that if tests assess basic skills and students have

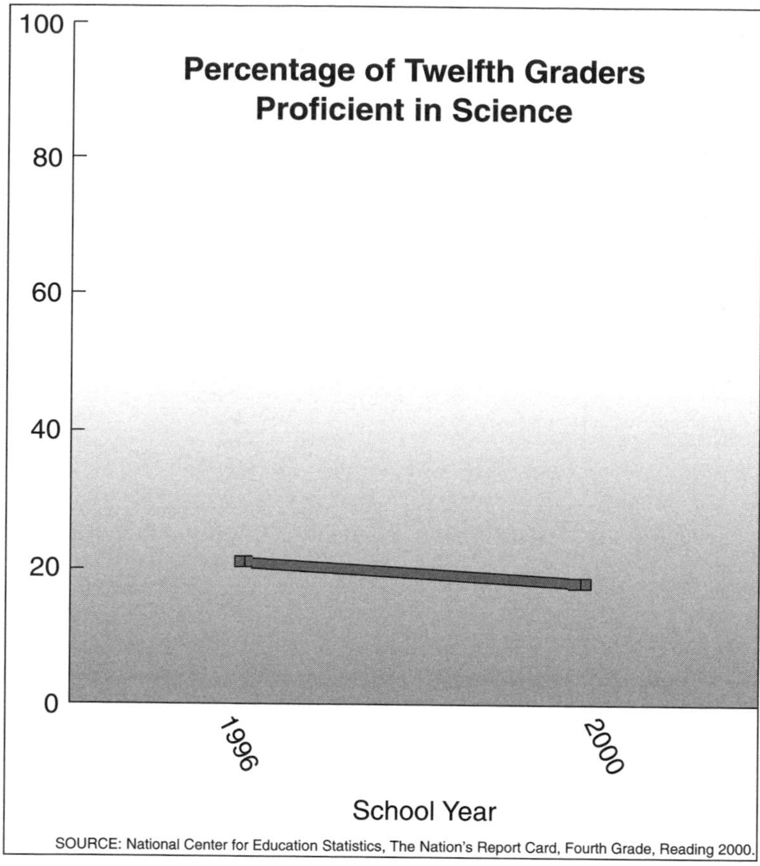

FIGURE 2.4

Percentage of twelfth graders proficient in science. (From National Center for Education Statistics.)

not mastered such skills to an acceptable level of proficiency, teaching to a reliable and valid test of necessary skills is desirable.

A theme that permeates both sets of legislation, *No Child Left Behind* and the *Education Sciences Reform Act*, is the need for greater emphasis on *learning*, not to the exclusion of other important educational outcomes but as the central goal of education. For example, the importance of promoting social and emotional development in preschool programs is openly acknowledged in the legislation, but the need to adequately prepare children for school during those crucial preschool years is emphasized. The assumption is that children will be emotionally healthier if they are successful academically, all other factors being equal, and that this can be accomplished in a supportive and nurturing environment. Although it seems illogical, much of the

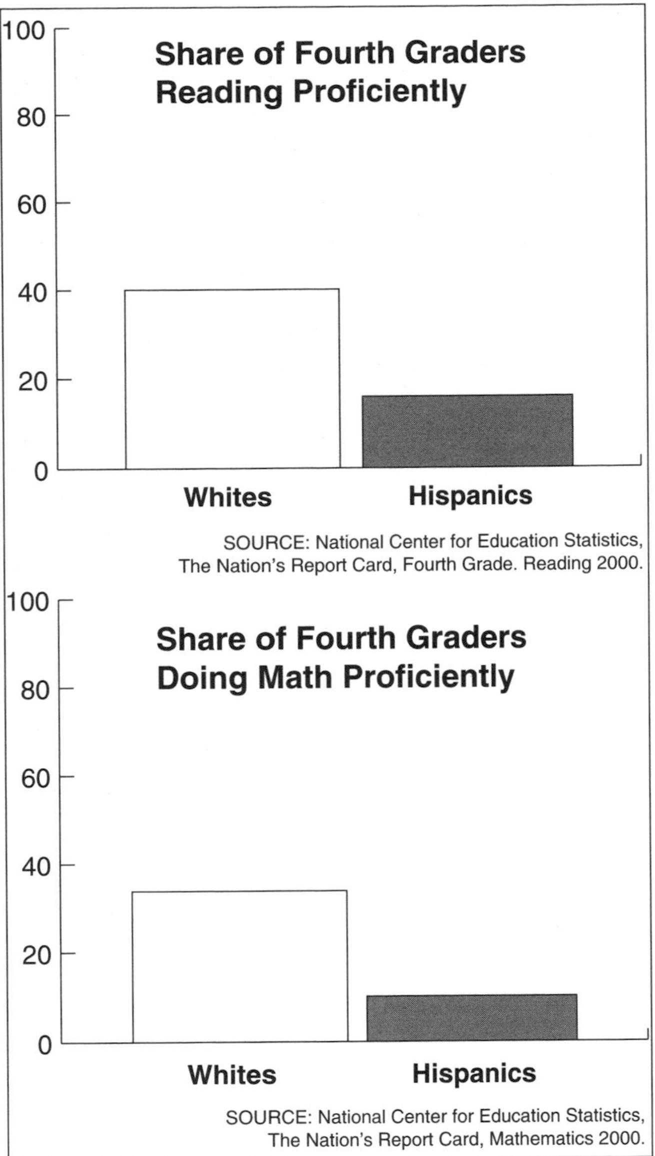

FIGURE 2.5

Percentage of white and Hispanic fourth graders proficient in reading **(A)** and in mathematics **(B)**. (From National Center for Education Statistics.)

research supported by the U.S. Department of Education heretofore has not focused on learning as a primary objective. Psychology departments, rather than colleges of education, and agencies other than those in education, have been the sources of much of the scientific evidence on learning and cognition relevant to education over the last several decades. (Readers should note that there are outstanding exceptions to this gross generalization.) Whether this trend will change as a result of the new legislation is debatable, but the need for interdisciplinary collaboration to address issues such as mathematics learning is straightforward; research has shown that better content knowledge of the disciplines in science and mathematics is associated with higher student achievement. Parents, students, and school personnel are unlikely to care whether the scientists who help students achieve adequate yearly progress are classified as psychologists, economists, mathematicians, sociologists, or some other discipline: The plural usage "education sciences" was intentional. Indeed, parochial concerns such as how much money has been "set aside" for researchers in colleges of education or for a specific type of research (e.g., qualitative research) regardless of the merit of individual proposals, will increasingly marginalize their proponents.

Thus, the four pillars of the *No Child Left Behind Act* are (a) accountability for results, (b) tempered by flexibility and local control, (c) increases in choices available to parents of students attending Title I schools that fail to meet state standards, and (d) an emphasis on educational programs and practices that have been clearly demonstrated to be effective through rigorous scientific research. The main components of the *Education Sciences Reform Act* are the replacement of the Office of Educational Research and Improvement with the Institute of Education Sciences, appointment of a director to serve a 6-year term (as opposed to terms tied to the coming and going of the administration), and the establishment of three divisions: the National Center for Education Research, the National Center for Education Statistics (reaffirming the old National Center for Education Statistics, better known as NCES), and the National Center for Education Evaluation and Regional Assistance. Two major changes that preceded the creation of the Institute of Education Sciences, but were carried over, were the development of peer review policies that more closely resemble those of other scientific research agencies and the transfer of substantial evaluation activities from other entities in the Department of Education to the research agency.

Enormously influential, the National Academy of Science's Committee on Scientific Principles for Education Research laid the groundwork for many of the aforementioned changes (Shavelson & Towne, 2002). Manuscripts of the Committee's report, and later the final published product, circulated during the period that legislation was under consideration, and dog-eared copies could be spied in the hands of key Congressional staffers and administration officials. The Committee concluded that educational research is subject to the same scientific methods as other fields and delineated the diverse approaches common to science. Sensibly, the Committee noted that methods should fit the questions posed in research: Descriptive research, based on objective measures, requires different methods than research seeking to establish cause-and-effect relationships. Cause-and effect questions require random assignment (whether comparisons are between or within subjects), which is, therefore, the gold standard for evaluating "what works." However, other kinds of data can narrow down hypotheses about what works, and what works is not the only important scientific question. Questions of mechanism—how a practice or program works—are a neglected area of research and are essential for generalizing proven practices to different contexts and populations (Reyna, 2004). Experimental designs are frequently used to test hypotheses about mechanism (see Bjorklund, 1995; Schwartz & Reisberg, 1991; Siegler, 1991). The Committee also made recommendations about research policy, pointing out that qualified researchers were necessary to staff, at least in part, a credible research agency. The Committee's efforts are currently being followed up by a distinguished panel of scholars under the leadership of the National Academy of Sciences. The Strategic Educational Research Partnership, or SERP, is also currently formulating recommendations for research in education. The President of the National Academy of Sciences has placed education at the forefront of concerns for this august body, and its formal involvement is maintained in the *Education Sciences Reform Act*.

The What Works Clearinghouse is another project that spanned the prelegislative and postlegislative periods (*wwcinfo@w-w-c.org*), both influencing and being influenced by the legislation. Building on the rationale for the Campbell Collaboration in the social sciences, which was, in turn, modeled on the Cochran Collaboration in medicine, the What Works Clearinghouse was intended to provide scientifically sound and independent reviews of practices and programs in education in a user-friendly format (Mosteller & Boruch, 2002). The statement of work soliciting competitive bids for the contract to implement a What Works Clearinghouse underwent numerous revisions to balance concerns about quality control and rigor with transparency and independence. The selection of a contract mechanism to accomplish this task indicates that the federal government, in this case the Institute of Education Sciences, will continue to exert control over the Clearinghouse. The primary contractors for the What Works Clearinghouse are the American Institutes for Research and the Campbell Collaboration, and include subcontractors such as Aspen Systems, Caliber Associates, and the Education Quality Institute (another organization, along with the Coalition for Evidence-Based Policy, that played a role in the impetus for evidence-based practice). The What Works Clearinghouse has completed the solicitation of public comment about procedures for applying scientific standards to evidence of effectiveness; procedures for adjudicating among claims of effectiveness are forthcoming.

Guiding the What Works Clearinghouse is a technical advisory group consisting of social science methodologists with the following:

- Significant records of accomplishment of peer-reviewed publications in high-quality journals
- Demonstrated proficiency in conducting and publishing empirical research
- Particular expertise in experimental and quasi-experimental designs, tests and measurements, and research synthesis

If education is to be based on evidence, such expertise is necessary (but not sufficient) for *any major policy recommendation* or any decision to adopt particular practices or programs.

SCIENTIFIC RESEARCH IN THE NO CHILD LEFT BEHIND ACT

Under section 9101 of general provisions of the *No Child Left Behind Act*, the definition of scientifically based research is given as follows:

> Except as otherwise provided, in this Act:
>
> (37) SCIENTIFICALLY BASED RESEARCH—The term "scientifically based research"
>
> (A) means research that involves the application of rigorous, systematic, and objective procedures to obtain reliable and valid knowledge relevant to education activities and programs; and
>
> (B) includes research that
>
> (i) employs systematic, empirical methods that draw on observation or experiment;
>
> (ii) involves rigorous data analyses that are adequate to test the stated hypotheses and justify the general conclusions drawn;
>
> (iii) relies on measurements or observational methods that provide reliable and valid data across evaluators and observers, across multiple measurements and observations, and across studies by the same or different investigators;
>
> (iv) is evaluated using experimental or quasi-experimental designs in which individuals, entities, programs, or activities are assigned to different conditions and with appropriate controls to evaluate the effects of the condition of interest, with a preference for random-assignment experiments, or other designs to the extent that those designs contain within-condition or across-condition controls;
>
> (v) ensures that experimental studies are presented in sufficient detail and clarity to allow for replication or, at a minimum, offer the opportunity to build systematically on their findings; and
>
> (vi) has been accepted by a peer-reviewed journal or approved by a panel of independent experts through a comparably rigorous, objective, and scientific review.

Scientists will recognize familiar notions of objective empirical observations, valid and reliable measures, appropriate experimental designs and controls, analyses that test hypotheses, replicability, and peer review. Although these methods have been available for centuries, and have been applied successfully to human learning (Schwartz & Reisberg, 1991), they have not been used consistently to inform educational practice. This has occurred despite worked examples being applied to educational research (Campbell & Stanley, 1963; Cronbach, 1982) and cogent appeals to educational researchers to enhance the credibility and impact of their work (Levin & O'Donnell, 1999).

Although professional wisdom will remain the source of many judgments about effective programs and practices simply because relevant evidence is unavailable, the onus is now on practitioners and other decision makers to use teaching methods with demonstrated effectiveness. Just as it is unimaginable to administer untested drugs to patients or, worse, to fail to administer proven life-saving treatments in favor of unproven ones, so it should become unimaginable to forego proven methods in education.

The *No Child Left Behind Act* does not rely on the discretion of researchers or educators but, rather, mandates the use of scientific research in various areas. In addition to the general provision to base practice on scientific research, as stated above, individual sections concerning a range of programs also mandate its use. For example, Title I assistance programs are *required* to use instructional strategies grounded in scientific research. School improvement plans, professional development, and technical assistance that districts provide to low-performing schools must also be based on strategies that have been proven effective. More specifically (from No Child Left Behind: A Desktop Reference, *http://www.ed.gov/offices/*OESE/*reference/*1*a.html*):

- States must assist school districts in developing or identifying high-quality, effective curricula aligned with state academic achievement standards and must disseminate such curricula to each district and school within the state.
- School districts are required to take into account the experience of model programs for the educationally disadvantaged and the findings of relevant scientifically based research as they develop their plans for services.
- Both school-wide and targeted assistance programs are required to use effective instructional methods and strategies based on scientifically based research.
- Schools identified for improvement must develop 2-year improvement plans that incorporate strategies based on scientifically based research. School districts must provide technical assistance to these schools, such as identifying and implementing professional development, instructional strategies, and methods of instruction that are grounded in scientifically based research and have been proven effective in addressing the specific instructional issues that caused the school to be identified.

• School districts identified for improvement must incorporate scientifically based research strategies in their improvement plans. State technical assistance to identified school districts must be based on scientifically based research.

• If a school district is identified for corrective action and a new curriculum is implemented, the state must provide professional development based on scientifically based research.

• School support teams, whose top priority is to provide assistance to schools subject to corrective action, are to be composed of persons who are knowledgeable about scientifically based research and practice on teaching and learning, as well as about successful school-wide projects, school reform, and improving educational opportunities for low-achieving students.

The Comprehensive School Reform (CSR) program builds on the Title I school-wide program by providing greater flexibility in the use of federal funds and by encouraging the implementation of effective strategies for all students in a school. The CSR program gives financial assistance to schools to implement whole-school reforms that reflect research on effective practices, helping students meet state academic standards. Grantees *must* rely on scientifically proven strategies; each CSR plan *must* include scientifically proven teaching and learning strategies.

Similar mandates are outlined for reading. *Reading First* is a formula grant program to states based on the number of 5- to 17-year-old students below the poverty line. States receiving grant awards from the U.S. Department of Education then make competitive grants to school districts. States must develop plans to assist districts in using "scientifically based" reading research to improve reading instruction and raise student achievement. The goal of *Reading First* is to ensure that every child can read at grade level (or higher) by the end of third grade through the implementation of instructional programs and materials, assessments, and professional development grounded in scientific reading research. More specifically,

• State education agencies or school districts must select professional development, instructional programs, and materials that focus on the five key areas that scientific reading research has identified as essential components of reading instruction: phonemic awareness, phonics, vocabulary, fluency, and reading comprehension.

• *Reading First* provides increased teacher professional development to ensure that teachers are able to teach scientifically based instructional programs.

The new *Early Reading First Program* extends the goals of *Reading First* to younger learners. It is a federally administered discretionary grant program in which the U.S. Department of Education makes competitive awards for up to 3 years to local school districts, other public or private organizations, or collaborations. These organizations apply for awards on behalf of preschool programs to strengthen the literacy components of early-childhood centers. Grantees must use *Early Reading First* funds to provide preschoolers with high-quality oral language and literature-rich environments, provide professional development to staff based on scientific research about methods that enhance linguistic and cognitive skills, and provide activities and instructional materials that are grounded in scientifically based reading research.

In some instances, preexisting programs were retained in the legislation but strengthened through mandates involving research. For example, the *Even Start Family Literacy Program* provides low-income families with integrated literacy services for parents and their young children (birth through age 7). *Even Start* is primarily a state-administered discretionary grant program in which states hold competitions to award subgrants to partnerships of local school districts and other organizations. *Even Start* programs have new requirements under *No Child Left Behind* to use scientifically based research evidence to design program activities, especially reading-readiness activities for preschool children.

Many of the programs in the legislation address the means by which skills and knowledge are attained, rather than the skills themselves. For example, educational technologies have proliferated in schools despite their expense, rapid obsolescence, and outstandingly poor record of inspiring competent scientific research on effectiveness in promoting learning (Reyna, Brainerd, Effken, Bootzin, & Lloyd, 2001). The legislation is aimed at improving this state of affairs by emphasizing the "implementation of proven strategies" and by requiring districts to base the strategies they use for integrating technology into curricula and instruction on reviews of relevant research. Specifically, the goals of the Educational Technology State Grants Program are to improve learning through technology in elementary and secondary schools and to assist every student in becoming technologically literate by the end of eighth grade. These goals will be achieved, it is hoped, by integrating technology resources and systems with teacher training and professional development to establish research-based instructional models. The program targets funds primarily to school districts that serve low-income students.

Other programs address research-based teacher training and development as a means of achieving better learning. These programs include *Early Childhood Educator Professional Development*, *Teaching American History*, *Improving Teacher Quality State Grants*, and the *Mathematics and Science Partnerships*. The *Early Childhood Educator Professional Development* program funds partnerships whose goal is to improve the knowledge and skills of early childhood educators who work in mainly low socioeconomic areas by basing professional development on scientific research and training those professionals to apply the best available research on early childhood pedagogy, child development, and learning. The *Teaching American History* program aims to increase students' knowledge of history by providing funds to school districts to design, implement, and demonstrate effective, research-based professional development programs. The *Improving Teacher Quality State Grants* program also stipulates the use of scientifically based professional development interventions. All activities supported with Title II funds must be based on a review of scientifically based research that shows how such interventions are expected to improve student achievement. As the Desktop Reference helpfully notes,

> For example, if a state decides to fund interventions such as professional development in math, the state must be able to show how the particular activities are grounded in a review of activities that have been associated with increases in student achievement.

Finally, the *Mathematics and Science Partnerships* program is a discretionary grant program that supports enhanced training and recruitment of high-quality math and science teachers. Grants are targeted to partnerships of high-need school districts and to science, mathematics, and engineering schools within universities, giving districts and universities joint responsibility for educating teachers. (Note that cognitive scientists—experts on student learning—are not mandated partners, but learning experts could help teachers more effectively transmit science content.) In years that the program receives more than $100 million, the U.S. Department of Education will allocate funds to states by formula so that they can award subgrants to partnerships of institutions of higher education and high-need local education agencies. Grants are awarded for 3 years and grantees must comply with the following:

- Institute reforms that are aligned with academic standards in mathematics and science.
- Engage in teacher training and learning activities that are based on scientific research.

The language of the section on Mathematics and Science Partnerships emphasizes the use of high-quality, research-based practices in instruction. Partnerships are authorized to conduct only those training activities that are based on scientific research. Whether this is construed as training that is broadly commensurate with research or for which formal evaluations of specific programs have been conducted remains to be seen.

Addressing learning and teacher training, the section on limited English proficiency reiterates some of the features of the broad definition of "scientifically based research" in the General Provisions. Foremost, language instruction curricula used to teach limited English proficient children must be tied to scientifically based research and demonstrated to be effective.

(The Institute of Education Sciences convened an expert panel of empirical scientists to review this literature, the National Literacy Panel on Language Minority Children and Youth; their preliminary report is expected in 2003.) School districts must use Title III funds to provide high-quality language instruction programs that are based on scientific research and that have demonstrated effectiveness in both improving English proficiency and student achievement. State education agencies have similar constraints. In addition, professional development must be informed by scientifically based research that demonstrates its effectiveness in increasing children's English proficiency or teachers' knowledge and skills.

Given the increased emphasis on students with limited English proficiency in many quarters, it is useful to note that specific language concerning multiple approaches to research is included in Section 3222 of the legislation. That is,

> (a) ADMINISTRATION—The Secretary shall conduct research activities authorized by this subpart through the Office of Educational Research and Improvement in coordination and collaboration with the Office of English Language Acquisition, Language Enhancement, and Academic Achievement for Limited English Proficient Students.
>
> (b) REQUIREMENTS—Such research activities
>
> (1) shall have a practical application to teachers, counselors, paraprofessionals, school administrators, parents, and others involved in improving the education of limited English proficient children and their families;
>
> (2) may include research on effective instruction practices for multilingual classes, and on effective instruction strategies to be used by a teacher or other staff member who does not know the native language of a limited English proficient child in the teacher's or staff member's classroom;
>
> (3) may include establishing (through the National Center for Education Statistics in consultation with experts in second language acquisition and scientifically based research on teaching limited English proficient children) a common definition of limited English proficient child' for purposes of national data collection; and
>
> (4) shall be administered by individuals with expertise in second language acquisition, scientifically based research on teaching limited English proficient children, and the needs of limited English proficient children and their families.
>
> (c) FIELD-INITIATED RESEARCH-
>
> (1) IN GENERAL—The Secretary shall reserve not less than 5 percent of the funds made available to carry out this section for field-initiated research conducted by recipients of grants under subpart 1 or this subpart who have received such grants within the previous 5 years. Such research may provide for longitudinal studies of limited English proficient children or teachers who serve such children, monitoring the education of such children from entry into language instruction educational programs through secondary school completion.
>
> d) CONSULTATION—The Secretary shall consult with agencies, organizations, and individuals that are engaged in research and practice on the education of limited English proficient children, language instruction educational programs, or related research, to identify areas of study and activities to be funded under this section.
>
> e) DATA COLLECTION—The Secretary shall provide for the collection of data on limited English proficient children as part of the data systems operated by the Department.

Last in this nonexhaustive review of programs that explicitly mention the use of scientific research is a program that does not directly address the acquisition of skills or the inculcation of training, the *Dropout Prevention Program*. The program is primarily a grant program to state education agencies and local school districts to implement research-based, sustainable, and coordinated school dropout prevention and reentry programs. As the researchers who spoke at the White House Conference on Character and Community on June 19, 2002 (*http://www.ed.gov/inits/character/*) pointed out, there is a nascent body of scientific evidence indicating that prosocial behavior can be fostered by school-based programs and important outcomes such as reductions in dropping out and drug use can be achieved using scientifically tested interventions.

IMPLICATIONS FOR EDUCATIONAL RESEARCH AND THE TRAINING OF EDUCATIONAL PROFESSIONALS

Other writers have presaged many of the implications of the *No Child Left Behind Act* and the *Education Science Reform Act* for the nature of research, and I will not attempt to recapitulate them here (e.g., Levin & O'Donnell, 1999; Shavelson & Towne, 2002; Slavin, in press). The bottom line of both pieces of legislation is that research in education must now satisfy the canons of science, just as scientific research in other fields has done for some time (guidelines in Campbell & Stanley [1963] and Cronbach [1982] remain timely). The *No Child Left Behind Act* mandates determining what educational programs and practices have been clearly demonstrated to be effective through rigorous scientific research. Federal funding will then be targeted to support the programs and teaching methods that improve student learning and achievement. How broadly these strictures are interpreted remains to be seen. However, it seems inevitable that the standards for research in education have begun to move upward, and practitioners and decision makers who adhere to high scientific standards will find that their programs and practices satisfy the law. Although there may be some programs and practices that slip by for which evidence is weak or nonexistent, the appetite for science will expand in the next decades for several reasons.

First, as more teachers, administrators, and policy makers become educated about the scientific method, they will become more skeptical consumers. Less snake oil will be sold and more medicine that is real will become available. As has happened in other fields when the flow of research information is facilitated and disputants accept that scientific evidence will be used to settle disputes, the good will drive out the bad. Signals of this attitude change in the schools include a far more receptive response to the use of random assignment to groups in school-based research. Only a year ago, it would have been accurate to assert that schools were philosophically opposed to "experimenting" with their students (see Reyna, 2004). Today, although still a minority attitude but one that is rapidly changing, more school personnel understand the rationale behind random assignment and recognize that, for important decisions about instructional programs or practices, random assignment to groups is essential for finding out what works. Rather than being unethical, in fact, experiments are the ethical choice for responsible educators who realize that they have an obligation to find out what works for the sake of the students.

Education faces a special challenge with respect to accepting scientific evidence as the basis for settling disputes. Educational researchers have often stooped to ad hominem personal attack in lieu of data, impugning the motives of those who disagree with them. The public and educators must learn to vehemently reject this form of argumentation. Journalists must begin to ask after every claim about educational mechanisms or effectiveness, what is the evidence for that conclusion? Because of the importance of journalism ("the press") in our constitution and in societal progress, all reporters must become science reporters to the extent that they understand the basics of scientific methods and can ask non gullible questions of advocates espousing particular programs or educational approaches. If such advocates are mistaken, their programs and approaches are not innocuous; they threaten the well-being of the nation's children. Schools of journalism should provide adequate preparation through coursework that exposes students to scientific methods and scientific skepticism, and through apprenticeships with empirical scientists during the training process. Much nonsense and damage could be avoided with better-informed reporting.

It is well known from psychological research that negative information has a greater impact than otherwise-comparable positive information (e.g., Nisbett & Ross, 1980). Science provides a practiced self-discipline in reining in such normal human reactions: We must accept that people with disagreeable motives can be correct just as those we admire can be wrong. We must accept that intuitive plausibility is not the same as evidence. The facts care little about how beautiful, compelling, or coherent our stories are or whether the scientist in question is a likeable person. Moreover, critical thinking must be applied to all educational claims. It is perhaps an indictment of our educational system that much of the debate in the pages of educational magazines and journals would not pass muster as "critical thinking" (see Halpern, 2003, for definitions and research on critical thinking). For example, a vocal minority has cast aspersions on one of the few comprehensive school reform programs with respectable scientific evidence indicating positive outcomes. *Success for All* is impugned as *Success for Some*, with much winking and nodding about how researchers have characterized their data. Unfortunately, the price of success in educational research is too often unsubstantiated attacks. However, it should be clear that no educational program is expected to achieve absolute 100% success and that the title conveys an ideal. Indeed, the researchers report less than perfect results. Why would such an aspersion have any appeal to a reasonably intelligent audience (it has been passed on with little critical comment in respectable outlets such as the *Washington Post*)? Similarly, I have heard educators and researchers debate whether a program should be described as "effective" because it is not equally effective with every student. Antibiotics are not 100% effective with every patient, and yet no one is seriously advocating that we should discourage their use when indicated or that they be considered ineffective because they fail to achieve "success for all." It seems that only in education would such ludicrous arguments be taken seriously.

Second, as the word gets out that there are superior instructional methods that are more likely to produce learning, educators will clamor to have access to the methods that yield "adequate yearly progress" as opposed to frustration, disappointment, and loss of federal funding. Funds will be increasingly directed to after-school and other programs that have been scientifically demonstrated to prevent drug use and violence among youths. As students, parents, and educators experience these outcomes, they will work to maintain and enhance them. The key to achieving these consequences of pressure to maintain effective programs, naturally, is that Congress and the administration must hold fast to their resolve to avoid fatal compromises that lower the standards for accountability.

Such experience with positive outcomes has characterized early reading interventions, which have been shown to reduce reading disabilities and, consequently, the need for costly special education. Early reading research has been a scientific success story that has inspired new requests for proposals for research in reading comprehension, mathematics learning, teacher quality, and other areas where more research is needed. In addition, there is widespread acknowledgment that, as noted in the description of the Cognition and Student Learning Program of the Institute of Education Sciences, "the most important outcome of education is student learning." The description goes on,

> In order for students to succeed in school, they must attend to, remember, and reason effectively about information, whether that information is provided by teachers, textbooks, or via computers. These three components of cognition are the basis for achievement in reading, science, mathematics, and other school subjects.

Because it encompasses the encoding, processing, and learning of information, *cognition is the basic science of education*. Thus, all educational professionals should be thoroughly conversant with research on how students attend to, remember, and reason about information.

Specifically, to be relevant to the practice of education under the new legislation, teacher-training programs should inculcate deep conceptual understanding of rigorous research on cognition and, for those who teach younger learners, on developmental differences in cognition. Topics in basic (attention, memory, and perception) and higher-order (reasoning, problem solving, and decision making) cognition are a must, and would include the following:

> Attention; working memory; learning processes (acquisition and retention); storage in and retrieval from long-term memory; interference and inhibition; executive function and monitoring; metamemory or memory strategies; meaning extraction (literal and figurative) for words, sentences, and discourse; inference and critical thinking (semantic, logical, and pragmatic inferences, situation models, and other mental representations); similarity, categorization, and analogic reasoning; nonverbal reasoning (e.g., spatial, scientific, and quantitative reasoning); domain-specific knowledge (e.g., biology, calculus, or American history) and conceptual development; and judgment and decision making.

Training for leadership or policy-making positions should also include teaching these topics as fundamental to understanding student learning. Conversely, those who lacked this crucial knowledge would not be adequately prepared to make decisions about instructional approaches, textbook adoption, or other policies or practices intended to produce learning. In addition, an intensive course or courses in statistics, assessment, research design, and methodology should be mandatory for teachers, leaders, and, ideally, policy makers. No one should graduate from a bona fide college or university with a degree in education without knowledge of what a valid and reliable test is and how that is judged. These topics are not the only subjects that educators should know about, but their importance is much greater given the new legislation. The topics have been successfully taught to these populations in the past, so arguments about feasibility ignore the fact that this has already been accomplished, albeit not equally well everywhere. Teaching important material well, however, ought to be the business of education.

As this discussion implies, many colleges of education will have to make changes to remain relevant to educational practice in the 21st century. Presidents and provosts of institutions of higher education should immediately assess whether their deans are knowledgeable and comfortable with scientific approaches to education. Those who are not comfortable with science are analogous to the buggy whip makers of the latter century at the dawn of the era of the automobile. It is often remarked that change in higher education occurs slowly. Few central administrators are acting on the realization that the train is moving rapidly forward without the deans and faculty of many colleges of education on board. A conversation with a respected president of a Research I university (a classification indicating a major research institution) illustrates the disconnect that is widely evident: In discussing potential candidates for a deanship of his college of education, the president remarked that he was leery of hiring an outstanding researcher because of his concern about being relevant to what really happens in schools, implying that research and practice were somehow antithetical. As the review of the new legislation indicates, high levels of research competence must now be viewed as minimum qualifications to be relevant to educational practice in schools. The changes made to the *Elementary and Secondary Education Act* as reauthorized by the *No Child Left Behind* legislation are a challenge, and they present numerous problems of appropriate implementation that would benefit from the dedication and experience of members of colleges of education. The changes are also an unprecedented opportunity to make progress on behalf of students and be central to a top national concern. If they rise to the challenge and respond, because of the emphasis on research in the legislation, colleges and universities can be more important than they have ever been in educational practice.

POSTSCRIPT: PROMISING OPPORTUNITIES, LOOMING OBSTACLES

Research has been published that fits the model I have described: Research that is rigorous, theoretically informed, and useful in the classroom (e.g., in mathematics learning, Ashcraft & Kirk, 2001; Carpenter, Fennema, Peterson, Chiang, & Loef, 1989; Nye, Hedges, Konstantopoulos; 2001; Siegler, 1988). These and many other studies provide a solid foundation for future work, including new research programs initiated under the aegis of *No Child Left Behind* and the *Education Sciences Reform Act* (see also the American Psychological Society *Observer*, 2003). One project, for example, infuses a Web-based science curriculum for middle and high school students with "desirable difficulties," counterintuitive ways of improving learning to maximize long-term retention. These desirable difficulties include spacing rather than massing study sessions, reducing feedback, and using tests as learning interventions. Intuitive plausibility would deliver a "thumbs down" for most of these interventions, and, yet, the evidence indicates that they have the potential to revolutionize the efficiency of learning. An educational researcher (Marcia Linn), who has worked in the "trenches" in schools, and a cognitive psychologist (Robert Bjork), who was inspired to translate basic research into practice, joined forces on this project to improve education. Sustained and sufficient funding is necessary to build a critical mass of such researchers, innovative and willing to tackle educationally significant issues. Although some think of educationally relevant research as mainly random-assignment evaluation studies that can be churned out formulaically with assured payoffs, it is crucial to focus the attention of the nation's best minds on educational problems. The best minds will not be drawn to doing unimaginative "piece work" performed at the government's behest. Furthermore, although formulaic evaluation can be highly useful, it is not the source of new ideas. Without innovative research, there will eventually be little to evaluate. Strictly basic research cannot be counted on to develop in the direction of educationally significant issues. For evidence-based education to become a reality, relevant research must be nurtured at each point along the continuum from basic to applied science, with improving learning the ultimate goal.

It should be noted that a major factor that will affect efficient progress toward evidence-based education is human-subjects regulations. Human-subjects regulations could be the undoing of the progress toward science enshrined in the *No Child Left Behind Act*. Because of what seems to be a sincere desire to protect human subjects, but without any realistic cost–benefit analysis of the burdens of regulations, regulations under consideration at this time may present an unreasonable burden to researchers. Regulations may become so onerous that many researchers, especially good ones, will refuse to conduct research in schools. According to the legislation, this would be a problem because conducting school-based research is in the national interest. On the one hand, most behavioral science research that is confidential and anonymous does not place subjects at greater risk than normal activities of living, but is nevertheless subjected to levels of bureaucracy that are incommensurate with its potential risk at great expense to the nation. Ironically, the ethics of such practices have been increasingly questioned. On the other hand, researchers must become more sensitive to valid concerns about privacy and interference with relationships within families, as expressed by members of Congress and others. For example, parents certainly have a right to prevent the solicitation of personal family information from their minor children. The use of informed parental consent, which is current practice, along with technology that strips personal identifiers from data but allows researchers to connect data records from the same individual may hold the key to rational compromise on this issue.

CONCLUSIONS

Scientists and policy makers have come to Washington in the past, worked very hard, and have had relatively little success in passing legislation or raising standards for educational research. (As with every statement I have made in this chapter, there are notable exceptions to this conclusion.) Within a short window of time, in contrast, spanning roughly the spring of 2001 to the fall of 2002, two landmark pieces of legislation were passed that could substantially change educational practice in the nation for the better. The most important aspect of this legislation was not any specific program or policy but, rather, the wholesale embrace of the scientific method for generating knowledge that will govern educational practice in classrooms across the nation. Scientific evidence is not sufficient to decide practice; human values and other considerations are also important. However, evidence is a necessary precursor to responsible decision making about issues that affect students' lives. Furthermore, because scientific hypotheses (e.g., about what works or how it works) are subject to empirical challenges, science is self-correcting. As inconsistencies develop, the conventional wisdom of the day (even when it is based on scientific evidence) can be overthrown with new, contrary data. Thus, science, like democracy, has within it the mechanism for renewal and progress, building on earlier knowledge to achieve even better results.

I have included quotations from the legislation to illustrate the detail and vigor with which the scientific method is advocated in the legislation, and that the method is one that real scientists would recognize and adhere to (with the usual quibbling that scientists are prone to). The quotations also illustrate the gamut of educational programs and practices that are now privy to constraints involving scientific evidence of effectiveness. The imperfections in the legislation are also apparent, but these consist mostly of issues of implementation rather than principle, in my view. The centrality of research for actual practice in schools, and, thus, of institutions that generate research, such as colleges and universities (but also foundations, federal agencies and other institutions) is plain. The urgent need for new and better training for educators and leaders (especially deans of colleges of education) is evident, but is presently virtually unmet.

Although researchers should feel encouraged that what they do is so strongly valued, there will no doubt be a tendency to defend past research, disciplinary turf, or the way things used to be. I should point out that there have been successes in the past. Administrators of the National Institute of Education, a previous incarnation of the Institute of Education Sciences, advocated some similar policies and created such noteworthy programs as "scholars in residence," an excellent idea for attracting successful and highly qualified scientists to government service. With that homage to the past, I would encourage researchers, educators, and policy makers to put aside narrow concerns and turn to the future. What are the assessments that ensure accountability, but also inform teachers about areas of learning that need attention, and place the lowest possible burden on the valuable instructional time of students? How do we foster content knowledge as well as reasoning or critical thinking, both essential in the modern economy? What kind of research education is necessary for practitioners to achieve conceptual understanding of learning so that they can successfully adapt effective practices to different contexts and populations? These are only some of the questions that could be asked, but they illustrate the lack of sound scientific answers about basic issues in education. Many researchers continue to urge the use of exploratory methods for hypothesis generation in education after decades of like research. I would submit that there is a surfeit of hypotheses, intuitive speculations, and plausible claims, and a corresponding scarcity of supportive empirical evidence. The most practical achievement of research at this time would be the development of empirically tested theories of learning that could be used to reliably predict which instructional practices will produce which outcomes for which students. Few agencies or foundations are supporting this kind of explanatory and predictive research. The *No Child Left Behind Act* and the *Education Sciences Reform Act* provide opportunities to harness the power of science, including predictive theory, to allow every student access to the American dream. Drawing from multiple disciplines, a new kind of researcher will be needed to achieve this goal, the *educational scientist*.

References

American Psychological Association (2002). Making a difference to education: Will psychology pass up the chance? APA *Monitor* Volume 33, No. 7 July/August.

American Psychological Society (2003). Science goes to school. APS *Observer* Volume 16, Number 4, April.

Ashcraft, M. H., & Kirk, E. P. (2001). The relationship among working memory, math anxiety, and performance. *Journal of Experimental Psychology—General*, 130(2), 224–237.

Bjorklund, D. F. (1995). *Children's thinking: developmental function and individual differences* (2nd ed.). Pacific Grove, CA: Brooks/Cole.

Campbell, D. T., & Stanley, J. C. (1963). *Experimental and quasi-experimental designs for research*. Boston: Houghton Mifflin Company.

Carpenter, T. P., Fennema, E., Peterson, P. L., Chiang, C., & Loef, M. (1989). Using knowledge of children's mathematics thinking in classroom teaching: an experimental study. *American Educational Research Journal*, 26, 499–531.

Cronbach, L. (1982). *Designing evaluations of educational and social programs*, San Francisco, CA: Jossey-Bass.

The Elementary and Secondary Education Act as Reauthorized by the *No Child Left Behind Act of* 2001; Public Law 107–110, Passed January 8, 2002.

Education Sciences Reform Act, Public Law 107–279, Passed November 5, 2002.

Halpern, D. F. (2003). *Thought and knowledge: an introduction to critical thinking* (4th ed.). Mahwah, NJ: Lawrence Erlbaum Associates.

Levin, J. R., & O'Donnell, A. M. (1999). What to do about educational research's credibility gaps? *Issues in Education: Contributions from Educational Psychology*, 5, 177–229.

Mosteller, F., & Boruch, R. (2002). *Evidence matters: randomized trials in education research*. Washington, DC: Brookings Institution Press.

Nisbett, R., & Ross, L. (1980). *Human inference: strategies and shortcomings of social judgment*, New York: Academic Press.

Nye, B., Hedges, L.V., & Konstantopoulos, S. (2001). The long-term effects of small classes in early grades: lasting benefits in mathematics achievement at grade 9. *Journal of Experimental Education*, 69(3), 245–257.

Reyna, V. F. (2004). Why scientific research? The importance of evidence in changing educational practice. In P. McCardle & V. Chhabra (Eds.), *The voice of evidence in reading research* (pp. 47–58).

Reyna, V. F., Brainerd, C. J., Effken, J., Bootzin, R., & Lloyd, F. J. (2001). The psychology of human computer mismatches. In C. Wolfe (Ed.), *Learning and teaching on the world wide web* (pp. 23–44). San Diego, CA: Academic Press.

Schwartz, B., & Reisberg, D. (1991). *Learning and memory*. New York: W.W. Norton.

Shavelson, R. J., & Towne, L. (Eds.) (2002). *Scientific research in education*. Washington, D.C.: National Academy Press.

Siegler, R. S. (1988). Strategy choices, procedures, and the development of multiplication skill. *Journal of Experimental Psychology: General, 117*, 258–275.

Siegler, R. S. (1991). *Children's thinking* (2nd ed.). Englewood Cliffs, NJ: Prentice Hall.

Slavin, R. E. (in press). Evidence-based education policies: transforming educational practice and research. *Educational Leadership*.

CHAPTER

3

Dissing Science: Selling Scientifically Based Educational Practices to a Nation that Distrusts Science

DIANE F. HALPERN
Claremont McKenna College

I was surprised and somewhat awestruck when, a few years ago, I was asked to present testimony to the U.S. House of Representatives Committee on Science. The topic of my testimony was "applying the science of learning" (Halpern, 2001, *http://www.house.gov/science/research/reshearings.htm*). The main theses of my presentation were clearly outlined, and as far as I was concerned, persuasively argued. I checked and rechecked data as I prepared to appear before this powerful group of elected officials charged with the immense task of formulating laws that would advance science at a time in history when science is more important than it has ever been before.

Because I had a short presentation time to advocate for the science of learning, I outlined a few main points that would make the strongest case for science. First, I explained that the study of human cognition is an empirical science with a solid theoretical basis. Second, although scien-

Empirical Methods for Evaluating Educational Interventions

tifically based knowledge of how people think, learn, and remember should be central to educational reform efforts, the sad reality is that there is a schism between the scientists conducting basic laboratory work in cognition and many of the applied practitioners—teachers, curriculum consultants, school administrators, educational policy makers—who tend to view laboratory findings as artificial and irrelevant to real-world education. My third point was that too many students are failing to achieve at an educational level needed for effective citizenship or a skilled work force, thus confirming the worst fears of the blue ribbon panel who, in 1983, described us as "A Nation at Risk" (National Commission on Excellence in Education, 1983) and the various expert panels who reconfirmed that 20 years later, we are still at risk (Peterson, 2003). I urged the Committee on Science to act quickly by affirming the need for empirically validated methods for instruction and creating opportunities for high-quality research that was designed to further our knowledge of how to make learning more effective and efficient. Finally, I launched into a short discourse about practices that enhance long-term retention and transfer and thanked them for their support of educational practices that were solidly grounded in science. The reception to these comments was even sadder than I had imagined.

On the way into the hearing room, a helpful legislative aide coached me about how to provide effective testimony to the Committee on Science. More than once she warned me not to present too many numbers because they tend to get bored and confused by data. A good story works best, she advised. Did I know someone who showed great gains in learning and then went on to be a solid citizen because a teacher changed to one of the methods I was advocating? I could not believe that I should tell anecdotes in an attempt to persuade the Committee on Science that educational methods supported by research findings were more likely to provide beneficial outcomes than those that are not. Wouldn't such an approach be insulting to the highest elected officials in the United States who are the national guardians of science?

I now know the answer to what I had intended to be a rhetorical question. When I completed my testimony, the first question I was asked was about Thomas Edison—did I know he filed 1,093 patents and that he had only a few years of formal education? Didn't Edison's phenomenal success prove that children need only to work harder to succeed? I countered that if Edison had lived today and had only 3 years of formal education, he would probably be working at a minimum-wage job—and he was a creative genius, not a model for formulating educational policies for the United States, a response that did little to endear me to the committee member who asked about Edison. The second question I was asked concerned finances. Why had the amount of money spent on education increased steeply over the last decade, while the percentage of children who were reading at a level of proficiency necessary for high-quality jobs remained flat? Of course, I really could not answer that question, but I speculated that the mismatch between spending and achievement was related to the large number of children for whom English is not their best language and the fact that a greater proportion of the population was staying in school longer than in previous generations. I do not know how many of the committee members considered this a plausible explanation. I learned some hard lessons that day, ones that both emphasize the difficulty that advocates for empirically based educational practices face and the genuine need to teach the value of and reasons for science to students at every level of education and to reinforce these messages throughout life.

LESSON 1: PUBLIC POLICIES ARE OFTEN MADE BY ANECDOTE

We like stories—they make abstract concepts come alive and provide flesh and bones to colorless data. Astute readers will realize that I began with an anecdote about how little the Committee on Science wanted to know about the science behind the science of learning. A single vivid example can often outweigh a huge body of data collected from a random sample of a population; whereas anecdotes are self-selected, based on a sample size of 1, subject to all of the biases of memory, and likely to be atypical because they would not be told if they represented an expected outcome. It seems as though humans cannot think about very large (or very small) numbers, possibly because the personal experiences of one's self and one's close friends were the only information available to humans to guide their decision making prior to the advent of mass media, so thinking about results from large samples is not a task that comes easily or naturally to most people.

Whenever politicians comment on the state of our nation, we can find evidence of the preference for and reliance on anecdotes. Communicators know that if they want to persuade an audience, they need to use vivid examples to "bring home" their point—the small-business person who went bankrupt, the children whose mother was killed in an accident, the sick person denied medical coverage, and so forth. Even people who know better find the appeal of an anecdote hard to resist. We can teach the public the difference between anecdotes and science and the reasons why we need science as a foundation for sound policies. This will not be an easy lesson to teach or learn because there seems to be a natural affinity for stories and distaste for science, but it can be done.

LESSON 2: POLITICAL PHILOSOPHY IS OFTEN STRONGER THAN SCIENCE

One of the main reasons why educational research rarely provides data that actually are used in decision making is that teachers, the general public, funding agencies, state and federal legislators, and just about every other potential consumer of educational research believes that they already know the correct answers. The representative who quizzed me about Thomas Edison's amazing accomplishments believed that personal attributes, such as the willingness to work hard, were far more important in determining academic success than anything that teachers do in school. Such a philosophy is part of a larger belief system that extends to what and how public funds should be spent, personal theories about intelligence, and where one falls on a spectrum ranging from endpoints that are sometimes (and erroneously) labeled "spend-thrift democrat" to "tight-fisted republican" and beyond. If data were to contradict one's personal belief system, the uncomfortable state of cognitive (and affective) dissonance would result, and it is far easier to discount, disregard, and disrespect data than it is to restructure one's system of beliefs. The "dissing" of science occurs at all points on the political philosophy spectrum. Few teachers or others are willing to engage in a research project that allows for the possibility that they are not having much effect on the children they teach or that some cherished belief about teaching and learning was not supported by research.

Consider these examples: Voters in California approved Proposition 49 in November 2002 in response to a campaign led by actor Arnold Schwarzenegger, who argued that children would benefit by the creation and expansion of after-school programs in schools around the state. Soon after Proposition 49 was voted into law, Schwarzenegger announced that he was running for governor of California in the recall election of then-Governor Gray Davis. Schwarzenegger's championing of after-school programs helped to establish him as a credible candidate, and he ran on a platform that emphasized his concern for children. Soon after the referendum on after-school programs passed, a meta-analysis that was funded at a cost of over $1 *billion* by the U.S. Department of Education was published (Dynarski, 2003), with the conclusion that after-school programs do not accomplish much. According to the findings from this very expensive, government-funded review of the literature, after-school programs had minimal effects on academic achievement, no reduction in the number of latchkey kids, no changes in feelings of safety or the likelihood that middle school kids took or sold drugs, and negligible impact on developmental outcomes. The large number of parents, teachers, and pro-Schwarzenegger politicos who believed that after-school programs must be good for children did not want to hear these results. The release of the report was followed by a flurry of press interviews in which the study was criticized as being flawed by many people with little or no science background. I doubt that they would have labeled the meta-analysis flawed if the data had supported the opposite conclusion.

Similarly, in California, voters passed Proposition 10, which placed a 50 cent–per-pack tax on cigarettes to fund programs that serve children from 0 to 3 years old—the years that were identified as critical for brain development (California Children and Families Commission, January 20, 2000). The main mover on this initiative (Proposition 10) was Rob Reiner, an actor and producer who has considered a run for governor or other political office. Research has suggested that ages 0 to 3, although important, should not be funded disproportionately more than other years of childhood, say 4 to 6 years (Bruer, 1999). This was more news that was not well received. Who can value science if it can provide unwanted (i.e., wrong) answers to questions we do not want to ask?

LESSON 3: GOOD INTENTIONS AND LOTS OF EXPERIENCE ARE OFTEN SEEN AS "BETTER THAN SCIENCE"

Everyone can and probably should thank those dedicated teachers who worked long hours and really care about student success. Most people can recall at least one teacher who believed in them and communicated this belief in a way that made a positive difference in their lives. Why can't we just rely on caring and experienced teachers to teach the way they always have? Borrowing from a pop culture quote from an old film (John Huston's 1948 Humphrey Bogart movie, "The Treasure of the Sierra Madre"), "We don't need no stinking" science if we have dedicated teachers. The belief that dedicated, caring teachers with many years of experience produce the best learning outcomes is pervasive. This belief is seen in the criteria for a national program to accredit high-quality teachers, which asks for, among other documents, a reflective essay on one's teaching. Reflection is good; it can lead to insights and testable hypotheses about methods that promote learning, but it is not a substitute for data showing that students are learning.

Unfortunately, many years of experience do not necessarily result in improvement because experience alone is a poor teacher. There are many examples showing that what people learn from experience is, in fact, systematically wrong. For example, some physicians believe that a particular intervention has worked when a patient improves after a particular regime; but of course, most patients will improve no matter what intervention is taken. If the patient does not improve, these physicians may reason that the patient was too sick to benefit from the good treatment. Similarly, most children will learn regardless of the teaching methods used, so one teacher's success with a particular method does not necessarily mean that the method is best, although many teachers believe that their methods are best because children usually learn when the methods are used. There are countless examples of this sort of erroneous thinking, where beliefs about the world are maintained and strengthened despite the fact that they are wrong, and people end up with great confidence in their erroneous beliefs. Confidence is not a reliable indicator of depth or quality of learning. In fact, research in metacognition has shown that most people are poor judges of how well they comprehend a complex topic (see Halpern & Hakel, 2003 for a review). We should not confuse experience with improvement or good intentions for success.

WHO CAN WE BLAME FOR THE LOW REGARD FOR SCIENCE?

The science community, the very people who are clamoring for more respect and for science-based methods of determining the effectiveness of instructional methods, must assume the blame (a fruitless activity) for the "dissing" of science. We have not done a good job of teaching the value of science or explaining why it is a critical thinking skill that can be applied to any empirical question and not the arcane activity of people in white coats and nerdy kids. Media images reinforce negative perceptions of science, so we are often fighting an uphill battle with negative images and personal preferences working against an appreciation for science.

The process of science is complex and, in many ways, counterintuitive. Few people understand why their personal experiences are not more valid than, or at least as good as, impersonal data collected from thousands of learners. Nor do they understand why the failure to find differences between two groups does not mean that there are no differences between the two groups, when we can conclude that there are differences when we find differences. I have taught statistics many times. Students always find this to be a difficult concept to understand, even when they can repeat it on a test. It is possible for students to be able to respond correctly on tests without altering their underlying conceptions about the phenomenon they are studying.

There are principles of science that the public does not understand and we need to address them with a public service educational campaign, with something like the vigor we have directed toward teaching about safe sex, the need to wear automobile seat belts, or anti-smoking campaigns. We are not likely to change ideas or attitudes without continued educational efforts directed at getting people to think better about important issues—use unbiased data, consider alternatives, support conclusions with evidence and reasons—the basics of critical thinking. These ideas need to be taught and reviewed multiple times in different formats before they are incorporated as a way of thinking.

IF SCIENCE IS SO OBJECTIVE, THEN WHY DON'T RESEARCHERS AGREE?

This is a commonly asked question. Debates among scientists cause the public to disregard all scientific findings because many nonscientists reason that if the researchers cannot agree on what is true, how can they trust the researchers or depend on anything they say? Of course, scientists know why we disagree. Sometimes the difference is between "good science" (random assignment, careful measurement, data that support conclusions) and "junk science" (there are too many examples of the way a study can be junk to know where to begin with an example). Sometimes scientists disagree because they have measured different variables (e.g., two different methods for teaching a concept) or sampled differently (rich kids or poor kids). The problem is that the public usually cannot understand how two credible researchers can end up with opposite conclusions. There is no easy solution to this problem. All we can do is be clear as to why there is disagreement and be specific as to what the disagreement is about.

Unfortunately, the media thrives on controversies and unusual findings, a fact well known to most of us who have been asked by reporters to comment on controversial issues. A reasoned response that explains why two researchers may get different results is rarely reported because it is far less interesting than inflammatory sound bites or "breaking news." Reasoned explanations of science outcomes do not sell newspapers or keep television watchers glued to their sets for their daily dose of news-light televised news. For example, the well-publicized debate over whether reading should be taught with a phonics approach or whole-language approach never communicated the fact that most children learn to read regardless of the method used, and the debate is only important for children who are having difficulty with their reading. The second truth, that both methods can be used together, was also rarely explained in the media, perhaps because it is more interesting to focus on the differences in a debate than to suggest a compromise.

WHY SHOULD WE TRUST THE ANONYMOUS RESULTS BASED ON PEOPLE WE DO NOT KNOW WHEN TEACHERS CAN SEE WHAT WORKS IN THEIR OWN CLASSROOMS?

It is very difficult to get anyone to disregard their own personal experience in preference for data collected on a large sample they do not know by someone they do not trust. The value of science is that it is less prone to biases and self-serving errors than one's own personal experiences. But, if science is never taught as a critical thinking skill (Halpern, 2003), it is not incorporated as a way of thinking through decisions, solving problems, and recognizing the pitfalls in other ways of knowing.

HOW CAN WE RELY ON STRONG EMPIRICAL METHODS FOR DETERMINING WHAT WORKS IN EDUCATION IF THERE ARE TOO FEW STRONG EMPIRICAL STUDIES ON WHICH WE CAN BASE OUR DECISIONS?

Causal statements in education are difficult to make because the gold standard for determining cause are studies that used the random assignment of students (or other participants) to different conditions (with adequate controls). It is very difficult, expensive, and time-consuming to conduct such studies, and not surprisingly, we do not have enough of them. It is embarrassing how few studies have used strong scientific methods given the huge number of people we need to educate. If a main thrust of the *No Child Left Behind Act* is that we are to rely on empirically strong research for educational methods, there must be financial support for the kinds of studies that permit causal analyses. These studies take time, and time is something that is in short supply in the early stages of academic careers where virtually all assistant professors have at most 7 years to prove that they should be tenured. The system by which faculty are hired and retained is not compatible with the type of strong research methods that the Department of Education is now requiring. But, the time constraints are only one of the variables why the ideals in the *No Child Left Behind Act* will be difficult to fulfill.

THE REWARDS SYSTEM OF HIGHER EDUCATION IS INCOMPATIBLE WITH HIGH-QUALITY EDUCATIONAL RESEARCH

The high-quality research that is demanded by the *No Child Left Behind Act* will usually require a team of university researchers, often working with graduate students, to plan, conduct, analyze, and disseminate usable results. The rewards system in higher education does not support long-term research projects. If professors invest years into one long-term, well-conceptualized study and that study fails to produce publishable results, the rules in this game stipulate that they leave higher education and move into the private sector for employment. If the study yields unpopular results, the researcher can expect negative consequences, yet few are prepared for the consequences of unpopular research findings, and he or she may find himself or herself alone in defending research methods to a public that is unhappy with the results.

Educational research needs multiple replications to ensure that the findings from any single study really do apply to other students in places other than the ones used in the original research. However, replications do not count as original research and are virtually ignored in the promotion and tenure process. Replication studies are often seen as an "added" cost, not a valuable investment. The best way to ensure that replication data are available is to build replications into the original research design. Yet, few grants will extend beyond their usual time frame to support replications, and few agencies are willing to commit funds to replicate findings that have not yet been found.

EDUCATIONAL RESEARCH IS LOW STATUS

The unfortunate phrase, "Those who do, do, and those who don't teach" is compounded in a way that makes it even worse when applied to those who teach others to teach. On virtually every campus, the status of professors in schools of education is above only those in former departments of physical education, departments that are now called kinesiology on many campuses. Failures in our public schools are seen as failures in the schools that prepare teachers. The focus on what is wrong with kindergarten through grade 12 (K–12) schools and low levels of student achievement have extended to schools of education, so that they are often included in a downward spiral of low prestige, which does not help to attract the best people. We will need a change in how and what we value as a society to remedy many of these educational ills.

IF ASSESSMENT IS THE ANSWER, WHAT IS THE QUESTION?

I have been an advocate for the assessment of learning outcomes for the past 15 years, which is most of my academic career (Halpern, 1987), so when I raise problems with assessment, it is in the spirit of an assessment advocate. The Department of Education has coupled its insistence on rigorous scientific studies of educational methods with the measurement of learning outcomes. This coupling is logical and desirable to those of us who see learning assessments as a way of providing information about what and how much students are learning. By shifting to a learning outcome model, we can determine what and how much students know at periodic intervals as they learn. McKeachie and Hofer (2001) demonstrated that one way to improve instruction is to improve testing. Good tests reflect learning goals and content and provide feedback to the student and the instructor. Good assessments also provide information to the many stakeholders in education assuring them that their money is being spent in ways that promote learning. They can also be used to identify what is not working so that revisions can be made in a timely manner so that students do not fall too far behind.

Despite all of the reasons for assessment, there are many vocal opponents. Testing is stressful, and it can have negative consequences if it is done badly. For example, a test that emphasizes only low-level thinking skills will likely lead to teaching that produces only these types of skills. Test information can be misused in dangerous and destructive ways—to punish and label children who are not achieving well instead of using the information to provide additional assistance. The many children for whom English is not their best language are concerned that they will be labeled as slow learners and tracked into low-expectation educational paths, when what they need most is improved proficiency in English. Teachers who already feel under attack with large classrooms dominated by a few disruptive children, a lack of quality materials for teaching, and too little autonomy in how to achieve their own goals for their students are concerned that low achievement levels by their students will be interpreted as poor teaching. There is also the complaint that education funds are being cut, so students have fewer resources to support learning, at the same time assessments are being created to measure student learning. The idea that assessment is a critical phase in the teaching–learning–assessing cycle, not an "add on" that is not relevant to the enhancement of learning, is a critical reason why there is so little support for assessing what students know and how well they know it. Teachers who teach children who are behind in their achievement at the start of the school year need to know that student assessments will be concerned with how well students are progressing—a value-added measure of learning—not the absolute level of achievement, although high overall levels are the ultimate goal.

Testing is also unpopular because many well-behaved students achieve fairly good grades in school as long as they follow directions, turn in neat work, and appear to be exerting the effort to learn. Standardized assessments do not care about these indicators of student effort and work habits, a fact that seems unfair to many who believe that effort and habit by themselves should be recognized and rewarded. One way to mitigate some of the negative feelings about assessments is to provide understandable information about the nature of the assessments, how they will be used, and how to understand what assessment is and is not. The emphasis should be on valid and meaningful assessments that can be used to improve teaching and learning. This sort of message should go a long way toward quelling concerns about the assessments that are at the heart of *No Child Left Behind*.

TOWARD IMPROVING THE QUALITY OF EDUCATIONAL RESEARCH

Fortunately, the quality of educational research can be improved and the public's attitude toward scientifically based educational methods can become more positive, but it will not be easy or quick. I have a few suggestions for helping teachers, parents, legislators, and everyone else to become supportive of the need for and desirability of empirically-validated research in education.

1. Make education about the need for and understanding of empirical research a national priority. Like any major educational undertaking, the message needs to be made repeatedly throughout the middle grades and well into college and graduate school. The strong preference for personal experience and anecdotes (I know a person who . . .) will not be easy to replace with the impersonal data of large-scale studies, but there is ample evidence that students can learn to use the principles of science, when they are taught in ways that generalize. We need to teach the value of good data and the reasons why decisions based on the best evidence available are preferable to "feel-good" decisions or other criteria. The National Educational Goals Panel (1991) had originally included the enhancement of critical thinking skills in college students as one of its goals for 2000. Unfortunately, it was never funded and seems to have died a quiet death. We desperately need to resuscitate this goal for all levels of education. We need to teach students at all levels about evidence, reasoning, and quality data.

2. The reward structure of higher education needs to support those who engage in the type of high-quality studies that provide credible data (Halpern, 2000). Promotion and tenure standards should be based on the quality of one's research, regardless of the outcomes, or for good progress on long-term projects before they are completed. This sort of change in rewards would permit more creative work, which by its nature involves greater academic risks.

3. The general (and unfortunate) perception that research on applied topics in education is a low-status activity will hinder progress toward understanding how people learn and using that knowledge in ways that show improved learning outcomes. Thus, theoretical and applied research designed to answer the question of how to improve student learning—one of the most critical problems for the United States at this time in history—is routinely ignored by many of our most outstanding research scientists, even in related areas such as human cognition, intelligence, learning (laboratory-based models), perception, attention, and social psychology. The social structure of American contemporary higher education is among the most class-conscious systems in history. This "unspoken problem" needs to

be acknowledged and addressed if we are to attract the best and brightest of our scientists to the difficult problems of applying what we know about human learning to real-life problems in college classrooms.

4. Create rewards for collaborations between departments of educational psychology and departments of psychology. There is a large body of research literature conducted under controlled laboratory conditions that needs to be translated into applied settings. Similarly, many interesting phenomena have been found in applied settings that await the controlled analysis of the laboratory.

5. The public does not understand why we need more testing, especially when the results are not favorable. We need to explain that when assessment is done well, it provides valuable information to all of the stakeholders in education, especially the children, teachers, and administrators most closely involved in making curricular and teaching decisions. Quality assessments have the potential for improving student growth, fostering faculty development, and accomplishing real educational objectives. We need to ensure the public (and ourselves) that the assessments will be valid, reliable, and used appropriately in ways that improve teaching and learning.

6. Continue the dialogue about how to conduct high-quality research in educational psychology and hold researchers accountable according to these general principles. We need to take seriously the commitment to high-quality educational research that we can use as a basis for decision making. We need to teach our students and the public about the need for credible research and the value of empirical evidence.

The future of education is the future of our country. The creation and maintenance of an educated workforce is critical to every aspect of life in the coming decades. We can do a better job of educating our citizens. Our future depends on it.

References

Bruer, J. T. (1999). *The myth of the first three years: a new understanding of early brain development and lifelong learning*. New York: Free Press.

California Children and Families Commission (2000, January 20). News release, available online at *http://www.ccfc.ca.gov/*PDF/110088*.pdf. retrieved September* 13, 2003.

Dynarski, M. (2002). *When schools stay open late: the national evaluation of the 21st century community learning centers program*, Washington, DC: U.S. Department of Education.

Halpern, D. F., et al. (1998). Scholarship in psychology: a paradigm for the 21st century. *American Psychologist*, 53, 1292–1297.

Halpern, D. F. (Ed.). (1987). *Student outcomes assessment: what institutions stand to gain*. San Francisco: Jossey-Bass.

Halpern, D. F., Smothergill, D. W., Allen, M., Baker, S., Baum, C., Best, D., Ferrari, J., Geisinger, K. F., Gilden, E. R., Hester, M., Keith-Spiegel, P., Kierniesky, N. C., McGovern, T. V., McKeachie, W. J., Prokasy, W. F., Szuchman, L. F., Vasta, R., & Weaver, K. A. (1998). Scholarship in psychology: a paradigm for the 21st century. *American Psychologist*, 53, 1292–1297.

Halpern, D. F. (2000). It will take more than a leap of faith to bridge the credibility gap in educational research. *Issues in Education: Contributions from Educational Psychology*, 6, 175–180.

Halpern, D. F. (2001, May 10). *Classrooms as Laboratories: The Science of Learning Meets the Practice of Teaching*. Testimony presented before the United States House of Representatives, Committee on Science, Testimony published in the United States Congressional Record for May 10, 2001. Available on line at *http://www.house.gov/science/research/reshearings.htm*.

Halpern, D. F. (2003). *Thought and knowledge: an introduction to critical thinking* (4th ed.). Mahwah, NJ: Erlbaum.

Halpern, D. F., & Hakel, M. D. (Eds.). (2002). *Applying the science of learning to the university and beyond. New directions for teaching and learning*. San Francisco: Jossey-Bass.

McKeachie, W. J., & Hofer, B. K. (2001). *Teaching tips: strategies, research, and theories for college and university teachers* (11th ed.). Lexington, MA: Heath.

National Commission on Excellence in Education. (1983). A *nation at risk*. Available at *http://www.ed.gov/pubs/*NatAtRisk/*risk.html*; retrieved: September 18, 2003.

National Education Goals Panel. (1991). *The National Education Goals Report*, 1991. Washington, DC: U.S. Government Printing Office.

Peterson, P. E., (Ed.). (2003). *Our schools and our future: are we still at risk*? Stanford, CA: Hoover Institute.

The Failure of Educational Research to Impact Educational Practice: Six Obstacles to Educational Reform

RICHARD E. MAYER
University of California, Santa Barbara

Educational practice should be guided by scientific evidence. This simple principle—which can be called *evidence-based practice*—has been the centerpiece of educational psychology since its inception more than 100 years ago. For example, the world's first educational psychologist, E. L. Thorndike (1906, p. 206) eloquently articulated the need for evidence-based practice:

> The efficiency of any profession depends in large measure upon the degree to which it becomes scientific. The profession of teaching will improve (1) in proportion as its members direct their work by the scientific spirit and methods, that is, by honest, open-minded consideration of facts, by freedom from superstitions, fancies, and unverified guesses, and (2) in proportion as the leaders in education direct their choices of methods by the results of scientific investigation rather than general opinion.

Similarly, in a recent report entitled *Scientific Research in Education*, leading educational researchers offer a consistent message in support of evidence-

Empirical Methods for Evaluating Educational Interventions

based practice (Shavelson & Towne, 2002, p. 1), "No one would think of getting to the moon or wiping out a disease without research. Likewise, one cannot expect reform efforts in education to have significant effects without research-based knowledge to guide them." Today's calls for evidence-based practice are in many ways consistent with earlier calls (Eisenhart & Towne, 2003; Levin & O'Donnell, 1999; Slavin, 2002).

Yet, in spite of the best intentions of the past 100 years, much of today's educational practice remains remarkably uninformed by scientific evidence—using instructional methods that are popular but largely untested. The purpose of this article is to explore the reasons why it has been so difficult to achieve this 100-year-old goal of basing educational practice on scientific evidence. In this paper, I examine six obstacles to educational reform based on research.

OBSTACLE 1: BASING REFORM ON SLOGANS

Sometimes educational reform appears to be based mainly on slogans. In my community, a school district has adopted the motto, "All students can learn." The words are posted on the district's Web site, in the boardroom, and on district stationery. The sentiments are laudable, and of course, any successful educator should believe that all students can learn. The problem, however, is that a slogan does not easily translate into effective educational practice. What is needed is an understanding of how students learn and evidence concerning how instructional practices affect student learning.

An interesting variant of the slogan-based approach to reform is what I call the *expert-says approach*. For example, reform may be based on the idea that "Vygotsky says that students need to work in groups." The problem with the expert-says approach is that it is not necessarily based on empirical evidence or an understanding of how people learn.

OBSTACLE 2: BASING REFORM ON DOCTRINE

A significant obstacle to educational reform occurs when reformers base educational practice on doctrine rather than evidence-based theory. Constructivism is, perhaps, the major doctrine currently driving educational practice, although constructivism comes in many forms (Phillips & Burbules, 2000). For example, some educators interpret constructivist philosophy—the idea that learners construct their own knowledge—to mean that students should learn by discovery (Mayer, 2004a). However, in a recent review of discovery methods, I showed that guided methods are generally more effective than pure discovery methods in a variety of contexts (Mayer, 2004). Thus, the major shortcoming of a doctrine-based approach is that it can lead to educational practices that lack research support.

OBSTACLE 3: BASING REFORM ON POLITICAL AGENDAS

A related obstacle to educational reform occurs when reformers seek to make changes for the sake of political rather than educational goals. For example, a school district may have a vision of equity in which bilingual and monolingual students should perform at the same level on standardized language tests, girls and boys should perform equally well in mathematics, or all schools in a district should have the same balance of ethnic groups. The problem with this approach to reform is that it fails to address the educational question of how to foster learning in all students. Similarly, in some cases, large-scale administrative changes—such as shifting to a year-round schedule, using block scheduling of classes, requiring school uniforms, or creating middle schools—are based on the personal agenda of the proposer rather than solid empirical evidence about how to help students learn. In short, good intentions are not the only requirement for successful educational reform.

OBSTACLE 4: FAILING TO BASE REFORM ON APPROPRIATE MEASURABLE GOALS

An important obstacle to educational reform concerns a lack of consensus on educational goals. Is it enough to visit a classroom and observe that good things are happening? Is it appropriate to ask whether an instructional program works? What does it mean to say that a particular classroom activity is worthwhile? These kinds of questions concern the goals of instruction and how to measure the degree to which they are being met.

Every year, schools in my community set goals for the coming year. For example, in the area of technology, a typical goal is, "All students will visit a computer lab for at least 45 minutes per week." This is a goal based on access. In the area of art, a typical goal is, "All students will visit an art museum or attend a play." This is a goal based on exposure. In the area of writing, a typical goal is, "All students will write a two-page persuasive essay." This is a goal based on activity. Although such goals are commendable, and also quite measurable, they fail to address the central issue in educational reform—fostering change in learners.

In his classic, *Principles of Teaching: Based on Psychology*, Thorndike (1906, p. 1) argued that the main goal of education is to create situations that foster useful changes in learners,

> The word education is used with many meanings, but in all its usages, it refers to changes. No one is educated who stays the same as he was. We do not educate anybody if we do nothing that makes any difference or change in anybody . . . In studying education, then, one studies always the existence, nature, causation, or value of change of some sort.

When educational reformers define reform in terms of access, exposure, or educational activities, they miss the central task of education—fostering learning outcomes.

Educational reform depends on being able to clearly specify and measure the knowledge of learners. Fortunately, there has been substantial progress—boosted by advances in cognitive science—in describing knowledge (Anderson et al., 2001; Pellegrino, Chudowsky, & Glaser, 2001). Cognitive scientists have developed useful techniques for conducting cognitive task analyses of various academic tasks, which allow for descriptions of the learner's knowledge (Mayer, 2003). There is also a growing understanding of how to design assessments aimed at "knowing what students know" (Pelligrino, Chudowsky, & Glaser, 2001, p. 1). Instead of tests that provide some vague general accounting of percent correct, knowledge-based assessments are aimed at determining the learner's specific strategies, procedures, concepts, facts, and beliefs.

For example, in a mathematics assessment concerning students' learning of how to solve word problems, a traditional approach would be to ask students to solve a set of 20 problems and then assign a score based on percent correct. A positive feature of this assessment is that it is an attempt to measure the learner's knowledge rather than some other aspect of instruction such as exposure to the lessons. A negative feature is that it does not provide a precise description of what the students know. Based on recent analyses of mathematical proficiency (Anderson et al., 2001; Kilpatrick, Swafford, & Findell, 2001), an assessment could focus on five kinds of knowledge:

facts—such as knowing that there are 100 cents in a dollar
concepts—such as knowing problem types, such as in total cost problems the underlying structure is (total cost) = (unit cost) × (number of units)
procedures—such as knowing how to add, subtract, multiply, and divide
strategies—such as knowing how to generate a solution plan by breaking a problem into parts and
beliefs—such as thinking that effort leads to solutions

Thus, a precise description of the changes in a learner's knowledge is a central component in successful educational reform.

OBSTACLE 5: FAILING TO BASE REFORM ON A METHODOLOGICALLY SOUND RESEARCH BASE

A serious challenge facing educational reformers interested in evidence-based practice concerns the quantity and quality of evidence. Initially, the emerging field of educational psychology lacked a sufficient quantity of research. For example, in the late 1800s, William James (1899/1958, p. 23) confessed to teachers that psychology did not yet have much to offer, "Psychology ought certainly to give the teacher radical help. And yet I confess that . . . I feel a little anxious least, at the end of these simple talks of mine, not a few of you may experience some disappointment at the net results."

In the ensuing 100-plus years, the amount of educational research has increased dramatically, but the challenge has shifted from quantity to quality of research evidence. The consensus among educational researchers is that "the reputation of educational research is quite poor" (Shavelson & Towne, 2002, p. 23). Levin and O'Donnell (1999, p. 177) refer to the problem of low-quality research as "educational researcher's credibility gaps."

A major factor contributing to low-quality research is the failure to use research methodologies that enable empirical tests of theory-based questions. In a clear and concise analysis of how to conduct useful educational research, Shavelson and Towne (2002, p. 3) ask researchers to "pose significant questions that can be investigated empirically" and "use methods that permit direct investigation of the question." In scientific research, "the final court of appeal for the validity of a scientific hypothesis or conjecture is its empirical adequacy" so "testability and refutability of scientific claims or hypothesis" are essential for educational reform (Shavelson & Towne, 2002, p. 3).

The quality of research is tied to the adequacy of the research methods—that is, the research methods must be able to help test the research hypothesis or question. A variety of methods can be used ranging from experimental methods to observational methods to cognitive neuroscience methods. The primary criterion for the adequacy of a particular method concerns the degree to which it can generate data that are useful in judging the validity of a claim or hypothesis.

When the goal is to determine whether there is a causal relation between an instructional method and a learning outcome, experimental methods are particularly well suited. For more than 100 years, educational psychologists have successfully used experimental methods to determine whether a particular instructional method works.

For example, consider a situation in which a funding agency wishes to test the claim that an after-school computer club improves students' literacy skills. One approach would be to conduct a design experiment (Brown, 1992) in which an after-school computer club is implemented and the designers observe the students and revise the club on the basis of what seems to be working and what seems to need changing. Overall, this approach involves a process of continually improving the club on the basis of observations. After several years, the club seems to be working fine. Anyone walking into the club would be able to see that good things are happening. What's wrong with this way of using a design–experiment approach? The problem is that it is not possible to determine whether participating in the after-school club fosters any useful cognitive changes in the participating students.

Alternatively, another approach is to conduct an observational study of the learning changes in club participants in which some students are videotaped every time they come to the club for a total of 20 hours. In addition, these students are interviewed intensively on a regular basis to pinpoint any changes. In analyzing the tapes, we can compare segments at various points in the student's participation and try to find changes in the student's behavior. What's wrong with this way of using an observational approach? The problem is that it does not allow us to attribute changes to participation in the club.

Overall, the most straightforward way to examine the cognitive consequences of participation in the club is to conduct a controlled comparison of students who were assigned to participate and equivalent students who were assigned to not participate. When we conducted such studies, we found convincing evidence that participants showed greater improvements in certain literacy skills than did nonparticipants (Mayer, Schustack, & Blanton, 1999).

Research can be methodologically sound but educationally irrelevant (Levin, 1994). Some of the classic psychological research on learning—especially animal research in contrived laboratory settings—has been recognized as educationally irrelevant. Recent research on highly contrived tasks in highly artificial laboratory settings may also lack educational relevance. Thus, a high-quality research base must meet the twin requirements of methodological soundness and educational relevance.

Although much of the educational research literature is filled with methodologically flawed or educationally irrelevant studies, there are also many examples of stunning success in producing high-quality research. For example, a combination of experimental and observational studies has shown that phonological awareness—knowledge of the sound units in English—is an important prerequisite for learning to read (Goswami & Bryant, 1990). Observational research has shown a correlation between phonological awareness skill and reading skills; experimental studies have shown that students trained in phonological awareness learned to read better than comparison students who did not receive phonological awareness training (Bradley & Bryant, 1985). Similarly, a combination of experimental and observational studies has shown that number sense—

knowledge of a mental number line—is an important prerequisite for learning arithmetic (Griffin, Case, & Capodilupo, 1995). Observational research shows a correlation between number sense and learning of arithmetic; experimental studies show that students who are given training in developing the concept of a mental number line learn arithmetic better than comparison students who are not trained (Griffin, Case, & Capodilupo, 1995). Finally, another success story concerns research on teaching of cognitive strategies, including strategies for reading comprehension, writing, and mathematic problem solving (Pressley & Woloshyn, 1995).

OBSTACLE 6: FAILING TO BASE REFORM ON AN EDUCATIONALLY RELEVANT THEORY OF LEARNING

Having a solid research base is not enough to implement educational reform because research findings cannot always be translated directly into educational practice. In his famous *Talks to Teachers* more than a century ago, William James (1899/1958, p. 23) correctly noted, "You make a great, a very great mistake, if you think that psychology, being the science of the mind's laws, is something from which you can deduce definite programs and schemes and methods of instruction for immediate classroom use." In recent years, educational psychologists have made important strides in building an educationally relevant, research-based theory of how people learn (Bransford, Brown, & Cocking, 1999; Bruer, 1993; Mayer, 2003).

For example, suppose that students learn better when illustrations are added to text explaining how lightning storms develop. This does not necessarily mean that illustrations should always be added to science lessons. Instead, it is useful to have a theory of how people learn from words and pictures that can help guide the use of illustrations with text. For example, my colleagues and I have developed a research-based theory of how people process words and pictures, including the idea that people have separate information-processing channels for words and pictures, that the capacity of each channel is limited, and that appropriate cognitive processing in each channel leads to meaningful learning (Mayer, 2001a). This theory of how people learn helps inform decisions about when illustrations might be helpful, for whom they might be helpful, and which kinds of illustrations might be helpful.

An educationally relevant, research-based theory of learning must be at the heart of educational reform because education is essentially a learner-centered process. Dewey (1938, p. 25) was one of the first to argue eloquently for a learner-centered approach in which "all genuine education comes about through experience." A theory of learning helps educators understand how various instructional manipulations can result in experiences that affect the cognitive processing of learners and ultimately the knowledge of learners. The call for learner-centered principles of learning remains as a centerpiece for educational reform (Lambert & McCombs, 1998).

The search of an educationally relevant, research-based theory of learning has a long history in psychology and education (Mayer, 2001b). During the first few decades of the 20th century, educational psychologists lacked the database to build a useful theory. During the middle decades of the 20th century, several grand theories—ranging from S-R connectionist theories to Gestalt theories—competed for dominance. However, the theories—often based on animal learning in contrived laboratory tasks—were far removed from the practical context of academic learning, and seemed to lack educational relevance. Finally, during the last few decades of the 20th century and continuing onward, educational psychologists have begun to build domain-specific theories of how people learn in various academic disciplines—what can be called psychologies of subject matter (Mayer, 2004b) These new theories of learning focus on how people learn to read, learn to write, learn to solve mathematics problems, or learn science. Unlike the grand theories that eventually failed to be of much use, the new psychologies of subject matter show strong potential to help guide educational reform.

QUESTIONS ABOUT REMOVING OBSTACLES TO EDUCATIONAL REFORM

The theme of this article is that educational reform should be guided by research that is evidence-based, theoretically grounded, and educationally relevant. Some non–evidence-based approaches are the slogan approach, the doctrine approach, and the political approach. Such approaches are unlikely to lead to useful reform. When evidence-based approaches are used, they may fail when the research is methodologically weak, lacks theoretical grounding, or does not adequately measure changes in learning outcomes. The call for evidence-based practice raises several questions, which I address in the following sections.

Should Educational Research be Experimental or Observational?

Perhaps the most contentious question in the field of educational research concerns what constitutes an appropriate research method. Experimental methods—which involve random assignment to treatments and control of extraneous variables—have been the gold standard for educational psychology since the field evolved in the early 1900s. The advantage of experimental methods is that—when properly implemented—they allow for drawing causal conclusions, such as the conclusion that a particular instructional method causes better learning outcomes. The major disadvantage of experimental methods is that they sometimes cannot be implemented in applied settings, because the requirements for random assignment or experimental control cannot be met. In real classrooms, it is sometimes not possible to neatly manipulate one aspect of practice while keeping all other constant, and it is sometimes not possible to treat students in a class differently.

If experimental methods are the gold standard for testing causal hypotheses, what is the role of observational methods? In my opinion, observational methods can play an important role in educational research when they are used to test research questions or hypotheses. Overall, a variety of methods can be used to help test predictions in a variety of ways. Observational methods can become a detriment when they are used inappropriately to justify causal conclusions.

As an example, consider the research issue of whether children's learning of computer programming improves their thinking—an issue that generated a sizable research literature in the 1980s and beyond (Mayer, 1988). The flurry of research on the cognitive consequences of learning computer programming was motivated in part by Papert's (1980) influential book, *Mindstorms: Children, Computers, and Powerful Ideas*. Papert argued that learning to program a computer would improve children's cognitive development, "In teaching the computer how to think, children embark on an exploration about how they themselves think" (p. 19) so that "powerful intellectual skills are developed in the process" (p. 60).

Papert's book represented an inspiring and enthusiastic advocacy for children's learning of programming by a well-respected expert. Yet, the proclamations of experts do not constitute credible scientific evidence. Papert's book was filled with fascinating descriptions of students' creative thinking with a computer programming language called LOGO. Yet, Papert's vision of what children could do with LOGO does not constitute credible scientific evidence. If the goal is evidence-based practice, scientifically credible evidence is needed to determine the cognitive consequences of learning computer programming.

First, let's take an observational approach. We can observe students as they learn to use LOGO, in which they give commands that result in drawing lines on a computer screen. A good starting point is to ask what students bring to the task, that is, what are their intuitions about computer programming? For example, Fay and Mayer (1987) introduced students in grades 4, 5, 6, and 8 to six LOGO commands and then asked the students to predict the outcome for four instances of each of the six commands. For example, the command RIGHT 90 means that the cursor on the screen (such as a turtle or a triangular shape) will turn 90 degrees to its right—that is, if the cursor is facing toward the bottom of the screen, after the command RIGHT 90 it will be facing toward the left side of the screen. Fay and Mayer found that students displayed one or more naive conceptions (or misconceptions) such as thinking that RIGHT 90 means face the right side of the screen or thinking that RIGHT 90 means turn and move. Thus, observational methods played a useful role by determining the misconceptions commonly held by beginning LOGO programmers. It is useful to know that students enter the LOGO environment with naive conceptions about spatial reference that conflict with LOGO's requirements.

Can we stretch this observation approach into a quasi-experimental study? As a follow-up, let's see what happens to students' misconceptions as they gain more experience in LOGO programming (Mayer & Fay, 1987). Beginning programmers in grade 4 participated in three sessions of LOGO learning and were tested after each session. Some students displayed misconceptions—such as thinking RIGHT 90 means face the right side of the screen—on all three sessions, indicating a lack of learning. These students also performed poorly on a LOGO posttest, and did not show pretest-to-posttest improvements on a test of spatial cognition. However, other students displayed misconceptions on the first session but correct conceptions on the final session, indicating they had learned something useful. These students performed well on a LOGO posttest and showed pretest-to-posttest improvements on a test of spatial cognition. This quasi-experimental study provides additional evidence that students who learn LOGO in a meaningful way (i.e., eliminate their misconceptions) can improve in spatial cognition skills but those who do not learn LOGO in a meaningful way (i.e., do not eliminate misconceptions) do not improve in spatial cognition skills. This is a quasi-experimental study because the students were not randomly assigned to groups.

Finally, consider the value added by studying LOGO learning using an experimental method. Suppose one group of students (control group) learns LOGO by completing five exercises, such as creating a drawing of a house. In contrast, another group (design group) learns basic design principles such as how to break a task into parts (modularization) and is asked to apply these principles on each of the same five LOGO programming exercises. Fay and Mayer (1994) found that students in the design group wrote better programs than those in the control group. By using a controlled experiment with random assignment of subjects to groups, Fay and Mayer were able to attribute the increased quality of LOGO programs to the design training given to the design group. Importantly, the design group also showed some improvements in an errand-planning task as compared with a control group, suggesting that LOGO learning can improve cognitive skills under certain circumstances.

Should Educational Research Use Quantitative or Qualitative Measures?

Measures should be chosen on the basis of how well they provide useful information for testing a hypothesis. Quantitative measures offer precision and are useful in making comparisons among treatment groups. In some cases, qualitative data can be converted to quantitative measures, such as counting the number of times a student asks for help in an instructional episode.

If precise descriptions of learners' knowledge are required for successful research, then what is the role of qualitative measures (such as with observational research described earlier)? In my opinion, qualitative measures can play an important role in educational research when they are used to test research questions or hypotheses. In some cases, quantitative measures may not be able to tap some of the more detailed aspects of learning and learning outcomes. In general, a richer vision of how to improve educational practice emerges through a multileveled set of measures, which may include both quantitative and qualitative measures. However, qualitative measures are a detriment when they are used solely to prove a point rather than to test a prediction.

As examples of qualitative and quantitative measures, consider the LOGO studies described in the previous section (Fay & Mayer, 1987). In seeking to describe the strategies used by beginning LOGO programmers, we created qualitative descriptions of their misconceptions. For example, for the command RIGHT 90, one misconception is to say that the turtle will face the right side of the screen and another misconception is to say that the turtle will turn 90 degrees to its right and start moving. The correct conception is to say that the turtle will turn 90 degrees to its right (i.e., clockwise from the direction it is currently facing). These qualitative descriptions are indispensable in understanding the conceptions that beginners bring to the LOGO learning environment.

How can quantitative measures be used to further the research effort? In our research, we counted the number of learners exhibiting each type of misconception to get an idea of how prevalent the misconceptions were (Fay & Mayer, 1987). We also examined the effects of LOGO programming experience on reducing the number of students who harbored each misconception—thus, creating quantitative measures derived from qualitative observations (Mayer & Fay, 1987).

Similarly, in examining the effects of design training on students' LOGO programming (Fay & Mayer, 1994), we developed some qualitative descriptions of the students' programming processes by examining their programming transcripts, such as determining whether they ran the program (i.e., verification) and whether they revised a program after running it (i.e., revision). We then built quantitative measures by tallying the number of times each student ran a program (i.e., number of verification attempts) and the number of times each student revised a program after running it (i.e., number of revision cycles). Interestingly, students who received design training scored higher on measures such as number of verification attempts and number of revision cycles as compared to the control group. Thus, qualitative measures were converted into quantitative ones and used to test the effects of instruction.

Should Educational Research be Basic or Applied Research?

In many ways, the distinction between basic and applied research makes little sense because high-quality basic and high-quality applied research can be the same thing. For basic research on learning to be of much use, it should aim to account for how people learn in real situations. It is not much help to build theories that account for learning on contrived laboratory tasks but not beyond. Thus, in many ways the demands of education help challenge educational psychologists to develop basic theories of how people learn in practical contexts.

Similarly, for applied research to be of much value, it should be transferable to new situations. It is not much help to know that method A works better than method B for a particular group of students in a particular school. What is needed, of course, is an instructional method that can be adapted to work in other settings. In order to make use of such methods, it is useful to understand how it helps students learn, which is also the goal of basic research. In summary, educational research on learning is basic research on how people learn in applied settings.

For example, some observers might consider our studies of LOGO learning (Fay & Mayer, 1987, 1994; Mayer & Fay, 1987) to be applied research—aimed mainly at determining the practical issue of how best to teach LOGO to beginners. Yet, at the same time, our studies of LOGO contribute to basic research on learning. Specifically, our LOGO studies show that learning is more than just adding information to memory; instead, learning can also involve conceptual change in which students' naive conceptions are replaced or reshaped into more productive conceptions. It also shows that transfer is limited to cognitive skills that are similar to those that were taught, thus contributing to evidence against theories of general transfer. Overall, our research on LOGO learning has both practical and theoretical implications. For applied research to be useful, it should have theoretical as well as practical implications, and for basic research to be relevant, it should have practical as well as theoretical implications.

Should Educational Practice Scale Up from Best Practice or Trickle Down from Theory?

In best practice scenarios, researchers find educational practices that are highly successful in one context and attempt to replicate them elsewhere. The problem with a description of best practice is that all it tells us is that method A works well for a particular group of students in a particular school. Blindly replicating successful practices from another context can be ineffective. To be effective in scaling up, it is also useful to know how and why the method helps people learn—that is, there is a need for basic research on the mechanisms of learning underlying the method in applied settings.

In trickle-down scenarios, researchers devise grand theories of learning for educators to apply. A recent candidate for an influential theory of learning is social constructivism, which many educators interpret as requiring students to learn in groups through discussion. What is wrong with the trickle-down approach? Blindly applying instructional methods on the basis of grand theories can be ineffective. To be effective in applying learning theories, it is also useful to know whether the proposed method actually works—that is, there is a need for basic research on how the method affects learning in applied settings.

In summary, there are serious flaws with both scaling up from the best-practices approach and trickling down from the grand theory approach. Both approaches need to be supplemented with basic research on how the instructional method affects learning in practical settings.

Is Constructivism a Bad Idea?

If doctrine-based approaches are harmful, does that mean that constructivism is a bad idea? In my opinion, constructivism can be a useful idea when it leads to a testable theory of learning. Many of the ideas in the various forms of constructivism are consistent with current theories of learning and can be subjected to careful empirical tests. However, constructivism is a detriment when it is portrayed as an agent that prescribes educational practice.

In summary, my thesis is that educational psychology has something useful to contribute to the struggle for educational reform. Educational psychologists are concerned with how instructional practices affect the process of learning and ultimately the learning outcome. To help foster changes in learners' knowledge it is useful to know something about how people learn, how to measure what they have learned, and how to determine whether instruction affects what they have learned. In short, educational reform should be based on evidence that is methodologically sound, educationally relevant, and theoretically grounded.

References

Anderson, L. W., Krathwohl, D. R., Airasian, P. W., Cruikshank, K. A., Mayer, R. E., Pintrich, P. R., Raths, J., & Wittrock, M. C. (2001). A *taxonomy for learning, teaching, and assessing*: A *revision of Bloom's taxonomy of educational objectives*. New York: Longman.

Bradley, L., & Bryant, P. (1985). *Rhyme and reason in reading and spelling*, Ann Arbor, MI: University of Michigan Press.

Bransford, J. D., Brown, A. L., & Cocking, R. R. (Eds.). (1999). *How people learn*. Washington, DC: National Academy Press.

Brown, A. L. (1992). Design experiments: theoretical and methodological challenges in creating complex interventions in classroom settings. *Journal of the Learning Sciences*, 2, 141–178.

Bruer, J. T. (1993). *Schools for thought: a science of learning in the classroom*. Cambridge, MA: MIT Press.

Dewey, J. (1938). *Experience and education*. New York: Collier.

Eisenhart, M., & Towne, L. (2003). Contestation and change in national policy on "scientifically based" educational research. *Educational Researcher*, 32(7), 31–38.

Fay, A, L., & Mayer, R. E. (1987). Children's naive conceptions and confusions about LOGO graphics commands. *Journal of Educational Psychology*, 79, 254–268.

Fay, A. L., & Mayer, R. E. (1994). Benefits of teaching design skills before teaching LOGO computer programming: evidence for syntax independent learning. *Journal of Educational Computing Research*, 11, 187–210.

Griffin, S. A., Case, R., & Capodilupo, S. (1995). Teaching for understanding: the importance of central conceptual structures in the elementary school mathematics curriculum. In A. McKeough, J. Lupart, & A. Marini (Eds.). *Teaching for transfer: Fostering generalization in learning* (pp. 123–152). Hillsdale, NJ: Erlbaum.

Goswami, U., & Bryant, P. (1992). *Phonological skills and learning to read*. Hillsdale, NJ: Erlbaum.

James, W. (1958). *Talks to teachers*. New York: Norton (originally published in 1899).

Kilpatrick. J., Swafford, J., & Findell, B. (Eds.). (2001). *Adding it up: helping children learn mathematics*. Washington, DC: National Academy Press.

Lambert, N., & McCombs, B. L. (Eds.). (1998). *How students learn: reforming schools through learner-centered education*. Washington, DC: American Psychological Association.

Levin, J. R. (1994). Crafting educational intervention research that's both credible and creditable. *Educational Psychology Review*, 6, 231–243.

Levin, J. R., & O'Donnell, A. (1999). What to do about educational research's credibility gap? *Issues in Education*, 5, 177–239.

Mayer, R. E. (Ed.). (1988). *Teaching and learning computer programming*. Hillsdale, NJ: Erlbaum.

Mayer. R. E. (1999). *The promise of educational psychology: learning in the content areas*. Upper Saddle River, NJ: Prentice Hall.

Mayer, R. E. (2001a). *Multimedia learning*. New York: Cambridge University Press.

Mayer, R. E. (2001b) Changing conceptions of learning: a century of progress in the scientific study of education. In L. Corno (Ed.). *Education across a century: The centennial volume. Hundredth yearbook of the National Society for the Study of Education* (pp. 34–75). Chicago: National Society for the Study of Education.

Mayer, R. E. (2003). *Learning and instruction*. Upper Saddle River, NJ: Prentice Hall.

Mayer, R. E. (2004a). Should there be a three-strikes rule against pure discovery learning? *American Psychologist*, 59(1), 14–19.

Mayer, R. E. (2004b). Teaching of subject matter. *Annual Review of Psychology*, 55, 715–744.

Mayer, R. E., & Fay, A. L. (1987). A chain of cognitive changes with learning to program in LOGO. *Journal of Educational Psychology*, 79, 269–279.

Mayer, R. E., Schustack, M., & Blanton, W. (1999). What do children learn from using computers in an informal collaborative setting? *Educational Technology*, 39(2), 27–31.

Papert, S. (1980). *Mindstorms: children, computers, and powerful ideas*. New York: Basic Books.

Pellegrino, J. W., Chudowsky, N., & Glaser, R. (Eds.). (2001). *Knowing what students know: the science and design of educational assessment*. Washington, DC: National Academy Press.

Phillips, D. C., & Burbules, N. C. (2000). *Postpositivism and educational research*. Lanham, MD: Rowman & Littlefield.

Pressley, M., & Woloshyn, V. (1995). *Cognitive process instruction*. Cambridge, MA: Brookline.

Shavelson, R. J., & Towne, L. (Eds.). (2002). *Scientific research in education*. Washington, DC: National Academy Press.
Slavin, R. E. (2002). Evidence-based educational policies: transforming educational practice and research. *Educational Researcher*, 31(7), 15–21.
Thorndike, E. L. (1906). *Principles of teaching: based on psychology*. New York: Seiler.

PART

II

Basic Issues When Addressing Human Behavior: An Experimental Research Perspective

CHAPTER

5

Can We Measure the Quality of Causal Research in Education?

JEFFREY C. VALENTINE AND HARRIS M. COOPER

Duke University

CAN WE SCALE THE QUALITY OF CAUSAL RESEARCH IN EDUCATION?

Imagine you are a parent reading a letter from your local parent-teacher association (PTA), suggesting the PTA might recommend to the school board that it adopt a "school uniform" policy for your child's school. As support for this policy, the PTA letter asserts that research evidence suggests school uniforms would have a beneficial impact on student achievement and conduct. Being trained in research methods, you decide to do some research on your own. In addition, being public spirited, you commit to writing up a review of that research for a general audience of parents and administrators. After examining the literature, you find that the studies vary in their quality (or, the confidence that you have in the validity of their conclusions). Your sense is that the higher quality studies suggest a different conclusion than the lower quality studies do. You believe it would be helpful for you to have a study quality scale to quantify this judgment and to help you convey this message to your audience in a way that they will understand.

Empirical Methods for Evaluating Educational Interventions

Does it make sense to try to scale the quality of studies attempting to make causal claims about some intervention, that is, claims about whether the intervention is effective? If so, can it be done in a way that is meaningful to audiences with only a cursory understanding of research yet still satisfies the demands of the most technically minded scholars? We address these questions in this chapter. We begin by introducing and defining the foundational terms "causality" and "control," and by briefly discussing the historical development of experimental research approaches in the social sciences. Then, we introduce and critique some efforts to develop quality scales for intervention studies and finish with a thorough presentation of a scale we developed as part of our work with the *What Works Clearinghouse*.

Causal Questions, Experimental Answers

Our example involving a school uniform policy poses an interesting research question: Does mandating that uniforms be worn in school have a *causal* influence on student achievement and behavior? To begin to address this question, we need to define what we mean by "cause." Unfortunately, this is easier aspired to than accomplished. Philosophers have tried for many years but have had a very difficult time defining the term "cause." Examining a dictionary's definitions of the terms "cause" and "effect" illustrates the point. If you were to look up "cause," you would probably see something like "the agent or force producing an effect or result." If you were to look up "effect," you would probably see something like "something brought about by some cause or agent" (Funk & Wagnall's, 1976). Although it is true that all dictionary definitions are circular (after all, words can only be defined using other words that also have definitions), it is rare for this circularity to reveal itself so quickly and clearly. This implies that the construct "causality" is very abstract; we share our understanding of it through denotation, or the repeated pointing out to one another of causal relationships when we see them, rather than through connotation, or its literal meaning. So, simply knowing the dictionary definitions does not get one very far.

Absent a solid definition for the term, scientists and philosophers have tried to be explicit about the conditions under which they are willing to say that something is a cause. In general, the view of causation practiced by most social scientists owes a great debt to the Scottish philosopher David Hume, especially as discussed in A *Treatise on Human Nature* (1739–1740/1978). A very distilled version of Hume's argument asserts that for something to be considered a cause: (a) The "cause" and the "effect" must covary (or correlate), (b) the "cause" must occur before the "effect," and (c) there must be no reasonable alternative hypotheses (or explanations) for why the effect occurred. To return to our school uniform example, for a uniform policy to be seen as having a causal influence on achievement,

Hume's rules would indicate that (a) there must be a relationship between whether or not a school has such a policy and how well students in the school achieve and behave; and (b) assuming that students in schools with uniform policies achieve and behave better, the improvement in achievement needs to have occurred after the start of the policy. Finally, the third criterion holds that the relationship between whether or not a school has a uniform policy and the desired outcomes must not be due to the influence of other variables (often called confounds) associated with the schools or the timing of the introduction of uniforms. For example, it would be a confound if schools that adopted a uniform policy also adopted new mathematic and reading curricula at the same time. We would not be able to tell if changes in achievement were due to the uniform policy, the curricula reforms, or both.

Mill's Methods

If Hume canonized the *rules* by which we judge causality, John Stuart Mill (1843/1973) provided the most influential early articulation of the *methods* by which scientific causes are elucidated. Mill argued that there are three primary modes of experimental inquiry: the method of agreement, the method of difference, and the method of concomitant variation (a fourth, the "method of residues," will not be addressed in this chapter). His influence was so great that these are routinely referred to as "Mill's Methods."

The *method of agreement* takes the form "If X, then Y," where X is a presumed causal agent and Y is some effect. Simply stated, if we find two or more instances in which X and Y are present together, X and Y might be causally related. Returning to the school uniform policy example, if researchers examined schools that adopted a school uniform policy and noted their number of disciplinary suspensions, they would be using the method of agreement.

Mill recognized that, on its own, the method of agreement is an insufficient basis for inferring causality. Recall that Hume noted that to be considered a cause, the effect of X on Y cannot be due to some other factor. The method of agreement provides no way of determining if the relationship between X and Y is *spurious* or due to a third factor that is related to both school uniforms and suspensions (for example, a strong principal in the school). That is, if some unknown variable Z causes both X and Y, we may be tempted to attribute causal properties to X even though X, in and of itself, has no effect on Y. The method of agreement does not allow us to untangle these relationships.

The *method of difference* takes the form "If no X, then no Y." That is, if X is the cause of Y, then Y should be absent whenever X is absent. For example, assume adopting a school uniform policy does affect student achievement. If researchers looked at several schools that did not adopt a uniform policy and noted no change in achievement, they would be using the method of difference.

By itself, the method of difference is also an unsuitable method for determining if some intervention has had an effect; it only works if X is the sole cause of Y. Few outcomes in education (or most any other complex area) are completely determined by a single variable. Thus, even if some cause X does affect some outcome Y, other variables also affect that outcome. Again, assume that school uniforms really do affect student achievement. Because they are not the only things affecting achievement (surely teacher quality matters too!), we could observe increased student achievement even in the absence of a school uniform policy.

The *method of concomitant variation* takes the form "Y *f*(X)," or Y is a function of X. The term "concomitant" means "occurring at the same time," so the term "concomitant variation" implies variation that happens at the same time. As an example, the method of concomitant variation would be used in a study in which students were assigned to 15, 30, 45, or 60 minutes of reading tutoring per week and then reading achievement was measured as an outcome variable. This design tests the assumption that reading achievement is a function of the amount of tutoring per week that the students received. The method of concomitant variation is very common in medicine (as in with doses of a drug), but is used less often in education.

What is used often in education, and in the social sciences in general, was called by Mill the *joint method of agreement and difference* (today we refer to it as the joint method). As you might guess, the joint method is the simultaneous application of the method of agreement and the method of difference. Researchers use this method whenever they compare the outcomes of some students who receive an intervention relative to students who do not receive the intervention. As an example, a good study of the effect of adopting a school uniform policy would solicit schools to volunteer to be part of a study and then randomly assign them to either adopt a school uniform policy or not (see the section "Ronald Fisher" below for a discussion of random assignment). This study is an exemplar of the joint method because it uses the method of agreement and the method of difference. The group that adopts the school uniform policy is being studied with the method of agreement, and is often called the "experimental" group. The group not adopting the policy is being studied with the method of difference, and is often referred to as the "control" or "comparison group."

How Does a Control Group Provide Control?

The term control has several different meanings: (a) to exercise dominating influence over, (b) to regulate or constrain, and (c) to check or verify (Boring, 1954). It is in the latter two senses that the term "control" is used when discussing research methodology in the social sciences. A "control group" in an education study is that set of students, schools, or whatever unit is being studied to which the effect of receiving an intervention is compared. Thus, the control group serves as a check or verification, in the third sense of the term control. It is meant to give us an idea about what *would likely have happened to the participants* if the intervention had not been applied, and is the standard of comparison against which the relative effects of an intervention are judged. In social sciences, this knowledge of what would likely have happened in the absence of an intervention is often termed the "counterfactual"; we're sure you recognize that it is also an application of Mill's method of disagreement.

The term control is also used in the second sense (to regulate or constrain), as when social scientists use the phrases "control over rival hypotheses," "statistical control," and the like. When used in this manner, it is meant that a study has been designed, implemented, and/or analyzed in such a way as to regulate or constrain the "causal influence" of plausible rival hypotheses. Thus, in a properly constituted experiment, the control group both serves as a source of comparison with the treated group and as a control over plausible rival hypotheses.

Experimentation

An experiment can be defined as a research design in which a researcher deliberately manipulates one or more variables. By "deliberately manipulates" we mean that the experimenter controls who will receive the intervention and who does not. If we are interested in the question "Does intervention X have a causal effect on outcome Y?"—or, more concretely, if a principal asks "If our school introduces a school uniform policy, can we expect achievement levels to rise?"—then experiments provide the best way of answering that question. Not all causes we are interested in can be manipulated, nor do all interesting questions pertain to causality. As a result, we are not arguing that experiments are the only way to acquire valid knowledge, nor do we mean to suggest that random assignment is synonymous with the scientific method. Rather, we believe there is a need to strike a balance between these indefensible positions and their equally indefensible opposites, specifically, denials that experimentalism in social science can result in any knowledge at all. Thus, we believe experimental research in social science should focus on a specific goal: to try to determine if some intervention causes changes in some outcome. For our purposes, the quality of a study's design and implementation hinges on the extent to which this determination can be made with confidence.

Quality

One problem with assessing the quality of scientific studies is that "quality" could refer to any number of dimensions. For example, critical commentaries from peers and measures of impact (like citation counts) may be appropriate ways of defining scientific quality (Shadish, 1989), depending on the purpose of the judgment. Therefore, the best way to operationalize "quality" depends at least in part on why the judgment is being made. Our concern in this chapter is with the ability of a social or educational experiment to provide trustworthy information regarding the causal relations between two variables. As the foregoing discussion implies, we will focus our search for indicators of quality on the designs used in education research and how these designs are actually implemented.

William McCall

From the standpoint of the social sciences, William McCall (1923) provided one of the earliest guides to assessing the quality of social experiments. His book, aimed at education researchers and students, was written in response to the "great amount of experimental literature which is appearing in magazine and book form" (xi). In it, he details three basic research designs: (a) the one-group method, (b) the equivalent-groups method, and (c) the rotation method. For each of these designs, McCall provided guidance about when they were most appropriate and described their strengths and limitations.

Researchers using a *one-group study* often compare students before and after receiving some intervention. An example of a one-group design would be if a researcher noted the achievement levels of students in a school both before and after a uniform policy was introduced. If the students' achievement changed, the researcher may be tempted to say that it was due to the policy. If their achievement stayed the same, the researcher may conclude that the policy had no effect. Unfortunately, any conclusions drawn from results based on this design are fraught with plausible rival explanations. The problem, of course, is that this design does not control for variables such as ordinary growth (e.g., students' test scores were trending upward before the introduction of uniforms), confounded treatment (e.g., the reading and math curricula were changed at the same time) or random fluctuations (e.g., achievement scores in the school were generally unstable) that might also account for the study's results.

Researchers using an *equivalent groups study* assess the effect of an intervention by comparing a group of students who received the intervention with a group of students who did not receive the intervention. However, these are not experiments because the researcher did not have control over who received the intervention. Overstating the case a bit, McCall wrote that a strength of the equivalent groups design is that "changes produced by . . . irrelevant factors, like maturing, cause no trouble provided the irrelevant factor operates equally under each [experimental condition]" (1923, pp. 30–31). He did recognize that arranging groups that really are equivalent can be a problem. However, he did not seem to appreciate the difficulties inherent in determining whether groups are equivalent, nor did he have access to methods for ensuring that they are (i.e., randomization, see the section "Ronald Fisher" below). Thus, the problem with the equivalent group's design—one that remains true today—is that we cannot be sure that the groups are truly equivalent. For example, assume we identify a group of schools that (independently and without our involvement) adopted a uniform policy. We can examine these schools' scores on variables we believe may influence students' postintervention achievement scores and behavior (such as their preintervention achievement) and compare them with schools without uniform policies to construct a control group that "matches" the uniform-policy schools. Researchers often conduct statistical tests of the group differences on important variable before the intervention, and as long as that test has enough statistical power (see the section "Statistical Conclusion Validity" below), it is a good procedure to follow. However, there is no way that researchers can assess the impact of unknown differences, differences they could not or did not think to measure, on the outcome measure. For example, the matched-control schools might be equivalent to the uniform-policy schools on preintervention achievement, but what about the quality of school leadership, the number of preexisting discipline problems, and the parents' level of concern regarding their children's achievement (and therefore their willingness to support this type of intervention)? While the two groups of schools might have equal preintervention achievement scores, they might not be equivalent on the quality of their leader, other discipline-related strategies, or level of parent concern, any one of which might plausibly be related to student achievement and therefore might "masquerade" as a school uniform effect. As such, even the best equivalent groups' designs still have a fair amount of ambiguity in their results.

The last design discussed by McCall (1923), the *rotation* or crossover design, can be used with any number of groups. The essence of the crossover design is that participants receive one level of an intervention and then another. To borrow McCall's example, if a teacher were interested in the effects of praising versus scolding students, he or she could first praise a student and note the effects. The teacher could then scold the student and note the effects. This could be done with several students. If implemented in conjunction with other features (e.g., using random assignment to determine which students receive which condition first), the crossover design presents a very strong basis for making inferences about an intervention's effectiveness. The crossover design is perhaps most often used in single-participant research. We refer the reader to Kratochwill and Levin (1992) for a more thorough exploration of these methods.

In addition to his introduction of the three types of research designs, McCall (1923) identified a number of potential problems that can jeopardize the validity of conclusions arising from a study. In general, he grouped these problems into three categories: (a) those due to the experimenter (such as when a researcher intentionally or unintentionally influences the responses of the research participants), (b) those due to the influence of other interventions (such as when multiple interventions are introduced at about the same time), and (c) those due to bias in outcome measurement (such as when an outcome measure "favors" one experimental condition over another). An example of the latter might occur when participants in an experimental group (but not the comparison group) are exposed during the intervention to information on the posttest.

McCall's concerns anticipated many of the developments that were to be influential in social scientists' later thinking regarding the quality of interferences that can be drawn from research. For example, his first concern above relates to what we now call "experimenter expectancy effects." These occur when, for example, a researcher holds a belief about a participant and, by sending nonverbal cues, elicits behavior from the research participant that is consistent with that belief. Expectancy effects can occur regardless of whether the researcher's belief is true or not (see Rosenthal & Rubin [1978] for a review). McCall also gave examples of some possible ways to avoid expectancy effects, such as ensuring that the experimenter does not know potentially biasing information about research participants.

Ronald Fisher

About the same time McCall was publishing his book on conducting research in education, Ronald Fisher was emphasizing the importance of random assignment, a mechanism for assigning study participants to study conditions. Fisher (1925, 1950) encouraged the use of random assignment to ensure the pre-experimental equivalence of groups (or experimental units). He asserted that it is "the essential safeguard" (1950, p. 19), or at the very least, an important prerequisite to valid data analysis.

When participants are randomly assigned to conditions, it means that each individual in the study has an equal probability of appearing in each of the study groups. Functionally, it means that groups are expected to be equivalent in all respects, on average, within the limits of sampling error. To carry out random assignment, researchers might flip a coin, roll a die, pick a number out of a dirty cowboy hat, use a random number table (available in the back of many research methods and statistics books), and the like, to decide which participants will be in which condition (intervention or control). With very small numbers of participants, it is actually rather unlikely that the group will be equivalent in all ways. However, the larger the number of participants, the less likely it is that meaningful systematic differences will be found.

As a result, social scientists place great value in the use of random assignment to reduce bias associated with differences between participants at the start of the study. However, preexisting differences are but one source of problems in a study's design and implementation that can affect the extent to which valid conclusions can be drawn from it. Many of the rest of these problems were given their most thorough treatment by Donald Campbell.

Donald Campbell

Today, a large number of social scientists exploring problems with the design and implementation of research rely on the work on Donald Campbell (1957) and colleagues (e.g., Campbell & Stanley, 1966; Cook & Campbell, 1979; Shadish, Cook, & Campbell, 2002). In the Campbell tradition, the idea of *validity* assumes a prominent place. Here, the term "validity" refers to the strength of evidence available to support an inference (or claim) about a causal relationship between a presumed "cause" and its supposed "effect" (Cook & Campbell, 1979; Shadish et al., 2002). An inference is said to be "valid" if the evidence upon which it is based is sound and "invalid" if that evidence is flawed. Of course, the judgment about validity is not dichotomous. Rather, different research designs and different implementation features lead to more or less valid inferences. Factors that might weaken the strength of the inference are called "threats to validity" or "plausible rival hypotheses." These factors can be placed into four broad categories: *internal validity*, *external validity*, *construct validity*, and *statistical conclusion validity*.

Internal validity refers to the validity of inferences about whether some intervention has caused an observed outcome. Threats to internal validity include any variable that might plausibly have caused the observed outcome in the absence of the intervention. As an example, the single-group design discussed above, in which the outcome variable is measured in one group of students before and after receiving some intervention, is said to be weak in internal validity. This is because any observed changes in the outcome may be due to numerous other plausible rival hypotheses. Take, for example, student maturation. If some change in the outcome might be expected over the course of the measurement period (and this is often the case in educational research), the design leaves no way to assess whether maturation, the intervention, or some combination of the two (not to mention other factors) may have been the actual cause of the change.

External validity refers to how widely a causal claim can be generalized from the particular realizations in a study to other realizations of interest. That is, even if we can be relatively certain that a study is internally valid—meaning we can be relatively certain that any observed changes in the outcome variable were caused by the intervention—we still do not know if the results of the study will apply to different people in different contexts with different variations on the implementation of the intervention. For example, if an internally valid study suggests that adopting a school uniform policy increased student achievement in a school district that was rural and poor, one might wonder if similar effects would be found in different settings with different types of students. It is possible that the processes leading to increased achievement in the rural setting (e.g., through enhancing students' motivation by developing a greater sense of community) may not occur or may even backfire with students from different environmental contexts. This is a question of external validity.

Virtually every study conducted in education, and in fact in the social sciences in general, is conducted with limited persons, with limited variations on the intervention, and the like. Thus, we will go out on a limb and say that few single studies have had excellent external validity. The vast majority of individual studies haphazardly sample very few of the possible variations in participants, contextual variations, intervention variations, and so forth that are of interest. As a result, the extent to which the results of any one study will apply to other participants, contextual variations, and so forth of interest is unknown.

However, there are two ways to increase our confidence in the external validity of the result. First, if one is interested in making it more likely that the results of a study taken on a particular sample will apply to the population as a whole, one could randomly select students from the population to participate in the study. Random selection ensures that the students selected for the study will be roughly equivalent, on average, to the students not in the study but part of the same population, within the limits of sampling error. Random selection requires that a population be defined, and that the "elements" (students, schools, etc.) of the population be known. A study using random selection to select participants allows for clearer inferences about the intervention's likely effectiveness for individuals who were not in the study but are in the *specified* population. The same holds true for using a random process to select intervention and contextual variations, although it is even more difficult for researchers to implement random sampling of these possible variations.

As an aside, please note that random selection and random assignment are *not* the same thing even though they both use a random process. As we discussed earlier, in random assignment a mechanism is used for determining which students are assigned to which study groups, regardless of how students were chosen to take part in the study. It ensures that the intervention and comparison groups are equivalent (again, within the limits of sampling error). In random selection, a random process is used to determine who will be in the study and who will not.[1]

[1] In the Campbell tradition, the threat to internal validity that arises from not using random assignment to allocate participants to groups is known as "selection," a label that further confuses students of research methodology trying to learn the difference between random selection and random assignment.

Another approach to external validity is to treat it as an empirical matter (the term "empirical" means relying on observation or experiment). That is, if a study on the implementation of a school uniform policy suggests it raised achievement levels in a rural, low–socioeconomic status district, the question "Will it also work for other types of students?" is one for further experimentation. Ideally, researchers will conduct independent studies on important questions like this one, each using somewhat different participants, somewhat different interventions, and so on. This allows a body of knowledge to accumulate that will help researchers and policy makers make evidence-based decisions about for whom and under what conditions the intervention is effective.

Ultimately, if enough studies exist on the same topic, scholars might be able to conduct a synthesis of the literature. Broadly defined, a synthesis is a systematic attempt to assess the state of a research literature. Often, a research synthesis involves conducting a meta-analysis, in which the results of studies are combined and analyzed statistically (Cooper, 1998). One strength of a research synthesis relative to other approaches is that the generalizability of results is often more thoroughly tested, because several studies with different types of participants using different realizations of the intervention are included. When results of studies are analyzed statistically, it is often possible to compare the effects of the intervention for separate groups of participants (e.g., boys vs. girls) and different intervention variations (e.g., parent- vs. administrator-initiated drive to implement school uniform policy; presence vs. absence of aid program to help low-income families purchase uniforms).

Construct validity refers to the extent to which the operational characteristics of interventions and outcome measures used in a study adequately represent the abstract categories for which they are supposed to stand. Researchers most often think of construct validity in terms of the outcome measures. As an example, a standardized achievement test is supposed to measure the construct of academic achievement, or the academically related knowledge possessed by the student. However, no measure is a perfect measure of achievement. Rather, all measures are imperfect measures, and indeed, we can argue over the appropriate content that defines academically related knowledge. Regardless, the more imperfect the instrument, the less accurate the label used to describe it.

Although fewer researchers think about it this way, construct validity also refers to the adequacy of other labels used in the study. For example, in our own research on mentoring (DuBois, Holloway, Valentine, & Cooper, 2002), we operationally defined mentoring (in part) as an activity that occurs with (a) an older mentor and (b) a single younger "mentee," that was meant to (c) focus on positive youth development in general, and that was meant to (d) occur over a relatively long period of time. We found a study in which the researchers said they had implemented mentoring in a way that did not seem to meet our definition of that term. Even though this study used an adult as the "mentor," the adult met with children in groups of two to three, their meetings focused on providing homework help, and the adult met with the students only a few times. Thus, the activity described by the authors—even though they used the term "mentoring"—did not seem like mentoring to us. This is an example of a construct validity problem because the authors used a label that—for us—did not seem to adequately capture their intervention. To return to our continuing example, would a school policy that banned blue jeans, belly button exposure, and baseball caps be considered a school uniform policy?

Statistical conclusion validity refers to the validity of statistical inferences arising from a study. You were probably exposed to statistical conclusion validity in an introductory statistics class, when the instructor discussed type I and type II errors. Type I errors (or, following Rosenthal & Rosnow [1992], errors of "gullibility") occur when an intervention is not effective but the researcher judges it to be effective. There are several statistical sources of type I errors, including when the assumptions of statistical tests are violated and when researchers conduct "too many" statistical tests without prior justification. Type II errors (or errors of "blindness") occur when an intervention really is effective but the researcher judges it ineffective. The major source of type II errors in education research is the lack of statistical power, which is a serious issue undermining education research in particular and social science research in general (Cohen, 1962; Levin, 1997; Sedlmeier & Gigerenzer, 1989). Statistical power refers to the ability of a statistical test to reject a false null hypothesis and is a function of three components: (a) the size of the sample, (b) the size of the intervention's effect, and (c) the type I error rate (or γ, usually set at 0.05). Power and these three components form a closed system, so that if one knows the sample size, the effect size, and the type I error rate, one knows the statistical power of that test. Similarly, if one knows power, the sample size, and the effect size, the type I error rate can be computed.

Our overarching goal for this first section of the chapter was to provide you with an understanding of how social scientists think about what issues must undergird any discussion of quality as it relates to making causal inferences. To this end, we discussed the rules Hume articulated for understanding when we can say that a relationship is causal. He nominated three: (a) The cause and the effect must covary, (b) the cause must occur before the effect, and (c) there must be no reasonable alternative hypotheses for why the effect occurred. We pointed out Mill's contribution in providing guidance about how to implement Hume's rules in practice, noting that the joint method is very common in the social sciences. We then described the contributions of three scholars who were influential in the evolution of the methods used by social scientists today, focusing on the work of Donald

Campbell and colleagues. Next, we turn our attention to attempts to formalize judgments of study quality.

SPECIFIC INSTRUMENTS TO ASSESS STUDY QUALITY

Given that a study's quality greatly affects the degree of confidence that can be placed in its results, it is not surprising that there have been attempts to develop systematic strategies for assessing how effectively a study's design and implementation permit drawing causal inferences. Most of this work has occurred in medicine. As an example, Moher, Jadad, Nichol, Penman, Tugwell, and Walsh (1995) identified 25 scales designed to measure the quality of studies using random assignment (called "randomized controlled trials" in medicine) that had been published through 1993. West et al. (2002) identified a somewhat different set of 25 quality scales for randomized controlled trials and another 12 scales for assessing the quality of observational studies.

Efforts in the social sciences have been generally less intensive than those in medicine. However, three are particularly prominent due to their use in relatively high-profile efforts funded by the U.S. government. The Maryland Scale (Sherman & Gottfredson, 1997) was developed to assess the effectiveness of crime prevention programs. The Center for the Study and Prevention of Violence developed a set of criteria meant to evaluate research on the effectiveness of violence prevention programs (available at *http://www.colorado.edu/cspv/*). The Substance Abuse and Mental Health Services Administration (SAMHSA, an agency of the U.S. Department of Health & Human Services) has developed an instrument to evaluate research on the effectiveness of drug abuse interventions (available at *http://www.modelprograms.samhsa.gov*).

Design of Quality Assessment Instruments

There are two general approaches to quality assessments in the social and medical sciences. The first approach involves a checklist, which is simply a list of features of a study's design and implementation that are considered important by the list's authors. Users applying the instrument will determine whether these features are present or absent. The second approach involves a study quality scale in which numeric scores or weights are assigned to study characteristics. Users assess the presence of the desirable characteristics, and the scores are then totaled to arrive at a single score representing the study's quality. For example, using random assignment to place participants into groups might be worth 15 points, and using a valid outcome measure might be worth 4 points. A study with both of these characteristics would be worth 19 points. Those points would be added to the points obtained from other characteristics, and the final total would represent the study's "quality."

Within these two general approaches, there is a great deal of variation in terms of what and how many different dimensions are considered to be important, and how weights are assigned to the various items. Some instruments focus on one aspect of study quality (usually internal validity), whereas others are more expansive, considering a broader definition of what constitutes quality. As an example, a few quality scales rate studies on an ethical dimension, such as whether the study had approval from an institutional review board.

Even when instruments share the same focus (e.g., two instruments focus solely on internal validity), there is little agreement on the specific features of study design and implementation that are considered important. Some instruments will spotlight a few key features, whereas others will take a more in-depth approach. Finally, even when instruments agree about the specific features that are considered important, they often disagree about the weights assigned to those items (see below).

Empirical Assessments of Quality Scales

Empirical evidence suggests that existing quality scales disagree about what quality is. In a demonstration of this disagreement in medicine (a field often thought to have greater consensus about research quality than education), Jüni, Witschi, Bloch, and Egger (1999) applied 25 different quality scales (the same scales identified by Mohr et al., 1995) to 17 studies reporting on trials comparing the effects of low-molecular-weight heparin (LMWH) with those of standard heparin on postoperative deep vein thrombosis. The authors applied the 25 quality scales to the 17 trials, and then performed 25 different meta-analyses examining in each case the relationship between study quality and the effect of LMHW (relative to standard heparin). Studies were divided into "high-quality" and "low-quality" categories, with the high and low categories defined by a quality threshold given by the original authors of the quality scales or by median split when such a threshold was not provided. Then, the authors examined the conclusions of the meta-analyses separately for "high-" and "low-" quality trials. For six of the quality scales, the high-quality studies suggested no difference between LMWH and standard heparin, whereas the low-quality studies suggested a significant positive effect for LMWH. For seven other quality scales, this pattern was reversed. That is, the high-quality studies suggested a positive effect for LMWH, whereas the low-quality studies suggested no difference between the two conditions. The remaining 12 quality scales resulted in conclusions that did not differ between high- and low-quality trials. In addition, there was no association in these studies between the overall quality score and effect size using any of the 25 quality scales.

Thus, Jüni et al. (1999) suggested that the clinical conclusion about the efficacy of the two types of heparin depended on the quality scale used. The scales appear to have been at best useless and at worst misleading (Berlin & Rennie, 1999). From the discussion above, it is not difficult to see why this result occurred. The 25 quality scales often focused on different dimensions and analyzed a differing number of dimensions (ranging from 3 to 34). Even when the same dimension was analyzed, the weights assigned to the dimension varied. For example, Beckerman, de Bie, Douter, de Cuyper, and Oostendorp (1992) allocated 4% of total points on their scale to the presence of randomization and 12% of the points to whether the outcome assessor was unaware of the condition to which participants were assigned (called "masking"). Brown (1991) very nearly reversed the relative importance of these two dimensions, allocating 14% of the total points to randomization and 5% to masking.

The scales reviewed by Jüni et al. (1999) also share a reliance on single scores to represent a study's quality. Especially when scales focus on more than one aspect of validity, the single-score approach results in a score that is summed from very different aspects of study design and implementation, many of which are not necessarily related to one another. For example, there is no necessary relation between the validity of outcome measures and the mechanism used to allocate participants to groups. When scales combine disparate elements of study design into a single score, it is likely that important considerations of design are being obscured. For example, a study with strong internal validity but weak external validity can get a score identical to a study with weak internal validity and strong external validity. If the quality of these studies were expressed as a single number, how would one know the difference?

These problems are not limited to scales used in medical settings. As an example, the Maryland Scale (Sherman & Gottfredson, 1997) is a checklist designed to help users rate the quality of group experimental and quasi-experimental studies aimed at reducing crime. It is made up of eight items that are generic enough to be applied to any area of social science research. The focus of the scale is broad: Three questions address internal validity, two address statistical conclusion validity, one addresses external validity, and one question addresses construct validity. A final question is used to assess the overall methodology of the study under review.

The scale has two notable positive properties. First, it is brief and can be applied with little time or effort. Second, despite its brevity, the scale addresses most of the fundamental issues associated with study quality. However, there are also several weaknesses inherent in the scale. One problem is the lack of specificity regarding the details of the coding categories. For example, although the scale asks raters to evaluate the reliability of the outcome measures, no guidance is provided about (a) what type of reliability should be focused on (internal consistency, test–retest, interrater) or (b) what constitutes acceptable reliability. Raters are left to their own devices to determine what is sufficiently reliable and what is not. Thus, two different scale users could choose different reliability cutoffs and rate the same study differently on this dimension, and a reader would have difficulty understanding why.

Even more problematic is how the overall score is arrived at. After completing the first seven questions, raters are asked to evaluate the overall methodology. Three categories are given: (a) no confidence should be placed in results; (b) methodology is rigorous in some respects, weak in others; and (c) methodology is rigorous in almost all respects. There is no necessary relation between the pattern of answers to the first seven questions and the answer to the final overall question. This final question might be based on criteria different from the first seven, or on the same criteria and each rater can bring their own idiosyncrasies to her or his answer. Further, there is a lack of transparency about the judgments made when completing the final question. Consumers do not know what elements of design and implementation were invoked here. In addition, the scale instructs raters to base their overall judgment on three critical issues, one of which (statistical power) is not addressed in the questions that comprise the scale. As a result, we believe the Maryland Scale is unlikely to solve the problems revealed by the Jüni et al. (1999) study and might have limited reliability and validity in its own implementation.

An Empirical Approach to Assessing Quality

One approach to the issue of the relation between the quality of design and implementation and a study's results is to investigate the matter empirically. However, primary researchers who want to know if their proposed design is of high quality are unable to adopt this approach; it does not help individuals who want or need to evaluate individual studies on their own merits. However, secondary users of data (such as meta-analysts) are often in a good position to empirically evaluate the relationship between study quality and study results. Meta-analysts often empirically investigate the associations between various quality-relevant features of study design and implementation and effect size. For example, in our meta-analysis of summer school programs (Cooper, Charlton, Valentine, & Muhlenbruck, 2000), we examined the roles of the assignment mechanism (i.e., random assignment vs. nonrandom assignment to programs), matching (i.e., within designs that did not use random assignment, whether or not researchers attempted to enhance equivalence of groups by matching experimental and control participants), and whether or not the summer school program was monitored for fidelity of implementation. We found that random assignment, matching students on achievement (when random assignment was not used), and monitoring the implementation of the summer school program were all associated with relatively larger effects for the summer school program.

In what is perhaps the ultimate exercise of this nature, Lipsey and Wilson (1993) examined the results of more than 300 *meta-analyses* in clinical psychology and education (broadly defined). Two results are particularly relevant to this chapter. First, the authors found that nonrandomized and randomized studies were associated with highly similar effect sizes. However, the variation in effect size estimates was much greater for nonrandomized studies. Second, 27 meta-analyses involved an explicit comparison of studies rated on their methodologic quality. Similar to the results obtained by Jüni et al. (1999), the effect sizes from the "low" quality studies were very similar to those of the "high" quality studies. This last finding could mean (a) on average, study "quality" (as defined by the quality scales) does not affect study results, or (b) the study quality scales were so poor that they obscured the real relation between study quality and study results.

Lessons Learned from Existing Quality Scales

What lessons can be learned from this review of study quality scales? We think there are at least four. First, study design and implementation need to be assessed on multiple dimensions. Internal validity is an important aspect of study quality, but it is clearly not the only one. Thus, we believe that a thoughtful approach to assessing design and implementation requires recognition of the importance of all four general classes of validity. Second, we believe that it is a mistake for scales that do focus on more than one dimension of study quality to attempt to summarize those dimensions using a single score. Doing so obscures important differences between studies and results in a number that is both useless and uninterpretable. Third, there is little justification or even agreement for complex schemes that weight items on quality scales and, once we abandon the single-score approach, the value of this exercise is greatly diminished. Fourth, assessments should be tied to explicit and transparent rules for relating the operational characteristics of studies to the judgments of quality. This way, the interjudge reliability of the scale will be enhanced and when disagreements about quality do arise, the source of the disagreement can be identified.

THE STUDY DIAD

Given the uninspiring empirical results quality scales have generated to date, one wonders if the entire enterprise is doomed. Can quality scales be designed and implemented more effectively?

Quality scales can serve an important function, namely helping to protect consumers of research from opinions, biased research, poorly conceived research, and ad hoc explanations parading around as scientific evidence (see Chapters 1 and 4). Because of their potential value, we undertook the task of trying to develop a better quality scale. The Study Design and Implementation Assessment Device (Study DIAD; Valentine & Cooper, 2003) attempts to avoid what we perceive to be the mistakes made in previous efforts. Specifically, it is used to assess study design and implementation on multiple dimensions, does not sum the scores of these dimensions to arrive at a single number representing a study's quality (but rather results in a study quality "profile"), and avoids a complex weighting scheme for the individual items. This is not to suggest that the instrument is perfect, but before discussing areas for improvement, we would like to lay out briefly its development and structure.

The Study DIAD was designed for the U. S. Department of Education's Institute of Education Sciences' *What Works Clearinghouse* (WWC). The WWC was established to provide educators, policy makers, and parents with a central, independent, and trustworthy source of evidence of what works in education. In addition to developing standards for reviewing and synthesizing educational research, the WWC reviews studies of interventions, will conduct research syntheses on interventions and practices when sufficient trustworthy evidence exists, and provides reviews of test instruments used in educational settings. More information on the WWC is available at *http://www.w-w-c.org*. The Study DIAD itself is under the "Standards" link on that page.

Development of the Study DIAD

We approached the development of the Study DIAD with two overarching goals in mind. First, we wanted to develop an instrument that could be understood (with a minimal amount of additional explanation) by a wide variety of audiences, such as policy makers, administrators, parents, and other research consumers as well as researchers themselves. Second, to ensure transparency and to enhance reliability, we wanted to base the Study DIAD on judgments about study design and implementation that would require very little inference on the part of the individuals applying it (so that their judgments were both reliable and open to the inspection of others). In response to both of these goals, we developed a multilayered, hierarchical instrument. At its core are a number of highly specific questions relevant to assessing the design and implementation of a study. These questions then feed into progressively more abstract levels of questions, culminating in four global, abstract questions about a study. These four global questions refer, not surprisingly, to the four classes of validity.

In addition to our overarching goals, we believe that much of what constitutes "quality" in a study is contextually dependent. That is, quality cannot be assessed without taking into consideration the topic under study and, to a lesser but still important extent, the research norms that become associated with studying the topic. As a result, we found it important to construct an instrument that allowed for topic-specific flexibility. As an example, we could not write a set of questions assessing the construct validity of an intervention that would be both transparent and applicable across domains. The operational components that define a school uniform policy will be different from those that define a curricular reform. Likewise, the number of participants needed to provide adequate statistical power for a study of school uniforms will be different than that needed for a study of behavior modification. These areas differ dramatically in the expected magnitude of their effect and the amount of control (in the "regulate and constrain" sense) they permit. For these reasons the Study DIAD requires that, before it can be applied, a number of context-specific questions must be answered. Examples of these questions include specifying the nature of the intervention (e.g., the operational definition of the intervention), the outcomes considered relevant by the user of the Study DIAD, and so on.

With these principles and goals in hand, the next difficult decision we faced was how to establish the content validity of the Study DIAD. That is, we had to answer the question "What aspects of design and implementation should be represented on the Study DIAD?" in a manner that would capture the broadest possible consensus. So, as part of its development, early drafts of the Study DIAD were shared with and comments were received from the WWC's Technical Advisory Group, composed of 14 highly regarded research methodologists. In addition, we sought input on the instrument at a public meeting, held at the National Academy of Sciences and attended by more than 150 people, and we accepted comments on a draft of the instrument through the WWC's Web site.

The Structure of the Study DIAD

As we mentioned earlier, the Study DIAD is based on a number of very specific questions about study design and implementation. These specific questions then feed into progressively more abstract levels of questions, culminating in four global, abstract questions about a study. These four questions relate to the four classes of validity from the Campbell tradition.

At the most abstract level, the Study DIAD uses four questions to address construct validity, internal validity, external validity, and statistical conclusion validity (Figure 5.1). As you can see, the four questions we ask (and answer) about study design and implementation are very abstract. While they may be generally understandable to audiences with little training in research methods, they certainly are not precise enough for the research

Relevance to the Review	Clarity of Causal Inference
Were the intervention and outcome measures relevant to the purpose of the review?	Did the research design permit an unambiguous conclusion about the intervention's effectiveness?
Generality of Findings	**Precision of Outcomes**
Was the intervention tested on participants, settings, outcomes, and times that were appropriate for this review?	Could accurate estimates of the intervention's impact be derived from the study report?

FIGURE 5.1
The four global questions of the Study Design and Implementation Assessment Device.

community. Further, if study quality ratings were actually made on the basis of these four questions, it would be very difficult for outside observers to replicate the judgments because the logic and considerations used to arrive at them are not transparent (rather, the judgments are based on the "cognitive algebra" unique to the judge). Still, we believe this level of the instrument is useful when used appropriately, especially to communicate research findings to audiences without research training.

At a slightly less abstract level, Figure 5.2 presents eight questions that we pose about the quality of study design and implementation. At this level, each of the four classes of validity is subdivided into two questions that are more specific. For example, the global question "Were the intervention and the outcomes relevant to the review?" becomes "Was the intervention relevant to the review?" and "Were the outcomes relevant to the review?" The global question "Did the research design permit an unambiguous conclusion about the intervention's effectiveness?" becomes "Were the participants (e.g., students, schools) in the group receiving the intervention comparable to the participants in the comparison group?" and "Was the study free of events that happened at the same time as the intervention that confused its effect?"

These questions are closer to the level at which judgments about studies are made. In fact, some instruments (e.g., Sherman & Gottfredson, 1997) use this level of analysis to make quality judgments. However, on the DIAD,

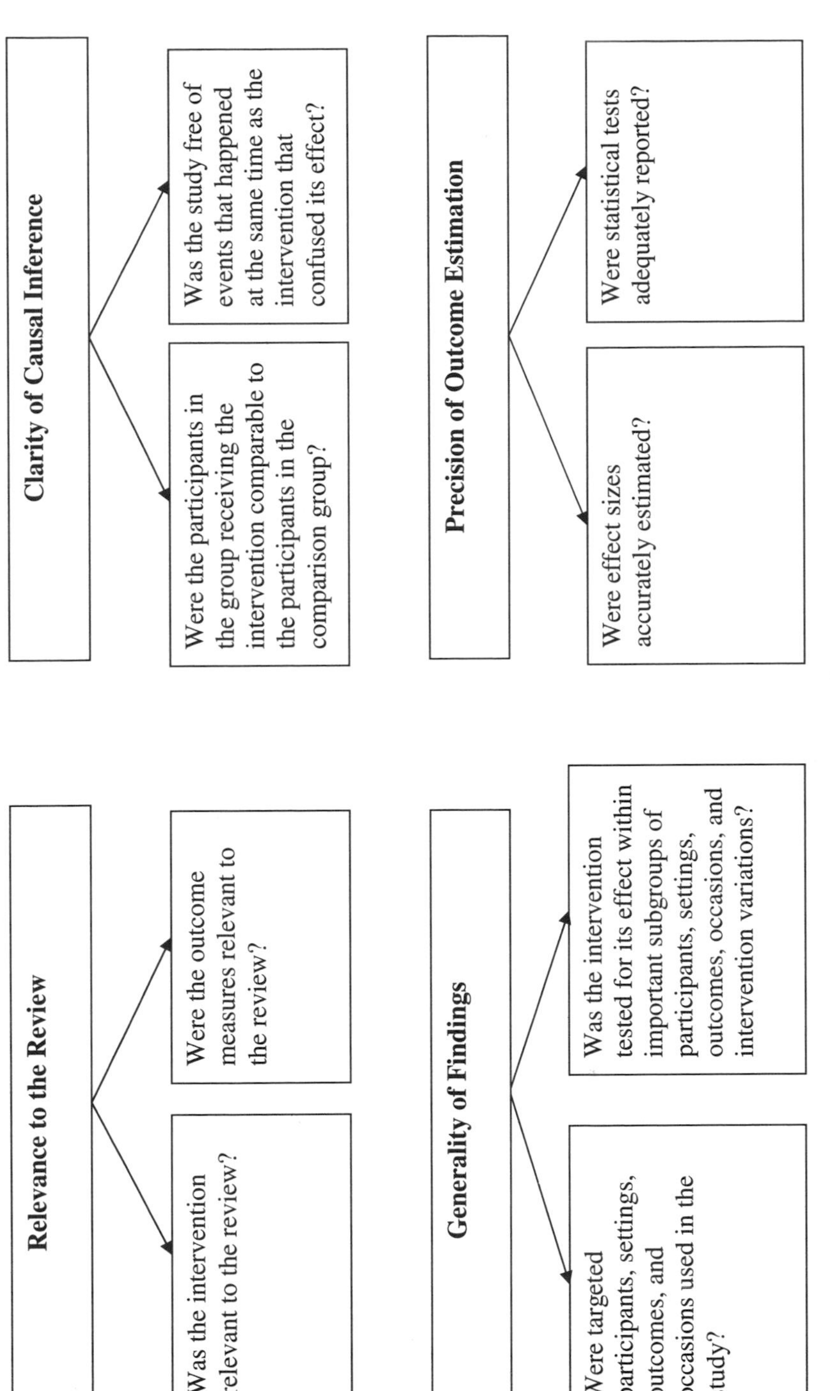

FIGURE 5.2
The eight composite questions of the Study Design and Implementation Assessment Device.

judgments based on questions at this level of abstraction still lack a sufficient degree of transparency. We refer to these as the "composite questions," as the term composite implies "having compounds," or "factors"—meaning that we believe these questions are still relatively abstract. In fact, this level of the Study DIAD is probably most useful for describing research findings to audiences with some, but still limited, knowledge of research methods.

At a more concrete level, the Study DIAD is based on approximately 35 questions about design and implementation (the exact number depends on the research design used in the study). We refer to questions at this level as the "design and implementation" questions. Figure 5.3 shows how these questions relate to the composite questions. As an example, consider the

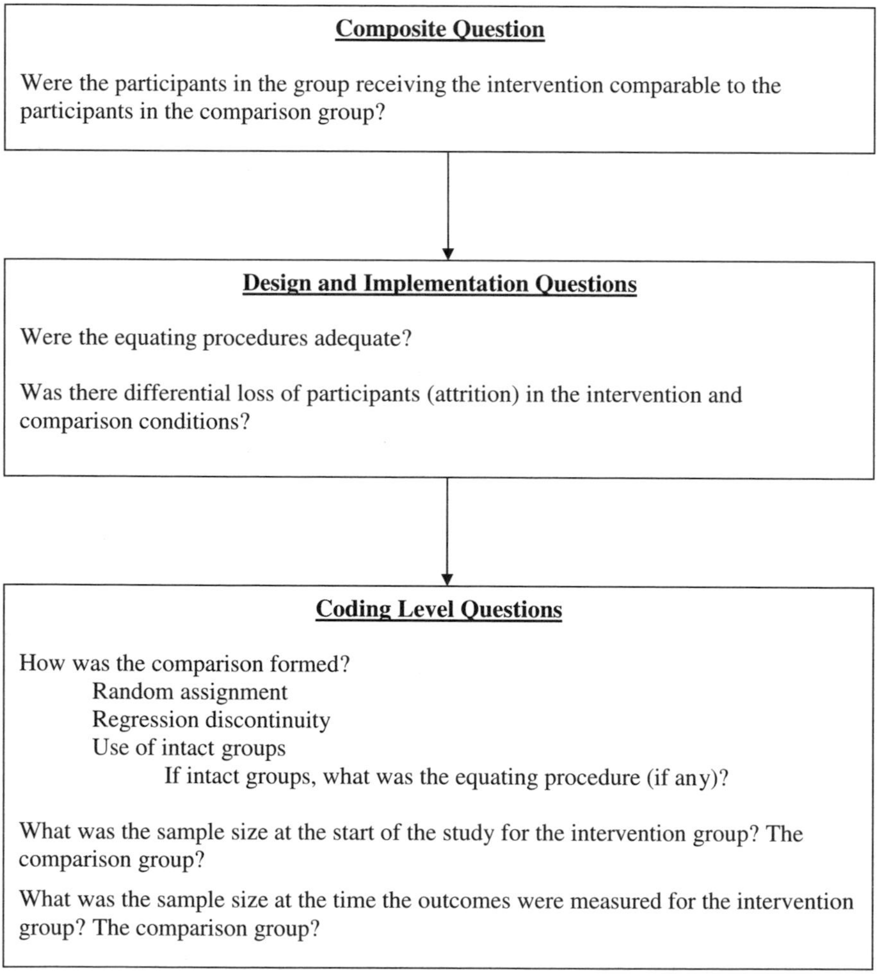

Composite Question

Were the participants in the group receiving the intervention comparable to the participants in the comparison group?

↓

Design and Implementation Questions

Were the equating procedures adequate?

Was there differential loss of participants (attrition) in the intervention and comparison conditions?

↓

Coding Level Questions

How was the comparison formed?
- Random assignment
- Regression discontinuity
- Use of intact groups
  - If intact groups, what was the equating procedure (if any)?

What was the sample size at the start of the study for the intervention group? The comparison group?

What was the sample size at the time the outcomes were measured for the intervention group? The comparison group?

FIGURE 5.3
How the composite question on fair comparison is answered.

composite question "Were the participants (e.g., students, schools) in the group receiving the intervention comparable to the participants in the comparison group?" For studies that do not use random assignment to place students into groups, we ask questions that address three specific issues: (a) "Were adequate procedures used to equate students?", (b) "Was there differential attrition?", and (c) "Was there severe overall attrition?"

Because these questions still involve some degree of judgment (e.g., what does "adequate" mean?), a final level of questions exists. We call questions at this level the "coding level" questions, and it is at this level that the information is extracted from the report and that judgments are made. For example, we do not ask individuals to make a judgment about whether the procedures used to equate students were adequate. Rather, what constitutes adequate matching is defined a priori (see below), and the coders examine the study to see whether the procedures used in the study were at least as good as the a priori definition. For example, in a study of school uniform policies, we might think it is important to match schools on pretest measures of the outcome variables and on socioeconomic status. Individuals coding studies would look to see if these procedures were carried out by the researchers who conducted the study.

Types of Judgments Made in the Study DIAD

The Study DIAD distinguishes three levels of agreement about what constitutes a good study. The first level involves those aspects of research design and implementation about which there is relatively strong consensus in the research community. For example, given that the Study DIAD relates to the trustworthiness of causal inferences and all else being equal, there is strong consensus that a well-implemented randomized experiment is better for making causal inferences than a well-implemented study using matching to equate study groups. These types of judgments are "hard-wired" into the instrument. The second judgment level involves the context of the research question. As we noted earlier (e.g., the operational definition of the intervention and the relevant outcomes), the Study DIAD permits flexibility on these, as it simply asks reviewers to be explicit about them, before undertaking to make judgments of quality. This might be considered the "software" of the DIAD. Finally, another level of judgments involves variables that seem like they could be hard-wired into the system, but lack consensus among experts about what the hardwiring should be. As an example, the most controversial of these seems to be attrition, so we will elaborate on it.

Attrition

Generally, attrition can be defined as the loss of participants from the study. Attrition problems can take two forms. First, differential attrition occurs when different conditions in the study lose different numbers of participants because they drop out of the intervention or control group or do not show up for the outcome measure. Differential attrition is particularly problematic. As an example, assume that 100 students are randomly assigned to summer-school and no summer-school conditions. During the course of the summer, however, 30% of summer-school students do not show up for class, move to another (unknown) district, or fail to show up for the posttest but only 10% of comparison group students are lost. In the presence of differential attrition, the assumption made by most researchers is that the characteristics of the remaining participants differ across the two conditions. Although this can be investigated empirically by examining postattrition group equivalence on measures taken at pretest (given a sufficiently powered statistical test), we can never know about group comparability on unmeasured variables.

Overall attrition can also be problematic. For example, consider a study in which 40% of the participants assigned to the intervention group and 40% of the students assigned to the comparison group leave. Like differential attrition, overall attrition (when it is severe) can lead to groups not being comparable after attrition has occurred, because we do not know if the characteristics of the students leaving the two groups are the same. Overall attrition also raises external validity concerns, as it makes it even less clear from what population of students the sample was drawn.

Thus, for both types of attrition, the primary concern is that attrition will introduce bias into the measurement of the intervention's effect. The problem is that attrition generally affects outcome measurement in largely unknown ways, and what we do know suggests that it is a complex phenomenon. For example, if the intervention has a very large effect, quite a bit of attrition of either type would need to occur before one would be led to a different conclusion about the intervention's effectiveness. If the intervention's effect is small (as it often is in education research), very little attrition can have a serious impact on the judgment of the intervention's effect.

Although the research community agrees that attrition can be a problem for studies, there is no consensus on how it should be addressed across studies. As a result, the Study DIAD is flexible about the strategies one could adopt to address these issues. Someone very concerned about the potential of attrition to bias effect sizes might choose to set a very stringent standard. If studies do not meet this stringent standard, their rating for internal validity is significantly downgraded. This strategy would likely minimize bias due to differential attrition, but also may lack sensitivity, as it seems likely that it would result in the downgrading of studies that are only minimally biased.

Another approach involves setting a very inclusive standard and then testing the relationship between attrition and effect size (our third strategy for assessing quality). All else being equal, if attrition is biasing effect size estimates, there should be a relationship (i.e., a correlation) between effect size and attrition. As we described above, this approach has a lot to offer, but it does not help the person who is trying to judge the merits of a single study outside the context of a meta-analysis.

Finally, another approach (and the one we generally recommend for individuals judging studies outside the context of a meta-analysis) involves setting a cutoff point that is relatively stringent. Studies with less attrition than the standard are assumed to be unbiased (at least with respect to attrition). For studies with more attrition than the standard, the burden of proof shifts, and reviewers would look for evidence in the study pertaining to the impact of attrition on group equivalence. For example, quality-evaluators might decide a priori that they will require a postattrition demonstration that the groups were equivalent on a pretest of the outcome.

Thus, even though there is little agreement among experts about how to handle attrition problems across studies, we believe the Study DIAD acts as a guard against researchers making arbitrary, post hoc decisions about how to address attrition that merely serve to support their preconceived beliefs (Gilovich, 1991). When consensus does not exist about what to hard-wire into an instrument on research quality, the Study DIAD allows the user enormous flexibility regarding how to proceed but requires a priori rule-based thinking that is open to the inspection of others.

Pilot Test of the Study DIAD

After using the above procedures to establish its content validity, we conducted a pilot test on the Study DIAD. To implement the pilot test, we chose studies from the prior review we had conducted on summer school (Cooper et al., 2000). Studies were chosen to represent various designs. Some studies were not relevant to summer school (to test whether the instrument and coders were sensitive to construct validity issues). In addition, we intentionally chose some studies that we knew would prove difficult to code. The same five coders coded all studies for the pilot test. All coders had earned a doctoral degree in a social science, but none had previous experience in research synthesis methodology.

Only two questions on the instrument were coded with relative unreliability. First, the coders often disagreed about the actual sample sizes reported in studies. This occurred because studies often report different sample sizes (e.g., the number of students selected to participate vs. the number of students agreeing to participate vs. the number of students actually completing the study vs. the number of students for whom scores are available on outcome measures). Second, coders often disagreed about whether or not effect sizes could be estimated for a given outcome. This occurred because translating study results into an effect size is not always a straightforward procedure and recognizing the possibilities often requires advanced training in statistics.

We believe the pilot test results were quite encouraging. It demonstrated that well-trained individuals can use the instrument properly, and it revealed out areas in which more in-depth training might be needed. In addition, the problems identified in completing the Study DIAD appear to be no different than those faced by individuals attempting to interpret the results of a study without the assistance of a study quality scale.

CONCLUSION

We hope we have accomplished several goals with this chapter. First, we introduced the notions of causality, control, and experimentation. While doing this, we asserted that questions of causality are best addressed through experiments. We then discussed the roles of McCall, Fisher, and Campbell in shaping our perceptions of what constitutes good experimental research. Next, we discussed structured attempts to measure study quality and argued that previous efforts had led to disappointing results. Finally, we discussed in detail an instrument developed to overcome many of the revealed shortcomings of other attempts to build quality assessment devices. The Study DIAD is meant to be a consensually based, multidimensional, transparent instrument for assessing the strength of causal inferences that can be drawn from a study. It is not perfect, partly because some issues in experimental design lack consensual answers regarding their impact on quality and partly because choices need to be made regarding what issues are most important to address. We hope the reader will take away from this discussion a clear picture of how the instrument operates, how it might evolve in the future, and what its limitations are. It is our hope that greater attention to the issues embodied in the Study DIAD will result in improved information becoming available for policy makers, administrators, teachers, and parents as they make evidence-based decisions about the education of children.

References

Berlin, J. A. & Rennie, D. (1999). Measuring the quality of trials: the quality of quality scales. *Journal of the American Medical Association*, 282, 1083–1084.

Boring, E. G. (1954). The nature and history of experimental control. *American Journal of Psychology*, 67, 573–589.

Campbell, D. T. (1957). Factors relevant to the validity of experiments in social settings. *Psychological Bulletin*, 54, 297–312.

Campbell, D. T. & Stanley, J. C. (1966). *Experimental and quasi-experimental designs for research*. Chicago, IL: Rand McNally.

Cohen, J. (1962). The statistical power of abnormal-social psychological research: a review. *Journal of Abnormal and Social Psychology*, 69, 145–153.

Cook, T. D. & Campbell, D. T. (1979). *Quasi-experimentation: design & analysis issues for field settings*. Boston, MA: Houghton Mifflin.

Cooper, H., Charlton, K., Valentine, J. C., & Muhlenbruck, L. (2000). Making the most of summer school: a meta-analytic and narrative review. *Monographs on Child Development*, 65, 1–118.

Fisher, R. A. (1925). *Statistical methods for research workers*. London: Oliver and Boyd.

Fisher, R. A. (1950). *The design of experiments* (6th ed.). London: Oliver & Boyd.

Funk and Wagnall's standard desk dictionary (Revised ed.), 1976. New York: HarperCollins.

Gilovich, T. (1991). *How we know what isn't so: the fallibility of human reason in everyday life*. New York: The Free Press.

Hume, D. (1978). A *treatise on human nature*. Oxford: Oxford Press (original work published in 1739–1740).

Jüni, P., Witshci, A., Bloch, R., & Egger, M. (1999). The hazards of scoring the quality of clinical trials for meta-analysis. *Journal of the American Medical Association*, 282, 1054–1060.

Kratochwill, T. R. & Levin, J. R. (Eds.). (1992). *Single-case research design and analysis: new directions for psychology and education*. Hillsdale, NJ: Erlbaum.

Levin, J. R. (1997). Overcoming feelings of powerlessness in "aging" researchers: a primer on statistical power for analysis of variance designs. *Psychology and Aging*, 12, 84–106.

Mill, J. S. (1973). A system of logic, ratiocinative and inductive, being a connected view of the principles of evidence and the methods of scientific investigation. In J. M. Robson (Ed.), *Collected Works of John Stuart Mill, Vol. 7*. Toronto: University of Toronto Press (Original work published in 1843).

Moher, D., Jadad, A. R., Nichol, G., Penman, M., Tugwell, P., & Walsh, S. (1995). Assessing the quality of randomized controlled trials. *Controlled Clinical Trials*, 16, 62–73.

Robinson, D. N. (1986). *An intellectual history of psychology*. Madison: University of Wisconsin Press.

Rosenthal, R., & Rubin, D. B. (1978). The interpersonal expectancy effect: The first 345 studies. *Behavioral and Brain Sciences*, 1, 377–415.

Sedlmeier, P., & Gigerenzer, G. (1989). Do studies of statistical power have an effect on the power of studies? *Psychological Bulletin*, 105, 309–316.

Shadish, W. R. (1989). The perception and evaluation of quality in science. In B. Gholson, W. R. Shadish, Jr., R. A. Neimeyer, & A. C. Houts (Eds.). *Psychology of science: contributions to metascience* (pp. 383–427). Cambridge, UK: Cambridge University Press.

Shadish, W. R., Cook, T. D., & Campbell, D. T. (2002). *Experimental and quasi-experimental designs for generalized causal inference*. Boston, MA: Houghton Mifflin.

Sherman, L. W. & Gottfredson, D. (1997). Research methods (appendix). In L. Sherman, D. Gottfredson, D. MacKenzie, J. Eck, P. Reuter, and S. Bushway (Eds.), *Preventing crime: what works, what doesn't, and what's promising* (pp. A1–A15). Washington DC: U.S. Office of Justice Programs.

West, S., King, V., Carey, T. S., Lohr, K. N., McKoy, N., Sutton, S. F., & Lux, L. (2002). *Systems to rate the strength of scientific evidence*. Washington DC: Agency for Healthcare Research and Quality.

CHAPTER

6

Measuring Learning Outcomes: Reliability and Validity Issues

JERRY D'AGOSTINO
University of Arizona

Conducting rigorous experimental research requires careful attention to the interdependencies among theory, research design, measurement, and statistical inference. Often students of educational research are misled into thinking that these components have little relation. Students typically take separate courses in these three areas during their graduate studies and never receive any formal instruction on how properties of one component can affect another. In this chapter, I discuss why sound measurement is a vital part of rigorous research, and how researchers can develop their measures to improve the strength of their studies.

Many of the issues and recommendations I present generalize across many, if not all, outcomes of interest to educational researchers. I focus, however, on measuring learning and achievement because those concepts have been the focus of most educational research over the past 100 years or so. Educational research has focused on these concepts for many reasons, but two are most salient. The mission of most federal education grants, such as education grants funded by the National Science Foundation, is to understand the conditions and interventions that foster student learning. If researchers desire to receive funding through one of these programs, they

Empirical Methods for Evaluating Educational Interventions

are strongly encouraged to include student learning as a primary outcome in their research proposal. Second, although schools are expected to offer students the opportunity to develop cognitive, affective, and psychomotor skills in a comprehensive manner, historically, the emphasis has been on developing students' academic skills. This priority is exemplified by the reliance on external achievement testing as the sole indicator of school performance. Consequently, researchers often focus on discovering effective ways to promote learning because it remains the primary goal of schools.

Although Campbell and Stanley (1963) and Cook and Campbell (1979) were clear that independent variable validity is equally as important as outcome validity, this chapter will address issues surrounding the latter in experimental research. I will discuss the importance of measuring learning reliably and validly in educational research. Without sound measures, the cogency of conclusions drawn from educational experiments would be compromised greatly. I then will turn to a discussion of how reliability and validity are assessed in general. The chapter will finish with some strategies for (a) integrating reliability and validity analyses into experimental designs and (b) bolstering the reliability and validity of learning outcomes to increase the rigor of research projects. As will be discussed, all forms of research validity are affected by outcome characteristics, underscoring the importance of sound measurement in high-quality experimentation. Generally, however, not all measurement validity concerns are at issue in a given study. The purpose of the study ultimately dictates the validity evidence required to defend its credibility.

THE CRITICALITY OF RELIABILITY AND VALIDITY IN EXPERIMENTAL RESEARCH

Measurement is the foundation of sound research. A rigorous research design and sophisticated statistical analysis will do little to correct a study based on poorly administered independent and dependent measures. Of the 36 threats to the four essential research validities (statistical conclusion, internal, external, and construct) explicated by Shadish, Cook, and Campbell (2002), 14 pertain either directly or indirectly to issues involving outcome measurement (Table 6.1). Measurement concerns are pervasive throughout the research process, from study conception, through research design development, to data collection, and continuing through data analysis and reporting.

The fundamental goal of experimental research is to document and understand cause–effect relationships. When we know what causes student learning to improve both in general and within various situations, we can develop or refine educational interventions to maximize future learning. It is important during the process of program formation to evaluate the cred-

TABLE 6.1
Threats to Four Main Research Validities (Threats in Bold Involve Outcome Measures)

Validity Types			
Statistical Conclusion	Internal	External	Construct
Power	Ambiguous Temporal Precedence	Unit Generalization	**Construct Explication**
Statistical Test Violation	Selection	Treatment Variation	**Construct Confounding**
Error Rate Problem	History	**Outcome Generalization**	**Mono-Operation Bias**
Measure Unreliability	Maturation	Setting Generalization	**Mono-Method Bias**
Range Restriction	**Regression**	Context-Dependent Mediation	**Construct Levels**
Treatment Implementation Unreliability	Attrition		**Treatment Sensitive Factorial Structure**
Extraneous Variance in Treatment Setting	**Testing**		**Reactive Self-Report Changes**
Unit Heterogeneity	**Instrumentation**		Experimental Situation Reactivity
Inaccurate Effect Size Estimation			Experimenter Expectancies
			Novelty
			Compensatory Equalization
			Compensatory Rivalry
			Resentful Demoralization
			Treatment Diffusion

Adapted from Shadish, W. R., Cook, T. D., & Campbell, D. T. (2002). Experimental and Quasi-experimental designs for generalized causal inference. New York: Houghton Mifflin Company.

ibility of the research that guided development. Study validity, or truthfulness of research inferences (Shadish et al., 2002), serves as the central focus of this evaluation endeavor. Two interconnected questions should drive study evaluation: (a) Are there other alternative explanations that can explain study results; and (b) are there any threats to study validity that delimit the cogency of study results? In reviewing a study, one considers potential validity threats as sources of possible alternative explanations. For instance, if a treatment group experienced a history event that could have influenced their outcome scores that was not experienced by the control group, the potential threat might explain the study results. Many validity threats are obviated by implementing a true experiment with randomization of participants to conditions, but randomized experiments alone do not eradicate all threats. Because measurement is involved in most threats, evaluating the quality of a study's measurement procedures is central to study critiquing. Let us now review those measurement issues that can influence each validity type.

Measurement and Statistical Conclusion Validity

Statistical conclusion validity pertains to (a) the degree to which a study is sensitive to detect covariation between variables, (b) the extent to which covariation reflects a cause–effect relation, and (c) the degree of covariation strength. Threats to statistical conclusion validity include violation of the assumptions of statistical tests, range restriction, conducting numerous statistical tests without γ corrections, unreliability of independent or dependent variables, inaccurate effect size estimates, within cell variance heterogeneity, and lack of statistical power. Some of these threats are interconnected, such as power and reliability.

In addition to hypothesis-testing assumptions, other properties of hypothesis testing play major roles in statistical conclusion validity. In the hypothesis-testing process, a null hypothesis is either rejected or not rejected, but the possibility of type I (rejecting a true null) or type II (not rejecting a false null) errors remain. A credible study possesses a good degree of statistical power, or the likelihood of rejecting a false null. Power can be increased by using certain techniques, such as reducing extraneous variability (e.g., by using blocking, analysis of covariance, or repeated-measures designs), increasing sample size, increasing the strength and variability of treatments, relying on repeated-measures designs, and conducting parametric statistical tests when the underlying assumptions are satisfied. Notice that measurement plays a vital role in many of these procedures, particularly the influence of reliability.

The concept of reliability is somewhat ambiguous in that multiple meanings exist. Reliability typically refers to the consistency of test results, but has at least two relevant factors: consistency of results over testing period (assuming no change on the latent variable) and consistency among scores on component test parts (e.g., internal consistency of test items). Although measures of these distinct consistency conceptualizations often are used and interpreted interchangeably, there is virtually no evidence documenting the relationship between the two. It is very possible that scores from a test are reliable over testing periods but test items are not internally consistent. The primary issue involving time consistency reliability is whether test scores are resilient to environmental and individual sources of error, such as weather conditions, mood, and motivation. At question is whether a child will score more or less the same on a reading test on a sunny day while happy compared with a rainy day after his or her parents were arguing that morning. Internal consistency relates more to item sample variations across parallel forms from the universe of items that comprises a domain. Often a test is split into two "parallel" forms to compute reliability because separate test forms are rather rare. This especially is the case in most studies that do not rely on standardized achievement tests as outcome measures. Usually one form of a test is made for research purposes.

Although each conceptualization of consistency reflects different error source concerns, the purpose of both is to decipher examinees' true placements on the attribute from their observed scores. Thus, the primary tenet of classical test theory, namely that the observed score is a function of true score and error, holds for both consistency models. The conventional standard error of measurement indicates the estimated standard deviation of an examinee's score distribution over repeated administrations of the same test or administrations of many tests comprising different items sampled from the same domain universe. Further, the conceptual definition of the reliability coefficient as the ratio of true score variance to observed score variance holds for both models.

In an intergroup comparison study, observed score total variation is partitioned into between- and within-group variances. Power is increased by maximizing between-group variability (mean differences) and minimizing within-cell error. As outcome measure reliability increases, a greater proportion of the total score variance is due to true differences among examinees. This tends to have little effect on between-group differences, but potentially sizable differences on within-cell variability, because measurement error typically is deposited within cells rather than between them. Increased reliability can shrink the error within groups, maximizing obtained test statistic results (Cleary & Linn, 1969; Cleary, Linn, & Walster, 1970; Shadish et al., 2002).

Because reliability estimates can vary across groups, the posttest estimates of reliability could differ between treatment and control participants. If the degree of posttest error is confounded with group membership, within-cell variances could differ artificially. If this difference was sizable, assumptions regarding the homogeneity of within-cell variability would be violated, causing a threat to the statistical conclusions drawn from most group-comparison tests.

Outcome properties also can play a part in range restriction issues. Often this phenomenon is due to sampling practices, such as sampling homogeneous individuals. However, if a test possesses many very easy and very difficult items, a leptokurtic total score distribution likely will result, with individuals' scores clustering around the mean. Likewise, untargeted tests containing too many easy items might lead to a highly negatively skewed distribution, and tests containing too many difficult items might lead to a positively skewed distribution. All three examples can facilitate range restriction apart from sampling issues. Tests comprising other item difficulty distributions can lead to other nonnormal total score distributions. Although parametric tests tend to be robust against normal distribution deviations when sample sizes are large, the item difficulty configuration of a test can increase the threat of statistical assumption violations.

Measurement and Internal Validity

Internal validity relates to the degree to which causal inferences can be drawn from the covariation among variables. Of the eight main internal validity threats described by Shadish et al. (2002), three pertain directly to measurement issues. These threats result from interpreting observed score differences as "true" effects rather than as extraneous changes due to characteristics of participants or measuring instruments. Testing is a threat due to changes in individuals rather than tests. Like the old saying, "you can never step in the same stream twice," taking a test once has an impact on how one approaches the test a second or third time. A testing effect would occur if participants' scores on a test were at least partially affected by their prior exposure to the test. After taking a test, one has the opportunity to discover if his or her responses were accurate to questions and seek additional information to "correct" mistakes. Or, people can talk about the test and receive help from others (or, of course, they can be misled). The simple fact of remembering how one completed the items initially changes the mental operations used to solve the same questions again, which also impacts negatively the construct validity of the second test score. For instance, if students remember their answers to multiple-choice mathematics questions on the first administration, they might simply circle their answers to remembered questions on a second administration and skip re-solving the questions.

Typically testing is a threat in longitudinal designs, such as when participants are administered the same measuring device at pretest and posttest. In experimental research, testing likely would have little effect on the mean differences between groups if equivalence is assumed a priori (i.e., through random assignment). There are situations, however, in which testing can have a negative impact on internal validity in an experimental design. If a treatment group, for instance, was sensitized to a test due to some unique experiences during an intervention, a testing by treatment interaction might ensue. One should pay careful attention to the transactions of each group to ensure that certain individuals were not provided undue practice on the types of items or item formats found on the outcome measures. This last statement might be misconstrued to mean that a measure should not tap into the construct for which the treatment was designed to address. At least one outcome should be tailored to the specifications of an intervention to ascertain the degree to which the primary treatment objectives were met. If a treatment group gets additional practice writing short answers to mathematics questions during an intervention designed to improve general mathematics skills, however, and perform better than a control group on a posttest that requires extensive constructed responses to mathematics problems, an observed effect might be due as much to the additional writing practice than improved mathematics learning. By including mathematics problems that do not require writing on the outcome measure, potential treatment effects would be better isolated. If, however, the intent of the treatment was to improve students' mathematics writing skills, then an argument could be made that detected effects were by design and not the result of an unintended practice effect.

When a treatment has negligible effects on testing, which is the more common situation, the magnitude of a testing effect likely will vary across individuals. In a mixed-design experiment (e.g., at least one repeated- and between-subjects factor), the person by test time interaction variance serves as the error term to test the statistical significance of the between-subjects factor. Thus, although testing usually does not impact the internal validity of experiments, it could reduce power by inflating error, which potentially could influence the statistical conclusion validity of results and interpretations.

Often researchers administer a parallel test at "Time 2" to mitigate possible testing effects. For two tests to be truly parallel, the observed-score means and variances must be equivalent, and the scores from both tests must correlate similarly with other variables. Examinees should have the same true scores on both tests, and the error variances on both tests should be equal for the tests to be considered parallel. Given these requirements, it is not an easy task to create parallel forms. Further, for the error variances to be equivalent, sources of error across the two tests must be similar, including error associated with domain item sampling and item formats. Parallel tests must measure the same content and contain items with similar formats. Thus, although identical items will not appear on each of two parallel forms, examinees might become familiar with the overall style of the test on a first administration, which will essentially prepare them for the test at Time 2.

Undoubtedly, however, using parallel forms can help reduce the magnitude of a testing effect (e.g., participants cannot simply remember specific test questions). An alternative strategy to creating truly parallel forms is to develop quasi-parallel or essentially τ-equivalent forms, which are forms that yield the same true scores for examinees (hence the term "tau" equivalent) except for an additive constant (see Allen & Yen, 1979). The error variances, means, and observed-score variances of essentially τ-equivalent forms do not need to be identical. Creating such forms would involve randomly assigning items with similar content and cognitive demand to one of two forms. This would result in two forms with matched content specifications. Half of each treatment and control group would be administered one form at pretest and the other form at posttest to control for any potential presentation order effects.

Another strategy is to administer a test with different content at Time 2. This strategy, which Cook and Campbell (1979) did not recommend, is susceptible to instrumentation effects (i.e., an observed change might be due to measuring different content at pre- and posttesting). If groups are considered equivalent initially, as would be the case in a true experiment, this potential issue subsides. However, the researcher must pay close attention to the primary construct measured over time. If one mathematics test is administered at Time 1 that contains mostly problem solving items, and a computation-laden mathematics test is administered at Time 2, the construct validity of "change" will be jeopardized. This potential problem is most pronounced when a series of vertically equated tests are employed in a long-term longitudinal study.

Constructs naturally vary in the degree to which their meaning changes over time. Take, for example, the concept of "geometry." In primary grades, geometry commonly is measured with items requiring youngsters to identify shapes. Visual memory processes come into play to a great degree to solve those types of items. Geometry becomes more formulaic in the middle grades (e.g., solve for the area of a triangle) and becomes proof oriented in high school grades. Logic is involved to a great degree to analyze proofs, which is quite distinct from the mental processes used to identify shapes. The content of other mathematics topics, such as algebra, change over time, but not to the same extent as geometry. Thus, due to an instrumentation problem, follow-up effects of an early education program designed to enhance students' mathematics skills might appear to fade over time when measured with a geometry subtest, but not when measured with a computation subtest. Often test developers use item response theory methods to create such tests (see Embretson & Reise, 2000; Hambleton, Swaminathan, & Rogers, 1991; Wright & Stone, 1979). They tend to spend considerably more effort choosing items based on vertical scaling properties (e.g., does this item serve well as an anchor between grades 3 and 4 tests?) than examining the fit of items and people to a unidimensional model. No matter which items are chosen, some concepts simply cannot be measured properly over time with one scale.

A regression artifact perhaps is the most discussed and misunderstood potential threat to internal validity. A common form of regression occurs when more extreme-scoring examinees move closer to the mean on a follow-up test administration. Initially low-scoring students changing the most and initially high-scoring students changing the least from pretest to posttest is an example of a regression effect. Typically, there is an "error" and "true" component of regression to the mean. More-extreme-scoring individuals often are measured with less precision (Wright & Stone, 1979), which leads to more positive error for high-scoring people and more negative error for low-scoring people. High-scoring people, therefore, tend to appear more proficient than in actuality, and low-scoring people are observed to be lower in proficiency given their "true" capabilities. These errors tend to diminish on a second test administration, so that initially high scorers are not as high and initially low scorers are not as low at Time 2 (see, for example, Campbell & Kenny, 1999; and for an empirical demonstration of the phenomenon, see Levin, 1993). Thus, much of the observed Time 1–to–Time 2 change is due to more measurement error at the tails.

Not all of an apparent regression effect is due to error, however. The relationship between prerequisite skills of initially extreme scorers and the substance of many interventions might contribute to an observed regression effect. Many general education programs are targeted for "average" students, so initially low scorers have more to learn from an intervention than middle- and high-scoring students. Hence, low-scorers might post larger pre–post gains on average because indeed they did have higher rates of learning on average relative to their peers.

Regression effects can be a serious issue in educational research because often programs and interventions are designed for extreme scorers (e.g., compensatory, remedial, special education, and gifted programs). If groups are not equivalent initially, a treatment effect can be underestimated or overestimated due to a group by regression interaction effect. This is a primary reason randomized experiments are so important in educational research. Initial group equivalence through randomization obviates most, if not all, the problems created by regression to the mean because measurement errors or differential learning rates based on initial status are balanced across groups. By designing an experiment, the researcher has guarded against any potential regression threats.

Measurement and External Validity

External validity is the degree to which research conclusions generalize across populations, settings, time, treatment variations, or outcomes. Studies based on one dependent variable suffer from concerns regarding outcome generalization. Even if multiple outcomes are used, but all cover a narrow width of the construct domain, generalization issues exist. This problem is most pronounced when outcomes are tailored specifically to an intervention or program. If positive results are found for the treatment, questions of whether students' academic skills have improved over all skills or only on those specific skills addressed by the treatment can linger. For example, Reading Recovery (Clay, 1985), which is a remedial tutor-based program for first graders, commonly has been evaluated based on outcomes designed for use in the program (the outcome battery is known as the "Observation Survey"). Although program students appear to outperform comparison students on these tailored measures, Reading Recovery critics have charged that participants do not perform much better than comparison students on standardized reading tests (for instance, see Hiebert, Colt, Catto, & Gury, 1992). A primary program goal is to increase a participant's overall reading achievement to the school or class average, which by definition, should generalize across many reading outcomes, not only those designed for the program. Outcome generalization involves more than the sheer number of outcomes used (the Observation Survey consists of six tests). It relates as well to comprehensive domain coverage given the goals of the intervention (for an additional discussion of the methodologic issues associated with research on Reading Recovery, see D'Agostino & Murphy, 2004).

Measurement and Construct Validity

Generally speaking, construct validity is the degree to which study operations match the vital characteristics of the theoretical constructs they were designed to represent. There are a number of common concerns addressed in research and measurement conceptualizations of construct validity, but there is one basic distinction. Measurement construct validity primarily relates to the quality of outcome measures, whereas research construct validity involves assessments of both independent and dependent measures. I will discuss construct validity issues surrounding outcomes, but many of the issues hold for both variable types. Often researchers attend more to ensuring construct validity of outcomes, but the validity of treatment conditions is equally important.

Most of the construct validity threats involving dependent measures relate to the outcome generalization problem. Although related, construct validity problems threaten the soundness of study results. The external validity of outcomes is the degree to which those results generalize across the universe of possible results in the domain. A universe of possible outcomes can be defined by certain key dimensions, such as content, operation format (multiple choice, essay, etc.), and method format (paper and pencil, computer, self-report, observation, etc.). Inadequate explication of a construct results when certain subfacets that an intervention is expected to affect are left unmeasured. Messick (1995) referred to this invalidity as construct underrepresentation. For example, it might occur in a Reading Recovery study if a vocabulary test serves as the sole outcome but the intervention was designed to improve several reading skills in addition to vocabulary, such as comprehension, phonemic awareness, and letter identification. It could also result if a program was designed to improve vocabulary skills, but the outcome measure comprised mostly nouns. Thus, an analysis of construct explication entails sketching out the subskills that an intervention is directly or indirectly designed to address, and matching outcomes to the final sketch. A study could indeed focus on an incomplete portion of the construct, but the researcher must temper conclusions accordingly. Hence, if a null difference is found on the noun-laden test, one can conclude that the program had little impact on improving noun vocabulary, not vocabulary in general.

A study likely would be susceptible to mono-operation bias (Campbell & Fiske, 1959) if the chosen outcome operations did not represent completely the anticipated mental skills an intervention was designed to address. An instructional program designed to improve only recognition skills, for instance, might be adequately assessed with a multiple-choice test. Many interventions, however, are explicitly or implicitly designed to develop students' skills in a more complex manner. Consequently, mono-operation bias would be a potential problem if one operation were used. If an instructional program were designed to increase students' recognition and recall, multiple-choice items alone would not be adequate. At least some constructed response items would be necessary to test recall.

Mono-method bias is another important potential threat that should be considered in an experiment. As is the case with content- and operations-related threats, the researcher should use the measurement method or methods that match the purposes of the intervention under study. Because a key goal of Reading Recovery is to improve students' oral reading skills, a study of the program based on paper-and-pencil outcomes only will not adequately address the effectiveness of the program in that subdomain of reading. For that reason, the Observation Survey consists of some oral tests, such as the running record, which involves a student reading aloud as the teacher records errors. It would be much more acceptable to use paper-and-pencil outcomes in a study of a program designed to address students' silent-reading comprehension skills.

The method of self-report is particularly problematic when attempting to gauge achievement or learning. Often people are aware they might be eligible to participate in a study, and they might have good reason to over- or underestimate their knowledge or skills to be selected for or to avoid program participation. If the selection measure is also used as a pretest, initial scores could be biased. Once selected, participants' motivational levels likely would change, leading to inaccurate change scores. Further, treatment participants often guess the purposes or hypotheses of a study, and subsequently, they might modify their reports either to uphold or to sabotage their beliefs regarding the expected outcomes. This might occur in a computer-based intervention course where treatment students exaggerate how much they learned in the hope of continuing the course.

All methods of collecting achievement or learning levels, for that matter, are subject to differing degrees of examinee motivation. A student could decide not to try very hard to pass a private school multiple-choice entrance examination because his or her friends planned to attend the local public school, and students might vary in how seriously they approach a standards-based high school graduation test. Undoubtedly, however, it is much easier to exaggerate one's achievement proficiency through self-report than through a conventional achievement test. Both methods might be equally susceptible to self-initiated underestimation of proficiency.

Somewhat opposite to the construct explication or underrepresentation problem is construct confounding, or what Messick (1995) termed *construct irrelevant variance*. Construct confounding occurs when scores on a test result from individuals' skills on multiple constructs, some of which were not intended. Requiring examinees to use science knowledge on a mathematics or reading examination would be an example of confounding. Because the goal of experimental research is to isolate causes and effects to understand their relationships, outcomes should be inspected closely for proper construct isolation. Construct confounding also can delimit statistical power (and hence, increase the threat to statistical conclusion validity), especially if the irrelevant variance is rather pronounced. For example, a reading intervention might appear less effective than in actuality if the outcome measure is driven to a great degree by participants' science knowledge, assuming that an integrated science and reading intervention is not under study. Conversely, a science intervention would appear less effective if the outcome measures depended heavily on students' reading proficiency. Yet, it is important to keep in mind that construct confounding is not a form of random error—it is systematic error that can lead to quite reliable test scores. Thus, whereas random error affects within cell variance, construct confounding can decrease between-group differences.

Often outcomes are selected that do not permit examinees to demonstrate their full capabilities on a construct because certain construct levels are not measured. A form of construct underrepresentation that frequently leads to range restriction, confounded construct levels of a learning outcome, results from testing a narrow range of the construct's cognitive complexity. Unlike construct explication, however, which pertains more to pertinent categories of the construct missing from the measure, the construct levels problem arises from not representing certain levels of a construct's cognitive demands.

For instance, construct level confounding could occur if a basic-skills mathematics test is used in a study of an intervention designed to increase both basic and higher-order thinking skills. If the program was no more effective than a comparison intervention at improving students' basic skills, but was much more effective than the comparison at developing students' higher-order skills, the outcome measure likely would fail to register such findings. Construct level confounding is relevant for outcomes only in situations in which the measured construct can be articulated by ordinal levels of complexity. Usually researchers rely on taxonomies of learning, such as Bloom's (Bloom, Engelhart, Hill, Furst, & Krathwohl, 1956), to elucidate the hierarchic levels to be addressed by interventions and measured through outcomes.

Many tests are designed on the basis of a multifactorial model. The factorial structure of a measure, however, can be altered as a result of an intervention. This phenomenon would be indicated by differing factor analysis results across treatment and control conditions on posttest, but not at pretest. For example, I have conducted factor analyses on a state's fifth-grade mathematics standards-based assessment (D'Agostino, 2004). The test was designed to measure six mathematics strands that comprise this particular state's mathematics standards. Confirmatory factor analyses based on the statewide data set revealed that a three-factor model yielded a fit to the data that was superior to the six-strand model of the standards. The three factors included a general mathematics skill factor, a geometric analysis factor, and a problem-solving factor. Assume that a program was developed to focus teaching on the academic standards. After the intervention, treatment students' conceptual understanding of mathematics quite possibly could be reconfigured to match the standards structure. This might result in the six-strand model fitting data best for treatment students but not for controls. If the researcher developed six subscales, one for each strand, the validity of the subscales would be questionable for students who did not receive the treatment. One way the researcher could rectify this problem would be to create subscales mapped to each separate factorial model, and then analyze intergroup comparisons across all developed subscales.

Clearly, outcome measurement is involved in many of the validity threats explicated by Shadish et al. (2002). The possible threats pertaining to outcomes are not specific to construct validity, as all four forms of research validity can be affected by outcome measurement issues. Some measurement issues relate to multiple threats, such as would be the case if a test were limited to measuring but a few construct levels: The construct validity of a test would be compromised, as would the score range, and consequently, the power of statistical analyses. This example demonstrates the interconnectedness of research components. Problems in one area can permeate to other research facets to jeopardize the overall soundness of the study. Let us now discuss how reliability and validity can be assessed.

ASSESSING RELIABILITY

As was previously mentioned, there are two distinct conceptualizations of reliability: (a) test consistency as overall score repeatability and (b) test consistency as the concordance of internal test components. The former reliability type relates to the degree to which test scores are resilient with respect to time-related sources of error. For instance, test scores would be circumspect if an examinee's mood or some environmental condition significantly alters a person's score on the test. Because mood and environmental condition rarely change during a single test administration, one must ascertain if a test is impervious to these error forms by administering the test on separate occasions. Notice that it is not the test that is reliable, but the examinees' scores rendered by the test. To be more specific, reliability is the interaction between examinees and test components. The same test might yield more reliable scores for second graders than first graders, for example, because younger children's moods and conditions tend to oscillate faster over time, and they tend to be more sensitive to mood and condition effects than older children. This is not to imply that a reliability coefficient is specific to every sample of examinees. Reliability data collected from inner-city first graders might generalize to similar schools in the same city, state, or perhaps country. It is the researcher's prerogative to determine the population for which reliability coefficients generalize.

Time-related reliability typically is assessed by conducting a test–retest study in which the test is administered to examinees, some period is allowed to elapse, and the test is readministered. The reliability coefficient is the correlation coefficient between Time 1 and Time 2 scores. The amount of time between administrations is critical. Ideally, the time should not be too short so that examinees easily remember item responses or can benefit too much from a practice effect. It also should not be too long so that examinees' position on the construct is altered through learning or some other change process. For example, I have witnessed some researchers who used fall and spring achievement test scores to represent test–retest reliability data. Given that examinees participated in schooling an entire school year and differential learning rates among students should have been assumed, using fall–spring scores as reliability data completely defeats the purpose of score consistency "assuming no growth." Typically, a 1-week to 1-month time interval is ideal to avoid remembering, practice effects, and differential learning, but the optimal interval depends mostly on the particular situation and test content. Preferably, data should be collected while examinees are not studying the topic of the test or related topics. Shorter intervals would be required if some learning of related topic was occurring. Test–retest data should always be collected before a group-comparison treatment-control study commences.

If the researcher is concerned about possible practice effects, a parallel form should be developed and forms A and B should be administered in a counterbalanced manner (half of the sample gets form A first, half take form B initially). Rarely do researchers go to such effort to avoid a practice effect due to the difficulty of creating a truly parallel form. Actually, researchers rarely conduct test–retest reliability studies mainly because procuring two separate testing times for the sole purpose of evaluating reliability is a difficult task indeed. Researchers frequently rely on data from one testing period to compute a number of internal consistency indices of reliability. Mistakenly, many will report those values as though time-interval indicators would be equivalent.

The basic purpose of internal consistency reliability is to evaluate whether examinees respond similarly at one administration to test components designed to measure the same construct. Sources of error that can occur within a test administration will lower internal consistency, such as varying test content, item artifacts, differential attention, and fatigue.

In a sense, internal consistency is equivalent to conducting a "test–retest–retest–and so on." study with little time interval in which single test items or components represent "tests." The more homogeneous or "parallel" that test items are to one another, the greater the score convergence. If items behave similarly, interitem correlations will be high. For this reason, the general case of the Spearman–Brown internal consistency estimate of reliability is a function of test length and average interitem correlation. Longer tests and those comprising items with higher intercorrelations tend to yield scores that are more reliable.

In addition to computing the average interitem correlation, the correlation is often computed between two test halves. To adjust for a reduction in overall test length, the Spearman–Brown double-length formula is applied to estimate the reliability of scores based on the full test length. Other internal consistency methods include the γ coefficient and the Kuder–Richardson formulas. Feldt (1989) and Nunnally and Bernstein (1994) explain the logic and statistical operations of these procedures. Most statistical software applications have built-in modules to compute several internal consistency estimates. It is useful to compute an array of indicators, because estimation variation should be anticipated.

Researchers relying on subjectively scored tests, such as essays and performance assessments, should use multiple raters who are trained to score student products using similar criteria. Interrater and intrarater reliability should be assessed and reported. The former term refers to the agreement between different judges and the latter term involves an analysis of individual rater consistency over time and students. Sources of error of concern for interrater agreement include differential scoring rubric interpretation, halo effects, and individual rater tendencies, such as gravitating toward central tendency responses. Rater drift is an example of an intrarater error issue, which involves raters changing their scoring criteria over time. Training raters to use scoring criteria in the same manner, followed by continuous refresher training, helps improve both forms of rater reliability.

ASSESSING VALIDITY

There are several definitions for test validity, but to synthesize many definitions, the term refers to the degree to which the interpretations and inferences of test scores or item responses used for a specific purpose can be supported with empirical evidence and logical analyses (Cronbach, 1971; Cureton, 1951; Messick, 1995). Notice that a test is not perceived as possessing a certain uniform level of validity. Rather than being an inherent property of a test, validity is seen as relating to the legitimacy of using test scores or item responses for given purposes. Scores can be valid to a great degree for one use, but meaningless or nonsensical for another. Also notice that test validity relates more to the interaction between test content and examinees' responses to that content (the scores) rather than to the test itself or the examinees themselves. This point is very important because it reveals that comprehensive validity analyses entail examining test content, examinees, and the interstice between the two. Further, it would be improper to ask the question, Are those test scores valid for that purpose? Validity is by degrees and is a continuous process of gathering evidence and formulating an argument to support score interpretations (Cronbach, 1971; Kane, 1992).

Test validity is one of the more confusing concepts in educational and psychological research. Conceptualizations and standards for validity evidence have changed over the last several decades, and measurement experts have continuously debated which forms of validity evidence should be gathered to support a test's usage.

A history of these issues is beyond the scope of this chapter, but good references for the interested reader include Shepard (1993) and Sireci (1998). A brief foray into the validity debate, however, is important to understand the role of validity evidence in experimentation.

It is not certain who actually coined the term "validity" or who first advocated for its analysis as a vital part of test development and use, but Edward L. Thorndike discussed the importance of the concept in what is often considered the first textbook on educational and psychological measurement (Thorndike, 1919). He did not use the term validity, but he did discuss the importance of deriving meaning for test scores by examining the association between a target measure and measures designed to indicate similar concepts. In a sense, Thorndike was describing procedures to gather what would become known as criterion-related validity evidence.

Shepard (1993) reported that criterion-related validity was the most common procedure for deriving test score meaning between 1920 and 1950. In its earliest form, this validity type involved examining the association between several measures of the same or like attributes, as Thorndike (1919) had described. As the concept evolved, criterion-related validity referred to the collection of evidence to support specific testing situations. One of these general situations is when tests are used to predict some outcome, or to select or place individuals in programs. To support the claim that a given test is useful for these purposes, one should gather evidence that using the test increases judgment accuracy. Criterion-related validity in these situations involves developing one or more criterion indicators of outcome success. For example, if a test were used for selecting students for graduate school, one would evaluate the test by first creating a measure of what it means to be successful in graduate school. Course grades, professors' appraisals, and self-reported degree of success might be some variables used as criteria.

Criterion-related validity is a term also used to describe the degree to which a test accurately depicts an attribute for which a directly observable indicator of the attribute exists. For instance, whether or not a person has influenza can be directly assessed through a blood test. There is little or no inference to be made: The virus is present in the blood or it is not. Let us assume that a physician does not want to wait for blood results to predict if a patient has influenza. The physician might develop a simple checklist of influenza symptoms, which are indirect indicators of the virus. A criterion-related study of the physician's checklist could be conducted to examine the degree of prediction accuracy by linking blood-test results to completed checklists for a sample of patients.

Ralph Tyler's (1934, 1949) work on curriculum and test construction in the 1930s had a dramatic impact on how validity was construed in educational measurement. Tyler discussed the importance of "mapping out" the objectives or aims of instruction in terms of what students will know and be able to do after instruction had taken place. Objectives represented actual student behaviors and ways of feeling that were the result of teaching, and to evaluate if instruction worked, tests were to be developed that allowed students the opportunity to display their attainment of objectives. Content validity emerged from this perspective on curriculum development and refinement, because it became imperative to document the universe of test items that could be used to represent each objective, and to ascertain if sampled test items were both relevant and representative of objective content domains (Cureton, 1951; Rulon, 1946).

But clearly defined content domains are not available for all learning and achievement outcomes that might be used in experimental research. A joint committee of the American Psychological Association, American Educational Research Association, and National Council on Measurements Used in Education (1954) recognized this issue, and essentially conceived another validity-type construct. Specifically, construct validity refers to the degree to which test scores or item responses represent the attribute for which the scores or responses are being used to indicate (Cronbach, 1971). This facet of validity has become predominant over the last 20 to 30 years as the major research emphasis in psychology and education shifted from examining behaviors per se to examining behaviors as signs of mental and cognitive processes (Messick, 1981). As this shift occurred, researchers started to construe that test performance was caused by some underlying latent construct within an individual rather than by some directly observable trait. Humans could not identify these constructs directly, but they could represent them through manifested behaviors and actions. So, what one was observing was not the entity being measured, but rather an inference of the entity under investigation. According to this perspective, measurement, and for that matter, science, progresses as the characteristics of these latent traits are elucidated to a greater degree.

The notion of test scores and item responses representing constructs also has led to confusion and divisiveness among validity scholars. One school of thought, known as the unitary perspective, ascribes to a perspective that only one "form" of validity is necessary, because validity always relates to making inferences from scores and responses to constructs. According to this viewpoint, there is no distinction between validity forms because content and criterion-related validities are subsumed under construct validity. Indeed, Messick (1989), a strong advocate of this perspective, argued that content-related evidence might not be validity evidence at all because it relates specifically to test item properties and not scores or responses of examinees caused by underlying latent attributes. Other researchers who have committed to this position, yet seemingly in a less extreme manner (LaDuca, 1994; Sireci, 1998), have claimed that content validity evidence is vital in many testing situations, and therefore, should not be unduly trivialized within a unitary perspective. These researchers, however, maintained that even content domains are constructs, so tests designed to represent objectives are as founded on inferences to abstract theoretical concepts as tests designed to measure mental attributes.

The trinitary perspective holds that construct, content, and criterion-related indeed are distinct validity forms that are relevant to separate testing purposes (see Thorndike & Hagen [1962] for an explication of this viewpoint). According to this position, content validity is not subsumed under construct validity because content domains are tangible entities with directly observable behaviors. Inferences, consequently, are not from examinee responses to constructs but from sampled items to a universe of items that represent a domain. Criterion-related validity, according to the trinitary view, also is distinct from construct validity because a test measuring one attribute might be a useful predictor of outcomes linked to other attributes. That is, a test used to select or place individuals does not necessarily have to tap into the attributes that comprise outcome success.

No matter which view one embraces, the key in experimental research is to articulate clearly the inferences that are made regarding the meaning of test scores and item responses. For example, if one were studying an intervention designed specifically to increase the number of single-digit multiplication facts a student can memorize without any intent to interpret test scores as signifying a mental attribute, then content validity evidence likely would suffice. A researcher studying the effects of an intervention designed to increase the scores reported by a state on a standards-based assessment serves as another example. As I mentioned earlier in the chapter, I could not garner adequate evidence supporting the position that a state's six-strand model of fifth-grade mathematics standards linked to mental attributes (D'Agostino, 2004). However, just because curriculum often is organized in a manner that does not map on directly to cognitive structure, is it not meaningful for schools and state education departments to identify student achievement according to curricular organization? One can make a strong argument that the six-strand subscores are as or more meaningful to educators than are scores driven by mental attributes. To develop interventions to increase scores organized by curricular content, a validity goal would be to collect evidence revealing how well sampled test items represented and were relevant to the universe of items within each strand. One must be careful not to overinterpret the strand scores as representations of student cognitive processes (LaDuca, 1994, explains that job-skill classifications might not align perfectly with cognitive-skill dimensions, but are meaningful nonetheless).

Likely, however, the purpose of most experimental research studies is to understand the underlying mental attributes that learners utilize to become more proficient. In these circumstances, content and construct validity evidence might be appropriate, but content evidence alone likely would not be sufficient. Because criterion-related validity of dependent measures is not usually as pertinent in true experiments (e.g., measures are used as outcomes, not to select or place individuals), its direct assessment usually is unnecessary. The concept of criterion-related validity, however, is very important in measuring learning and achievement outcomes. The ultimate goal of most educational interventions, either stated or implied, is not to increase student achievement, but to improve the life prospects of participants. Achievement outcomes are seen as critical to open up opportunities for students, such as getting into competitive colleges, and as indicators of important life skills. Consequently, achievement rarely is construed as an end measure itself, but as a means of reaching goals that are more important. Within that context, it is important for researchers to document that a student achievement measure indeed predicts critical life outcomes. Several studies have revealed that young students who fall behind their peers academically are at great risk for failing later in life (see Mayer & Peterson, 1999) and for dropping out of school prematurely (e.g., Battin-Pearson, Newcomb, Abbott, Hill, Catalano, & Hawkins, 2000). Far fewer predictive validity studies have been conducted to document that specific achievement test scores can be used to forecast life events, such as attending college, obtaining gainful employment, or avoiding criminal activity or unemployment.

Content-Related Validity Evidence

Researchers desiring to examine content validity evidence of test scores will be faced with a rather difficult conundrum. The most rudimentary form of content validity analysis is to conduct a "face" validity study. There is no systematic procedure for studying this type of validity, other than perusing through items to search for problems with content domain underrepresentation or irrelevant item content. If possible, content experts should be provided a clear definition of the content domain and then asked to modify or reject any items that do not fit the domain descriptions. Most measurement experts would not consider this rather informal and unsystematic procedure sufficient to document content validity. More sophisticated and accepted procedures, however, can be time consuming, require considerable resources, and typically are outside the scope of most experiments. If one is adopting an existing outcome designed specifically as an indicator of some domain, one should investigate if validity evidence exists based on a more formal content analysis method. Unless one is engaged in a very comprehensive experiment, it is doubtful that a more systematic method would be used, primarily because it is difficult to incorporate such methods into the design of an experiment. Construct validity can be explored much more readily within an experimental design.

One of the reasons content validity analyses are difficult to conduct as part of experiments is that most methods rely on subject-matter experts (SMEs) to evaluate test items. Consequently, test scores rarely serve as the primary data of content validity analyses. Some validity analysts, however, have developed procedures to examine the congruence between test content structure and item response patterns (see Deville [1996] for an example). These methods combine the results from SME judgments with examinee item responses to study simultaneously both content and construct validity evidence, and thus, are framed within a unitary view of validity.

SME judgmental methods designed to examine the alignment between test items and content tend to focus on item–objective linkages, content relevance, or content representation. When the goal is to ascertain the degree of alignment between individual items and objectives comprising a domain, a facet of item validity is under investigation (Hambleton, 1984). Relevance is studied by ascertaining the degree of importance or necessity of items as indicators of the domain, and representation is the degree to which sampled items taken together represent the universe of possible items that defines the domain. Notice that one must define characteristics of the universe in question to examine representation.

The matching and rating procedures are the two most commonly used methods to ascertain item–objective alignment. In the matching procedure, SMEs are provided the objectives comprising the domain or test specification document, and test items. After reviewing those materials, SMEs are asked to match up test items to objectives based on test content, cognitive demands, or both. The researcher then computes "hit" rates for each item by computing the proportion of judges that chose the objective for which the test item was designed to measure. Two arbitrary decisions must be made by the researcher: (a) What item hit rate constitutes adequate item alignment and (b) what proportion of items on the test must be considered "aligned" for the entire test to be deemed "adequately aligned?"

The main problem with the matching procedure is that one is not sure if SMEs considered all objectives as potential matches with each item. Judges might have overlooked certain objectives that potentially would have been good matches for items. If there are few items and objectives to be aligned, the method of Rovinelli and Hambleton (1977) mitigates this problem. In their procedure, SMEs are asked to consider each objective as a potential match with each item. They developed an alignment index to quantify congruence, although one has to decide on a cut-score that defines "adequate match."

In the rating method, SMEs are asked to rate the degree of content or cognitive demands (or both) congruence between items and the objectives the items were designed to measure. Measures of central tendency and variation are computed for each item across all SMEs, and arbitrary cut-scores must be set to determine "adequate alignment." This method tends to be more efficient than the matching procedure because SMEs do not spend their time searching through objectives to find a reasonable match for each item. SMEs are provided the designed item–objective pairs for review. This advantage of the rating method also is its greatest limitation. The technique could subtly persuade SMEs to overestimate item–objective alignment by presenting to them the planned item–objective pairings. Indeed, Moahi (2004) found that a group of SMEs judged alignment to be higher when asked to use the rating method than a SME group that used the matching procedure. One way to minimize the possibility of an experimenter effect when using the rating method is to present some "bogus" pairings (objectives matched with items designed to measure slightly different objectives) for judges to rate. This method has not been tested to my knowledge, however.

Content relevance typically has been assessed by asking SMEs to rate the importance of each item as an indicator of the tested domain. A number of relevance indices have been developed as sole indicators (Aiken, 1980) or as facets of content validity (Klein & Kosecoff, 1975; Morris & Fitz-Gibbon, 1978). Representativeness has been evaluated using a multitude of approaches. Cronbach (1971) proposed a content validity method in which test developers work independently to create tests using the same domain specifications. Examinees can be asked to take both forms so convergence can be examined. Obviously, this technique requires resources that might not be available in many experimental situations, but it might be appropriate if a researcher wishes to develop two test forms to avoid, for example, a testing effect.

Data reduction and scaling procedures, such as factor analysis, cluster analysis, and multidimensional scaling, have been used to ascertain the match between items and content domains based on SME judgments (for example, see Sireci & Geisinger, 1992, 1995). SMEs commonly are asked to rate the degree of similarity between items, and the similarity data are analyzed to examine how judges as a group organized items. The judges' item clustering then is compared with the organization depicted in a test blueprint, table of specifications, or other domain representation to check for fit between judges' and test developers' conceptualizations.

The advent of standards-based assessment in the last decade facilitated a boom in item and content validity evidence collection procedures. Because most state tests are designed to measure rather well-defined domains (embodied by state standards), collecting such validity evidence is appropriate. Most of these more recently developed methods are based on judgments made by SMEs using either rating or matching exercises, but some newer methods are distinct from past efforts.

The Survey of Enacted Curriculum (SEC) model (Blank, Porter, & Smithson, 2001) was developed primarily to examine the alignment between academic standards and enacted curriculum, but it has been used to study the three-way congruence among standards, instruction, and assessment. The model makes use of a matrix-matching procedure in which reviewers code the content and cognitive demands of each standard objective and test item. Content maps are developed from the reviewers' results that graphically display the degree of emphases in two-dimensional space (content by cognitive demand) of the standards and tests separately. Darker areas of the maps indicate greater emphases. Maps also can be developed to depict teachers' instructional emphases derived from survey data. The maps are visually compared to examine congruence; however, no quantitative results are produced indicating the degree of alignment. One must decide the degree of alignment by inspecting the maps, which makes the procedure susceptible to the vagaries of individual interpretation.

Webb (1997, 2001) developed a multistage process that relies mainly on a direct-matching procedure. SMEs code the cognitive demands of items and match them to up to three objectives. Webb examines four facets of alignment: categorical concurrence, depth-of-knowledge consistency, range-of-knowledge correspondence, and balance of representation. Categoric concurrence is met if, on average, reviewers identify at least six items that correspond to each standard strand, on the basis of logic that six items would yield minimally acceptable reliability estimates if strand subscale scores were to be computed. To judge depth-of-knowledge alignment, at least 50% of the items matched to an objective must be at or above the cognitive demand level of the objective, and at least 50% of the objectives from each standard must match at least one item for range-of-knowledge to be met. A balance of representation index is computed for each standard by taking the proportion of total objectives for the standard with matched items (values near one indicate good balance, whereas values near zero reveal poor balance). Reviewers are asked to flag any items with cognitive demand requirements not matching a chosen objective for reasons such as cultural bias or specialized knowledge. Such items are reviewed for source-of-challenge problems.

Rothman, Slattery, Vranek, and Resnick (2002) developed a multistage alignment procedure based primarily on the rating-scale method. Their procedure focuses on assessing four alignment facets: content centrality, performance centrality, challenge, and balance and range. The first stage of their process requires a senior reviewer to develop a test blueprint and compare it to the one created by test developers. Items might be matched with different objectives than specified by the original test blueprint in this stage. After a revised blueprint is confirmed, SMEs rate content and performance centrality. Content centrality is the degree of congruence between the content embodied in the objective and item, and performance centrality is the degree of match between the cognitive demands of the item and objective. In the second stage, SMEs rate the source of challenge, and they provide a written evaluation of the challenge level of each item using a series of question prompts. In the third stage, reviewers judge the balance (the match between standard emphases and test emphases) and range (proportion of total objectives mapped to a standard measured by at least one item) of test items.

Construct-Related Validity Evidence

Content validity procedures rarely require the use of actual item or test scores to gather validity-based evidence. Only test objectives or other domain specification information and test items are necessary to examine alignment, relevance, and representation. Contrarily, to conduct most, if not all, construct validity methods, actual item or test scores are required. Keep in mind that the goal of construct validity, as opposed to content validity, is to get beyond the "surface" features of test items to understand the mental processes actually invoked by items or test components. Thus, if a researcher demands evidence that outcome items pique the anticipated examinees' mental skills, even if the outcome was based on a clear set of objectives, content evidence alone would not be sufficient. The researcher would need to gather construct validity evidence as well. Many construct procedures can be integrated well into an experimental study, which saves the researcher from conducting a separate measurement analysis.

Campbell and Fiske (1959), Cronbach and Meehl (1955), and Nitko (2004) described several ways of gathering construct validity evidence. Perhaps the method most suitable for experimental research is to rely on group-difference evidence. If individuals representing certain groups are expected to possess more of the tested attribute than other groups, then one should demonstrate mean differences on a test purported to measure the attribute. In experimental research, one tests the effectiveness of an intervention by introducing the treatment to an initially equivalent group, withholding the treatment from a control group, and comparing mean differences on an outcome designed to measure the anticipated treatment effects. Thus, in a way, basic experimental research results also can serve as construct validity evidence. A treatment is designed to improve individuals' levels of an attribute, and so if an outcome truly measures the attribute, posttreatment mean differences should be detected.

This particular line of reasoning could be considered circular, however. Evidence for the effectiveness of a treatment is grounded in outcome results that derive meaning through anticipated treatment effects. Thus, the evidence to support treatment effectiveness is found in outcome differences, which in turn are supported by treatment properties. Even though this approach appears tautologic, it is predicated on theoretical expectations, connected to reality via operational definitions of both the treatment and outcomes, as well as verified by statistical testing. The decision to conduct a group-difference examination likely was based on a theory of why groups should differ, and the abstractions of the treatment and outcomes are brought to life through the operations that comprise the variables. When a null hypothesis is rejected on the basis of statistical grounds, the likelihood of group differences occurring due to chance is small. Consequently, the evidence would indicate that treatment group attribute changes indeed occurred by an outcome that tapped into the attribute. Hence, statistical significance supports both treatment and outcome construct validity simultaneously. In terms of supporting outcome construct validity, therefore, it makes sense to use at least some outcomes tailored to the purposes of the intervention.

Another construct validity approach related to the group-difference strategy is to examine expected individual change over time. Besides studying anticipated cross-sectional changes with the group-difference methods, one could examine longitudinal growth expectations on the measure. For instance, the construct validity of a series of vertically equated mathematics tests would be suspect if students who attend school regularly show no mathematics skill improvement over a 3-year period. However, growth on the measures is not the only way to demonstrate good construct validity evidence. It depends on the expected change patterns that can be attributed to an intervention. For example, many special education interventions are expected to wane if treatment ceases. Thus, if participants' scores continue to increase after treatment stops, the construct validity of the outcome would be jeopardized. In a repeated-measures treatment-control group design study, construct validity evidence for the outcome would be supported if each respective group demonstrates average changes based on theoretical expectations.

Construct validity is most relevant when there is no clear universe of operations to define the measured attribute, and when abstract mental activities predominately represent the construct. Thus, chosen operations should invoke the expected mental operations that the researcher desires to measure. To address this goal directly, one can study the mental processes that examinees engage in while addressing test questions or components. Perhaps the most popular strategy for conducting process studies is to ask a sample of examinees to think aloud as they solve questions (Van Someren, Barnard, & Sandberg, 1994). The examinees' verbalized thoughts are recorded and content analyzed for evidence that the targeted mental operations were used by examinees. The presence of construct-irrelevant mental operations also can be assessed in an effort to elucidate the degree to which items isolate the expected construct. Although the think-aloud method addresses the core of construct validity for many test purposes, it has two major limitations. First, the mere process of verbalizing one's mental operations can alter the mental operations that would occur if done without oral description. Hence, the technique is based on an assumption that what people say they are thinking is equivalent to what they would think if not asked to explain their thoughts. Second, think-aloud data are often very rich and difficult to analyze objectively. Content analyses usually yield descriptive results rather than a priori decision rules regarding whether an adequate degree of validity is supported by the findings (compared to the group-difference method in which statistical significance can be used as an objective decision rule). For these reasons, and the laborious nature of analyzing think-aloud data, it is not relied on frequently to examine construct validity. Additional methodologic work is required to develop more structured data analysis and interpretation methods.

Two additional construct validity methods involve analyzing the structure and patterns of test score performance, both within and between tests. Perhaps the most common construct validity method is to examine the factorial structure of items comprising a single measure. Factor analysis should support the purported dimensionality of a test, be it a unidimensional or multidimensional device. In terms of summative construct validity analysis, confirmatory factor analysis (CFA) is more appropriate than exploratory factor analysis (EFA) because one should have some notion of a test's apparent structure before using it in a study. CFA entails testing the fit of the purported factorial structure to the observable patterns of examinees' performances across items that comprise each expected dimension. EFA is more appropriate in a test-development phase that involves discovery of test dimensions. Simple item–total and item–subtotal correlations also can be used to study the internal structure of a test. One would expect to find higher item–subtotal correlations for items on their expected subscale than item–total correlations or item–subtotal correlations for items with other subtotals.

Besides studying the internal pattern of item and subscale interrelations, one could examine the pattern of correlations between outcomes and other variables of interest. This strategy dates back to the seminal piece by Cronbach and Meehls (1955) on developing and testing nomologic networks. According to them, construct validity of a measure can be supported by developing a theory of how the construct should interrelate with other constructs within a web of variable relations. By gathering data on measures of these other constructs, and examining the relations among measures of constructs within the network, one can examine the degree of confirmation of the theorized web. A few years later, Campbell and Fiske (1959) devised a method to test the expected relationships among constructs, adding that method variance might also influence test performance. Using their convergent and discriminant validation matrix approach, one measures a set of constructs using a variety of methods. If tests actually measure constructs, then the correlations between measures of the same attributes using diverse methods should be rather high, assuming that method variance should be present but not predominate. The correlations among measures of different constructs should follow theorized expectations. If rather unrelated or opposing constructs are included in the matrix, correlations among measures of those constructs should be small or negative. Correlations among measures of like constructs should be rather high.

Few researchers ever conduct a convergent and discriminant validation matrix. This is due to 2 things: 1) the difficulty of developing various measures of the same construct and other constructs that rely on different methods; and 2) the need to collect data on all measures. The general notion of examining convergent and discriminant validation has not waned, and indeed lives on with other methods, such as structural equation modeling (SEM). An extension of CFA, SEM is used to examine the fit of a purported nomologic network to observed data. For example, in an experiment, one might hypothesize that two measures of science knowledge will be interrelated, and science test scores will be affected by two compatible interventions: one geared toward increasing parents' participation in science-related home activities and one focused on increasing teachers' science teaching skills. Assume that a cumulative interaction also is expected. That is, students taught by teachers who participated in the in-service training and whose parents participated in the home activities will score higher on both science measures than those who were the recipient of only one intervention or no interventions. SEM could be used to analyze the fit of the expected model to the data.

It is also possible to add process variables to an experimental design to understand why interventions work or not and to bolster the construct validity of measures. In the science study example, one might further hypothesize that on the science outcome that was more conceptual in nature, students with parents who provide them more thought-provoking questions might outperform their peers whose parents provided fewer higher-order thinking questions. Parent–child interactions could be recorded and included in the SEM model to test the degree to which it improves overall model fit. Such analyses not only enrich the quality and substance of the study findings, but also provide better evidence for the construct validity of outcomes. In this way, a nomologic network analysis is built-in to the research design process. I now summarize some methods to design studies so that outcome reliability and validity evidence can be documented as part of the research findings.

INCREASING RELIABILITY AND VALIDITY IN EXPERIMENTAL DESIGNS

In Table 6.2 I list seven strategies that serve to (a) fortify the reliability and validity of outcome scores and (b) produce reliability and validity documentation. Using some or all of them will help reduce certain threats to all four types of research validity. Experimental designs are extremely suitable for building in reliability and validity checks.

Use Multiple Time Points

Several methodologists, including Raudenbush and Bryk (2001), Rogosa, Brandt, and Zimowski (1982), and Venter, Maxwell, and Bolig (2002) have discussed the importance of including more than two data collection time points. Adding more time points increases statistical power and can minimize the effects of regression to the mean. For example, if individual growth curves are computed as part of a hierarchical linear model, an examinee's initial status (i.e., scale placement at Time 1) usually is not his or her observed score, but a prediction of where he or she likely would have scored

TABLE 6.2
Ways to Increase Reliability and Validity in Experimental Research

A. Use multiple time points for outcome data collection
B. Use multiple outcome measures
C. Employ measures that adequately capture growth
D. Gather validity evidence that supports test-score inferences
E. Have experts review test content
F. Study processes that provide construct validity evidence

when error is taken into account. A three-point growth "curve" is actually not a curve but a straight-line regression analysis. Hence, a person's initial status is the y-intercept of the prediction line. The y-intercept is influenced not only by the person's score at the first administration, but also by the pattern of performance over multiple time waves. In a pretest–posttest design, it is not possible to compute a straight-line regression to capture change, and so a person's pretest score is the best estimate of initial scale placement. By adding more time points, the researcher can use postdiction to "work backward" toward a more accurate initial status. Capturing performance with multiple time points allows for a more accurate account of "true" attribute change.

Furthermore, at least two data collection time points should precede the introduction of a treatment. Shadish et al. (2002) recommend having the same time interval between the two pretests as between the second pretest and a posttest. Although this strategy would be useful in quasi-experimental research, the fundamental goal of double pretesting within an experimental design is to examine the time-interval reliability of one's outcome measures. Consequently, the time interval should be no more than a few weeks or that amount of time in which no examinee construct change is expected. This strategy allows the researcher to gauge time-related reliability of the sample's scores (rather than relying on published reliability indices that may or may not generalize to the sample) and to compute more stable estimates of pre-treatment status.

Use Multiple Outcome Measures

Whenever possible, researchers should use multiple outcome measures. The amount of useful information to be gleaned from multiple outcomes dictates the type of variation that should exist among these measures. For example, it makes little sense to have three mathematics tests that measure more or less the same mental skills and subject matter. Three paper-and-pencil mathematics tests that capture different subtopics or that measure a diversity of cognitive processes is more meaningful and will provide a deeper and broader understanding of potential program effects. Perhaps a better design, if possible, is to vary the item or method format of outcomes. Including open-ended questions, or direct observation, for example, helps enrich the outcome battery and allows for effect generalization to be examined.

If resources, time, and permissions permit, perhaps the best strategy for developing a battery of outcomes is to follow the logic of the multitrait–multimethod approach. Constructs for which a treatment was designed to affect could be measured with two or three diverse methods, and other constructs that are expected to either converge or diverge with the target construct can be measured in multiple ways. Some of these nontargeted constructs can have little to do with a treatment. Outcomes could be included that are tailored to the program specifically, while other measures might capture broader elements of the targeted attribute. The purpose of having an array of outcomes is to study the generalizability of effects across the targeted domain, study if the program met its direct purposes, and to examine the external structural validity of key outcomes. On some outcomes, no or opposite effects should be hypothesized. If null or opposite findings are detected on measures of these unrelated constructs, the overall study results are strengthened.

Use Measures That Capture Growth

If learning is to be adequately captured over time, a researcher must develop or adopt a measuring device that properly measures longitudinal change. With advances in item response theory (IRT), vertical scales are now rather straightforward to develop (see Embretson & Reise, 2000; Hambleton, Swaminathan, & Rogers, 1991; Wright & Stone, 1979). Vertical scales, however, can be susceptible to floor or ceiling effects as much as other scaling procedures because item properties drive proper measurement more than scaling methods. Another advantage of administering pretests, even in experimental designs, is to examine whether items are properly targeted at examinees. Items should be slightly too difficult on average for examinees initially, and items should be included that represent attribute capability that is beyond the most high scoring examinee's reach. On the low end of the scale, items should be present to capture accurately the lowest scoring person's initial attribute level. This spread of items will avoid floor and ceiling effects at pretest and at other time points in the study. If very difficult items are not included, the most capable students could "outgrow" the measure if the treatment is rather powerful, which would reduce the observed program effect.

Collect Validity Evidence That Supports Test-Score Inferences

The specific validity evidence to gather should be driven by how test scores will be interpreted (Joint Committee on Standards for Educational & Psychological Testing, 1999). If the researcher intends test scores to signify specific mental attributes, then content and construct validity evidence likely should be gathered. If the researcher intends test scores to indicate the degree to which an examinee mastered a specific body of knowledge and skills, content validity evidence alone might suffice. Undoubtedly, the notion of validity is very confusing, particularly because psychometricians have not been very clear on what actually constitutes "constructs." It is clear, however, that one must understand the limitations of the inferences that can be drawn from the test scores given the validity evidence available. In a sense, making proper test score interpretations is an external validity, or generalizability, issue.

Ask Experts to Review Test Content

Often researchers examine content validity by "face" validating items themselves. Although this procedure has some merit, evidence gleaned from it is not sufficient to document content validity. Researchers set on using a certain scale might overlook misalignment problems, and researchers cannot be experts on all topics they examine through experimental research. A much better approach is to ask some content experts to review items. This technique is more time consuming, and obviously, requires the researcher to identify individuals who are knowledgeable about the content and willing to participate. Nonetheless, the information yielded from a more formal content alignment analysis is far superior to a self-conducted face validity assessment. Reviewers using an alignment analysis method can identify poor items for potential removal before any pretest data are collected, which will save the researcher valuable time in the end.

Study Processes to Examine Construct Validity

When there are no stipulated objectives that define an attribute domain, content alignment analysis is not possible. Researchers must rely on construct validation methods. As stated, a detected group difference, either based on a cross-sectional or longitudinal design, is validity evidence. Nevertheless, this information alone typically is not sufficient to document construct validity. Mental process analysis, internal structural assessment, and external structural evaluation are other methods that should be used, either singly or together, to verify that the essence of key attributes is being captured by outcome indicators. Among these methods, external structural evidence is the best to gather within an experimental design given its ease to collect and the quality of validity evidence obtained. Instead of conducting "black-box" group-comparison studies, causal process analysis can be conducted that not only provides construct validity evidence, but much richer explanatory information. Theory should guide the selection of variables to be measured as part of the anticipated casual network.

CONCLUSION

Selecting and documenting the quality of one's measures are some of the most important research activities. Many students are led to believe that choosing standardized, "off-the-shelf" measures always is superior to designing measures for the purpose of a study. At times, standardized measures will work best, but in many situations, it is far better to develop one's own outcomes. The reliability and validity information of standardized measures often is incomplete or based on samples that differ dramatically from the samples of many research projects. Also, rarely do standardized measures match the student learning skills that treatments are designed to improve. Rigorous research that balances internal and external validity involves employing a battery of outcomes, some of which are tailored to the goals of the intervention under examination and some of which are more general in nature.

The different facets of a research project are interdependent. Good measurement will not overcome the problems of a bad research design, and a good research design will be plagued with problems if little care and effort were devoted to developing a proper outcome set. The credibility of educational research will not improve until more rigorous research models, such as those explained by Levin and O'Donnell (1999), become more predominant in the field. A cornerstone of all rigorous research is sound measurement, which is bolstered and documented through reliability and validity analyses. Methods were presented in this chapter to improve the quality of outcomes and to integrate reliability and validity evaluation into rigorous research designs.

References

Aiken, L. R. (1980). Content validity and reliability of single items or questionnaires. *Educational and Psychological Measurement*, 40, 955–959.

Battin-Pearson, S., Newcomb, M. D., Abbott, R. D., Hill, K. G., Catalano, R. F., & Hawkins, J. D. (2000). Predictors of early high school dropout: a test of five theories. *Journal of Educational Psychology*, 92, 568–582.

Blank, R. K., Porter, A., & Smithson, J. (2001). *New tools for analyzing teaching, curriculum, and standards in mathematics and science: Report from Survey of Enacted Curriculum project. Final report*. Washington, DC: Council of Chief State School Officers.

Bloom, B. S., Engelhart, M. D., Hill, W. H., Furst, E. J., & Krathwohl, D. R. (1956). *Taxonomy of educational objectives: the classification of educational goals, handbook i: cognitive domain*. New York: David McKay Company.

Campbell, D. T., & Fiske, D. W. (1959). Convergent and discriminant validation by the multitrait-multimethod matrix. *Psychological Bulletin*, 56, 81–105.

Campbell, D. T., & Kenny, D. A. (1999). *A primer on regression artifacts*. New York: Guilford Press.

Campbell, D. T., & Stanley, J. C. (1963). Experimental and quasi-experimental designs for research on teaching. In N. L. Gage (Ed.), *Handbook of research on teaching* (pp. 161–246). Chicago, IL: Rand McNally.

Clay, M. M. (1985). *The early detection of reading difficulties* (3rd ed.). Portsmouth, NH: Heinemann.

Cleary, T. A., & Linn, R. L. (1969). Error of measurement and the power of a statistical test. *British Journal of Mathematical and Statistical Psychology*, 22, 49–55.

Cleary, T. A., Linn, R. L., & Walster, G. W. (1970). Effect of reliability and validity on power of statistical tests. *Sociological Methodology*, 2, 130–138.

Cook, T. D., & Campbell, D. T. (1979). *Quasi-experimentation: design and analysis issues for field settings*. Chicago, IL: Rand McNally.

Cronbach, L. J. (1971). Test validation. In R. L. Thorndike (Ed.), *Educational measurement* (2nd ed.) (pp. 443–507). Washington, DC: American Council on Education.

Cronbach, L. J., & Meehl, P. E. (1955). Construct validity in psychological tests. *Psychological Bulletin*, 52, 281–302.

Cureton, E. E. (1951). Validity. In E. F. Lindquist (Ed.), *Educational measurement* (1st ed.) (pp. 621–694). Washington, DC: American Council on Education.

D'Agostino, J. V. (2004). *The internal structural validity of a state's standards based assessment*. Unpublished manuscript.

D'Agostino, J. V., & Murphy, J. A. (2004). A meta-analysis of Reading Recovery in United States schools. *Educational Evaluation and Policy Analysis*, 23–38.

Deville, C. W. (1996). An empirical link of content and construct validity evidence. *Applied Psychological Measurement*, 20, 127–139.

Embretson, S. E., & Reise, S. P. (2000). *Item response theory for psychologists*. Mahwah, NJ: Erlbaum.

Feldt, L. S., & Brennan, R. L. (1989). Reliability. In R. L. Linn (Ed.), *Educational measurement* (3rd ed.) (pp. 105–146). Washington, DC: American Council on Education.

Hambleton, R. K. (1984). Validating the test scores. In R. A. Berk (Ed.), *A guide to criterion-referenced test construction* (pp. 199–230). Baltimore, MD: Johns Hopkins University Press.

Hambleton, R. K., Swaminathan, H., Rogers, H. J. (1991). *Fundamentals of item response theory*. Newbury Park, CA: Sage.

Hiebert, E. H., Colt, J. M., Catto, S. L., & Gury, E. C. (1992). Reading and writing of first-grade students in a restructured Chapter 1 program. *American Educational Research Journal*, 29(3), 545–572.

Joint Committee of the American Psychological Association, American Educational Research Association, and National Council on Measurements Used in Education (1954). Technical recommendations for psychological and diagnostic techniques. *Psychological Bulletin*, 51, 201–238.

Joint Committee on Standards for Educational and Psychological Testing (1999). *Standards for educational and psychological testing*, Washington, DC: American Educational Research Association.

Kane, M. T. (1992). An argument-based approach to validity. *Psychological Bulletin*, 112, 527–535.

LaDuca, A. (1994). Validation of professional licensure examinations. *Evaluation and the Health Professions*, 17, 178–197.

Levin, J. R. (1993). An improved modification of a regression-toward-the-mean demonstration. *The American Statistician*, 47(1), 24–26.

Mayer, S., & Peterson, P. E. (Eds.). (1999). *Earning and learning: how school matters*. Washington, DC: Brookings Institution Press.

Messick, S. (1981). Constructs and their vicissitudes in educational and psychological measurement. *Psychological Bulletin*, 89, 575–588.

Messick, S. (1989). Validity. In R. L. Linn, (Ed.), *Educational measurement* (3rd ed.) (pp. 13–103). New York: Macmillan.

Messick, S. (1995). Validity of psychological assessment. *American Psychologist*, 50, 741–749.

Moahi, S. (2004). *The validity of the Botswana Junior Certificate Mathematics Examination over time*. Unpublished doctoral dissertation, University of Arizona.

Nitko, A. J. (2004). *Educational assessment of students* (4th ed.). Upper Saddle River, NJ: Pearson Prentice Hall.

Nunnally, J. C., & Bernstein, I. H. (1994). *Psychometric theory* (3rd ed.). New York: McGraw-Hill.

Raudenbush, S. W., & Bryk, A. S. (2002). *Hierarchical linear models: applications and data analysis methods* (2nd ed.). Thousand Oaks, CA: Sage.

Rogosa, D. R., Brandt, D., & Zimoswki, M. (1982). A growth curve approach to the measurement of change. *Psychological Bulletin*, 90, 726–748.

Rothman, R., Slattery, J. B., Vranek, J. L., & Resnick, L. B. (2002). *Benchmarking and alignment of standards and testing*. CSE *Technical Report* 566. Los Angeles: UCLA Center for the Study of Evaluation.

Rovinelli, R. J., & Hambleton, R. K. (1977). On the use of content specialists in the assessment of criterion-referenced test item validity. *Dutch Journal of Educational Research*, 2, 49–60.

Rulon, P. J. (1946). On the validity of educational tests. *Harvard Educational Review*, 16, 290–296.

Shadish, W. R., Cook, T. D., & Campbell, D. T. (2002). *Experimental and quasi-experimental designs for generalized causal inferences*. Boston, MA: Houghton Mifflin.

Shepard, L. A. (1993). Evaluating test validity. In L. Darling-Hammond (Ed.) *Review of research in education* (pp. 405–450). Washington, DC: American Educational Research Association.

Sireci, S. G. (1998). The construct of content validity. *Social Indicators Research*, 45, 83–117.

Sireci, S. G., & Geisinger, K. F. (1992). Analyzing test content using cluster analysis and multidimensional scaling. *Applied Psychological Measurement*, 16, 17–31.

Sireci, S. G., & Geisinger, K. F. (1995). Using subject-matter experts to assess content representation: an MDS analysis. *Applied Psychological Measurement*, 19, 241–255.

Thorndike, E. L. (1919). *An introduction to the theory of mental and social measurements* (2nd ed.). Lancaster, PA: New Era Printing.

Thorndike, R. L., & Hagen, E. (1962). *Measurement and evaluation in psychology and education* (2nd ed.). New York: John Wiley and Sons.

Tyler, R. W. (1934). *Constructing achievement tests*. Columbus, OH: Ohio State University.

Tyler, R. W. (1949). *Basic principles of curriculum and instruction*. Chicago, IL: University of Chicago Press.

Van Someren, M. W., Barnard, Y. F., & Sandberg, J. A. (1994). *The think aloud method: a practical guide to modelling cognitive processes*. San Diego, CA: Academic Press.

Webb, N. L. (1999). *Alignment of science and mathematics standards and assessments in four states*. *Research Monograph* No. 18. Madison, WI: University of Wisconsin-Madison, National Institute for Science Education.

Webb, N. L. (2001, November). *Alignment analysis of State F Language Arts standards and assessments grades 5, 8, and 11*. Paper presented at the meeting of the Technical Issues of Large-Scale Assessment Group of the Council of Chief State School Officers, Washington, DC.

Wright, B. D., & Stone, M. H. (1979). *Best test design: Rasch measurement*. Chicago, IL: MESA Press.

CHAPTER

7

The Micro and Macro in the Analysis and Conceptualization of Experimental Data

JOHN T. BEHRENS
Cisco Systems, Inc., San Jose, CA

DANIEL H. ROBINSON
University of Texas, Austin

Experimental methods are well described in many aspects, including the logic of validity statements (Shadish, Cook, & Campbell, 2002; Krathwohl, 2003), the computation of analysis of variance sources (Kirk, 1995), and the multiplicity of models available (Maxwell & Delaney, 2003). In this chapter, we emphasize two goals that complement these already-existing emphases in the experimental literature. First, we argue for data analysts to augment the most common techniques with a microlevel focus on the data that provides intimacy and understanding beyond the standard sums-of-squares computations. One way to accomplish this is to use techniques from exploratory data analysis (Behrens, 1997a; Tukey, 1977), and so this approach is summarized. Second, we argue that experimental analysis needs to be conceptualized and analyzed in the context of the landscape of studies aimed at examining similar phenomena. Conceptually, this means emphasizing programmatic research. Computationally, this means exploiting the power of meta-analysis for information integration and modeling. The combination of these conceptualizations and techniques, along with the standard toolbox, can potentially improve the way we currently analyze experimental data.

GRAPHICAL AND EXPLORATORY TECHNIQUES TO OFFER INTIMACY WITH THE DATA

In this section, we discuss activities designed to help researchers develop intimacy with their data. The explosive growth in understanding experimental design and statistics in the first half of the 20th century was equally well matched with emphasis on understanding the theoretical and empirical nexus in which a study occurred. R. A. Fisher, the father of modern experimental design and such techniques as the analysis of variance (ANOVA), frequently lamented the emerging isolation of statistical and "scientific" expertise:

> I have been frequently impressed with the advantage that a worker has gained, especially in self-confidence and resourcefulness, by being confronted, malgré lui, with problems of the so-called applied or practical character, which in reality are problems requiring exploration and judgment rather than the application of a ready-made formula (Correspondence to J. R. Baker, November 1940, in Bennett [1990, p. 344]).

Had Fisher lived past the 1960s, he would likely have mourned the continued trends toward data isolation exacerbated by automated computing and increasingly complex statistical analysis. Although we think the use of complex statistical formulations is important (e.g., a correct model that accounts for appropriate levels of hierarchy and intraclass correlation), we want to raise a flag against statistical complexity that leads to an unfamiliarity with the phenomena under study or interpretations based on assumptions about the object of study that do not hold.

To counter these difficulties, John Tukey (1977; Mosteller & Tukey, 1977) developed a tradition called exploratory data analysis (EDA). EDA seeks to supplement the more common traditions of hypothesis and significance testing with techniques aimed at revealing structure, providing rich description, and avoiding being fooled by the data or the statistical models being used. In all these ways, EDA seeks to develop intimacy with the data in the context of the discipline being studied.

EDA was first formulated by Tukey in his 1977 book entitled *Exploratory Data Analysis*, published the same year as Mosteller and Tukey's *Data Analysis and Regression: a Second Course*. These two books are classics; many of their themes and techniques remain highly relevant and continue to influence the field. More recent treatments of the EDA tradition in psychology and education include treatments by Behrens (1997a; Behrens & Smith, 1996,

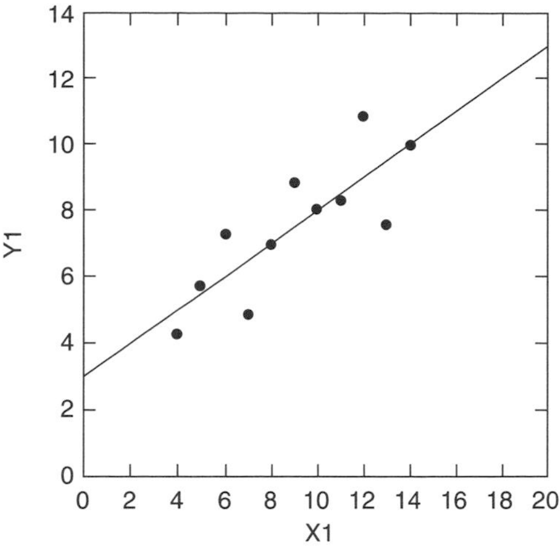

FIGURE 7.1
A set of bivariate data with a mean and standard deviation of 9 and 3.3 in X and 7.5 and 2.03 in Y, a slope of .5, and intercept of 3, and a correlation of .83. (From Anscombe, 1973)

Behrens & Yu, 2003), Leinardt and Leinardt (1980), Wainer and Velleman (2001), and Wilkinson (1999).

The main themes of EDA are frequently described as the four Rs (Hoaglin, Mosteller, & Tukey, 1983): Revelation, Residuals, Resistance, and Reexpression. Each of these main themes will be introduced briefly, with some examples of how educational and experimental data may be interpreted more intimately using these techniques.

Revelation

Revelation concerns the use of graphical techniques[1] to reveal patterns and structure and to suggest to the data analyst "what we never expected to see" (Tukey, 1977, p. vi). Although there are numerous illustrations of the value of graphics, and indeed a broad field of scientific visualization has emerged from similar goals, one particularly compelling set of data was presented by Anscombe (1973). Anscombe presented the reader with a set of bivariate data with a mean and standard deviation of 9 and 3.3 in X and 7.5 and 2.03 in Y, respectively. A classical regression (ordinary least squares) suggested a slope of 0.5, an intercept of 3, and a correlation of 0.83. These data are presented in Figure 7.1. If the reader was able to create such a pattern in his

[1] Graphic here is meant in the sense of charts and graphs and statistical graphics. This should not be confused with the use of graphic models (Almond, 1995; Edwards, 2000) based on graph–theoretic notions of objects and edges.

or her mind's eye, it is a testament to the normal patterns of data often seen in books and data sets used in statistical training. At the same time, it is a testament to the isolation of many books and instructors from the complexity of real-world data, which are often more complex and messy (c.f., Micceri, 1989). In addition to relating these statistics as coming from the data portrayed in Figure 7.1, Anscombe also presented data sets with these identical summary statistics as being generated from patterns shown in Figure 7.2. Interestingly, these patterns are seldom predicted or anticipated by students with standard statistical training.

This common failure to understand the possibilities of pattern and anticipate the multiplicity of underlying distributions points to several myths that arise in "normal" statistical analysis. First, the common assumptions about underlying statistical distributions (normal in the population) are often confused with both the empirical reality (skewed in the population) and the presentation in the sample (skewed in the sample). If our own interest is in the differences in means between groups in the population, we are likely to dismiss the skew as irrelevant because the sampling distribution is likely to be normal because of the central limit theorem. However, if our concern is to understand the data and the underlying generation processes, we should focus not only on how our long-term decisions about means may be misled, but also how our conceptualizations and understandings may be misled.

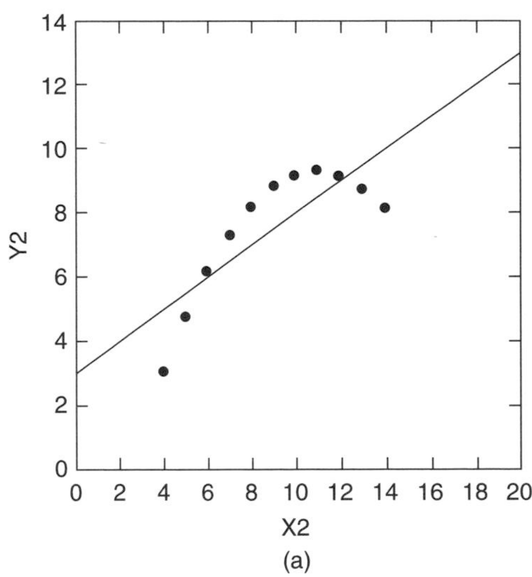

FIGURE 7.2
Three more data sets with identical summary statistics as those in Figure 1.

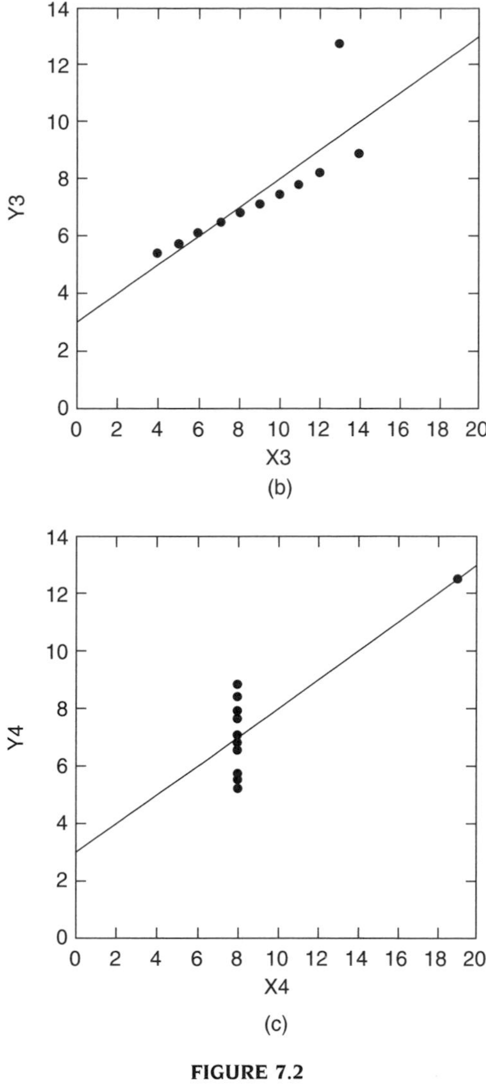

FIGURE 7.2
Continued.

For example, Behrens (1997b) reported a meta-analysis and multiple confirmatory factor analyses that suggested considerable problems with the interpretation of the White Racial Identity Attitude Scale (Helms, 1990) because the high interscale correlations suggested a single underlying factor for the purportedly multifactor scale. In reply, Helms argued that Behrens' conclusions were invalid because Behrens' use of classical statistical methods would require normal distributions whereas her theory suggested that the distributions would be skewed. Behrens and Rowe (1997) responded that this criticism was easily assessed by plotting the data and referred readers to one-, two-, and three-dimensional plots of the raw data provided on the World Wide Web at that time. In this way, the scientific dialog could be advanced quickly and publicly by the use of detailed graphics.

Behrens (1997a), Behrens and Smith (1996), and Behrens and Yu (2003) have worked through a number of examples that show the value of graphics to reveal the unexpected and to change our thinking regarding the underlying cause of the statistical summaries we see. Consistent with those papers, we recommend that researchers graph their data at many levels, including down to single distributions when appropriate.

Residuals

EDA is primarily inductive insofar as it looks for patterns and suggests descriptions (but see Behrens & Yu [2003] for a treatment of its abductive nature). At the same time, to promote modification to the induction and provide an evaluative tool for assessing the quality of quantitative descriptions, EDA emphasizes the use of tentative models and examination of the patterns of misfit between models and data—the pattern of residuals. Although many readers will be familiar with residuals from their use in regression analysis, EDA follows a model-building philosophy with a ubiquitous emphasis on residuals in general and individual patterns of residuals.

In most experimental analysis, residuals are summarized by overall size and compared against variation associated with the model using sums of squares, F ratios, and related techniques. This is satisfactory for testing specific hypotheses alone, but unsatisfactory for looking intimately at more detailed patterns. From an EDA perspective, the data analyst does not simply want to know how the model fits on average, but where in the structure of the experiment did the model fit and where did it not? Where were the cell means (or medians) higher than expected, and where lower? Were there a few cells with large residuals and a common feature that should be considered in future endeavors? Were the residuals too small because of some aberrant overfitting process? The appropriate question will vary with the context at hand; however, the open and suspicious attitude of the data analyst needs to remain constant throughout.

Consistent with the notion of models and residuals, the EDA tradition has a number of techniques to decompose multilayer structure as represented in factorial tables of values (means or medians) or multivariable regressions. In each case, the general logic is the same: Suggest a tentative hypothesis, fit a model to it, look for residuals that point out patterns of lack of fit in the data, and add additional terms to the model to account for the pattern if appropriate. Here again, the decision of appropriateness would not be only statistical optimization, but rather conceptual and pragmatic fit with the understanding of the phenomena and the goals of the analyses.

Resistance

Resistance[2] concerns the use of statistical summaries that are not easily distorted by unusually distributed data. This suggests using summaries that are based on location in the distribution, such as the median, rather than summaries based on means or sums of squares. The mean has a smaller sampling distribution than the median, and so is often preferred to the median for statistical inference or estimation. At the same time, however, outliers from skewed processes or methodological contamination easily affect the computation of the mean. Accordingly, the resistant summaries are generally required in EDA as a precursor to statistical inference to help understand the data, gauge any possible violation of statistical assumption, and create a descriptive model that is unfettered by the vagaries of extreme values. If the data are well understood using resistant methods, a second stage of analysis could follow that emphasizes efficiency of the statistic as measured in the standard error.

Another approach to building resistance into analysis is to use trimmed estimates. A trimmed mean, for example, would be a mean calculated after excluding some percentage of the extreme values of the distribution. For example, a 95% trimmed mean omits 2.5% of each tail of the distribution. If the shape of the distribution is not too far from Gaussian, the trimmed mean will be very much like the untrimmed means. On the other hand, extreme values will be omitted and will not improperly influence estimates aimed at understanding the center of the distribution. This approach can be used on any statistic since it concerns the data that are subject to the computation of the statistic.

Using location-based summaries and trimmed summaries reflects the skepticism that is an important aspect of EDA. Not all data come to us as we expect, and so it is important to protect our summaries from unknown influences. This is similar to the process used in some Olympic judging, where the lowest and highest score are dropped (trimming the extremes). This is not about massaging the data, but rather about deciding to use a process in which extreme values do not unduly influence our summary estimates about the bulk of the data.

In practical analysis and the reporting of results, the principle of resistance is often best accomplished by the simultaneous reporting of resistant

[2] Resistance concerns how summaries may resist fooling us into misperception because of extreme or rough data values. A closely related concept is robustness, which typically concerns the efficacy or consistency of statistical decision making under violations of particular assumptions.

and classical summaries. When means and medians do not vary, we have consensus supporting a single understanding of the center of the distribution. When they vary, a more nuanced understanding is required and researchers are forced to consider more carefully what they consider "the center." For example, Behrens (1997b) reported the results of a meta-analysis regarding subscale correlations for the White Racial Identity Scale. To guard against the criticism that the average correlation over a series of studies might have been unduly influenced by a few extreme results, he reported both the trimmed and untrimmed means. Consistent results suggested that a few anomalous studies were not of interest to the broader inferential question. At the same time, such extreme values represent model residuals that call out for individual attention and closer follow-up.

Re-expression

Re-expression concerns finding an appropriate scale transformation to express the data in a way that matches your statistical assumptions and understanding. In many educational situations, data come already reexpressed in "standard normalized" units from a Gaussian distribution, or some common variation based on its cumulative density function, including deciles, percentile ranks, or normal curve equivalents.

While the z score from a well-formed Gaussian distribution is likewise well behaved, z scores from non-Gaussian distributions can be quite misleading and mapping them back to areas under the curve are not supported. The common use of the percentile rank can likewise be problematic because this transforms scores into a scale with a fixed upper and lower boundary. This leads to scale compression in the tails that makes it difficult to properly compare shifts in performance at different parts of the distribution. A gain of 5 percentile points around a start value of the 50th percentile is easier than a 5 percentile point improvement starting at the 70th percentile. A logistic transformation, or return to the scaling of the original z scores, is more appropriate.

In the context of experimental data and analysis of variance, many writers recommend variance stabilization reexpressions, consistent with the EDA literature. One common approach is to calculate the means and standard deviations for each cell of the design and plot them to determine their ratio. Subtracting this ratio from one provides a value that is matched to the closest value in the set of -1, $-^1/_2$, 0, $^1/_2$, and 1. This corresponding value becomes the exponent to which the value of the original data is raised and on which the statistical analysis is computed. If the value is equal to zero, the recommended transformation is the log of the data. Other values suggest a reciprocal (-1), reciprocal square root ($-^1/_2$), square root ($^1/_2$), or no reexpression (1). Behrens (1997a) worked through a detailed example of how failure to re-express experimental reaction-time data led authors of a *Journal of Experimental Psychology* article to be seriously misled by the severe non-Gaussian shape in many distributions. Such difficulties are exacerbated in the multidimensional space of multiple regression. However, the combination of the four Rs of EDA can suggest important aspects of the structure of data that can help researchers improve their understanding and modeling of the phenomenon under investigation.

An Example of the Application of Exploratory Data Analysis

To illustrate the concepts described here, we examine the data reported by Griffin, Robinson, and Rittschof (in press). In this study, the authors randomly assigned undergraduates to one of four conditions where they viewed either a geographic map or list containing feature markers that were either names or icons. Students then read a text that described features of the map. Free-recall tests were used to measure students' learning of the text content.

Because the study uses an analysis of variance conceptualization of the study's structure, the authors aim to make inferences about possible differences among group means as measured relative to the variation within groups. Accordingly, from an EDA perspective, it is important to depict and model both the within-group variation and the between-group structure. The analyses shown here are only a small part of a larger toolbox that is available to a researcher. The reader is referred to Behrens (1997a), Behrens and Smith (1996), Behrens and Yu (2003), and Hoaglin, Mosteller, and Tukey (1991) for additional examples and analyses.

As described above, a first step would be to create appropriate graphics suggesting structure of the data. Because this will be done using a computer, rather than by hand, an important preliminary step is the visual analysis of the raw data that will be imported into the computer. At this stage, the analyst should seek to build a mental model of all the different possible aspects of the data: What is the apparent range of the different variables? Are all the variables in approximately similar order of magnitude? Do any observations or variables have missing data? Is there any unusual formatting that may cause difficulty for computer importing? A typical approach to answering these broad questions about the experimental context is to create a gallery of univariate distributions as shown in Figure 7.3. Note how even the identification (ID) variable is presented. We notice the independent variables of feature representation and display type are categorical with levels of one and two. The measures of nonrepresentational text and text match have some mild negative skew whereas representational-text recall is quite Gaussian in its shape. The measure of encoding label text is strongly negatively skewed whereas label location is surprisingly uniform. Spatial placement is dichotomous, with levels of zero and one.

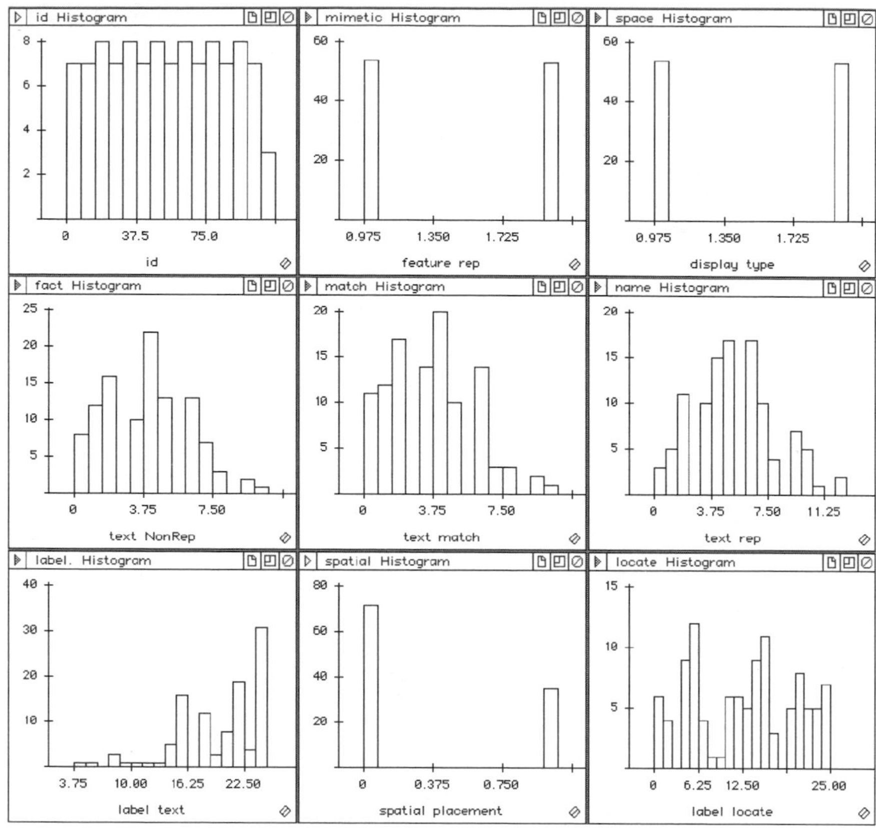

FIGURE 7.3
Univariate displays of data from Griffin, Robinson, and Rittschof (in press).

These activities are not intended to form the basis of strong inferences, but rather to offer a cordial introduction to the numeric context. We have encountered many situations in which researchers have skipped these steps; failed to observe typographical, recording, or computing errors; and performed analyses on inappropriate data only to have to go back and reconduct the analyses. Likewise, we have seen researchers whose knowledge of their own data was so obscure that they unjustifiably assumed their dichotomous nominal data were represented in a binary scale when they were not, leading to quite a bit of confusion after otherwise straightforward computation was added. We believe these introductory steps are especially important in the modern computing age where researchers do not meet each observation directly as they did in former days of hand computations. The hand no longer forces intimacy with the data; it must be created with the eye.

To assess the levels of central tendency and variation (or location and spread as it is called in the EDA literature), a common display is the box-plot that summarizes five key locations of a distribution: the median, the 25th percentile, the 75th percentile, and either the minimum and maximum or an extreme value after which individual values are indicated as outliers deserving particular, and often qualitatively distinct, attention. Figure 7.4A depicts multiple box-plots of the four groups of the 2 × 2 ANOVA design used by Griffin et al. (in press). The vertical axis represents the scale of the dependent variable (the number of representational text items recalled), with locations along the horizontal scale indicating group membership. Box-plots higher in the graphic indicate the distributions are higher in score values. Long boxes and long extending lines (called *tails*) indicate wide spread in the center and tails of the distribution, respectively. The bottom, middle, and top of the boxes represent the 25th, 50th, and 75th percentiles, respectively. Lines extend from the boxes to indicate the range up to a cutoff point after which individual observations are given greater prominence. Typically, the lines extend 1.5 times the interquartile range. Figure 7.4B shows a dot-plot in which individual observations are shown. The dot-plot is another depiction of the data presented in Figure 7.4A. It benefits from the detail of showing exact values, but suffers from hiding overlapping observations at the integer levels of the response variable. The combination of the dot-plot and box-plot provides a valuable complement.

Figure 7.5 presents multiple box-plots for several more independent variables. In the top panels, the reader can see that the boxes are relatively similar in location with a general indication of greater spread in groups that received the list treatment and higher location for scores from the icon conditions. As suggested from the univariate distributions presented in Figure 7.3, the label text variable presented in panel C is highly skewed, with the

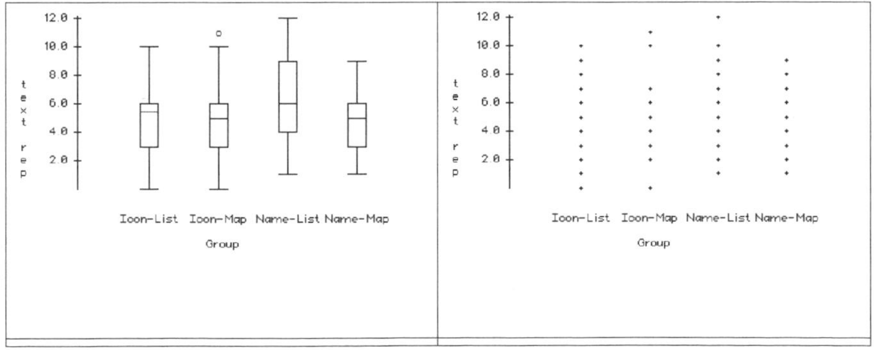

FIGURE 7.4A–B

Box-plot and dot-plot of outcome data from a 2 × 2 design.

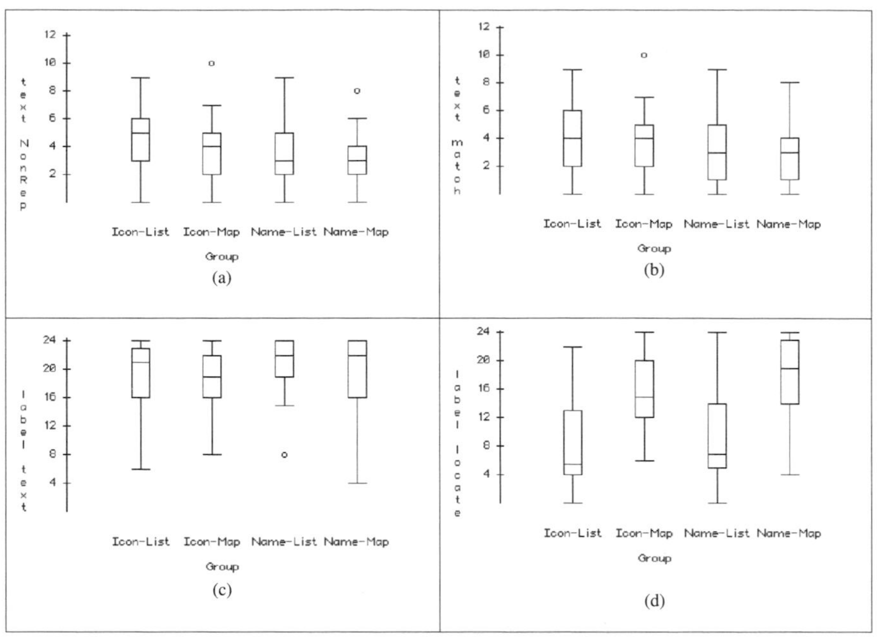

FIGURE 7.5 A–D

Multiple box-plots for several independent variables from Griffin, Robinson, and Rittschof (in press).

skew being more pronounced in groups receiving the name condition. Boxes in these groups have no tails because the top 25% of their data occur all at the value of 24, representing both the location of the 75th percentile and the maximum. These shapes suggest a ceiling effect that might be artificially compressing the variability in the measures.

Panel D of Figure 7.5 depicts the box-plots from a validity check that indicates that individuals in the map-reading condition were better able to construct and place labels on a map than individuals were able to construct and place labels in a table. This pattern reflects a strong main effect of display.

These analyses provide no smoking gun that cries out "the inferences were lost because there was no EDA." However, they do provide an important layer of rich description with which to understand the data. Effects that exist are generally subtle, spread in distributions is large and seems to be related to condition, and some dependent variables are strikingly skewed. All these observations are easily discernible in the graphics presented, whereas they may be easily overlooked in summaries too focused on single summaries and a singular focus on statistical significance. The reader is referred to Behrens (1997a) for striking examples of the failure to use EDA in previously published experimental work.

The World and the Data

It is important to keep in mind that the goal of EDA is not simply intimacy with data, but rather to support intimacy with the phenomenon to which the data are pointing. Accordingly, there is no understanding of data outside of an understanding of the semantics of the data and its link to constructs in the world.

For example, Robinson and Funk (in press) randomly assigned college students to groups that either read a short summary of the research on corporal punishment or not. Students then were administered the Corporal Punishment Attitude Scale that measured their (a) knowledge of corporal punishment's effectiveness, (b) consistency between the evaluation of corporal punishment attributes and their beliefs about its effectiveness at home and at school, and (c) behavioral intent in terms of whether they planned to use corporal punishment as a parent. Students who read the summary, as compared with those who did not, increased their knowledge about the issue of corporal punishment, increased their consistency between how they felt about it and how effective they thought it is in the home and at school, and a larger proportion (0.22) indicated on the postquestionnaire that they would not use corporal punishment as a parent than did those in the control group (0.07).

Because they found that the treatment group's affective–cognitive consistency changed from pretest to posttest whereas the control group's consistency did not change, Robinson and Funk (in press) decided to take a closer look at the data to determine if this change in consistency was mainly due to the eight persons in the treatment group who indicated a change in behavioral intent regarding using corporal punishment as a parent, and then to compare these eight people in terms of affective–cognitive consistency with the other 48 persons in the treatment group who did not change their behavioral intent. What they found indicated that the change in consistency for the treatment group was influenced mostly by those eight people who also changed their behavioral intent. Those eight persons became more consistent from pretest to posttest for both corporal punishment use in home (1.42 to 0.42) and in school (2.13 to 0.54). However, the other 48 persons in the treatment group who did not change their behavioral intent also did not change in terms of consistency, 1.26 to 1.24 (home) and 1.32 to 1.34 (school).

Thus, it appeared that the reason why persons change their behavioral intent of whether they will use corporal punishment is related to their affective–cognitive consistency. If what they read increases their knowledge about the ineffectiveness of corporal punishment to a degree where their affective–cognitive beliefs become more consistent (i.e., both affective and cognitive are negative toward using corporal punishment), then they will be more likely to change their behavioral intent concerning whether they would use corporal punishment as a disciplinary measure. This finding, which suggests a profile in terms of the type of person who is most likely to be swayed by reading a summary of corporal punishment research, would have remained obscured had Robinson and Funk (in press) not looked more closely at the data and instead relied on only overall group means and *p* values.

In summary, most common statistical techniques provide information at a middle level of detail that aims at statistical testing in a way that can overlook other important aspects of understanding and learning from data. Supplementing such approaches with EDA to provide additional detail and data-analytic intimacy is frequently richly rewarded by increased awareness and avoidance of untenable assumptions.

CONCEPTUALIZING RESEARCH IN THE LARGER LANDSCAPE

In the previous section, we emphasized a local and idiosyncratic view of research: Researchers should have great intimacy with their data, understand unexpected patterns, and relate the patterns in data back to scientific notions. At times this should be done down to the level of the individual observation when appropriate (as is often the case). In this section, we jump to the opposite end of the micro–macro continuum and argue that the results of individual studies are never properly considered by themselves. Rather, each individual study should be conceptualized as one trial among many that are systematically planned for in programmatic research and analyzed using the conceptualization and computational methods of meta-analysis. This argument centers on the idea that meta-analysis concerns conceptualizing and understanding long-run statistical phenomena, and not simply making summary statements for literature surveys. In this way, it supports and integrates programmatic research.

Meta-Analytic Logic

We take as our starting point the foundational work of Glass (1976), in which the basic approach to modern meta-analysis was discussed. Looking back over the previous 70 years of statistical work in sampled data, Glass recognized three fundamental limitations in the common use of small-sample statistical inference. First, the fundamental fact of sampling fluctuation meant that individual results were, by themselves, always wrong to some degree. Second, the binary decision rules common in most applications of statistical tests can suggest greatly misleading results when aggregated. Moreover, this distortion is amplified as increasing numbers of results are attained and small samples are used. For example, several underpowered, Type II error–prone studies that conclude no advantage for one educational treatment over another are more misleading than only one of those studies because people tend to believe that more studies equals more confidence. Third, the common practice of using raw scale scores for reporting results made research synthesis more difficult.

To address these issues, Glass (1976) recommended that the conceptualization of statistical tests shift from a binary decision approach to an approach based on standardized effect sizes whose computation incorporated information regarding the sample-to-sample fluctuation related to sample size. This would counter the binary decision problem by moving the discussion from a decision-making issue with difficulties related to "vote counting" to a problem of statistical estimation along a continuum. Glass showed how this estimation approach could be extended in a comprehensive way by considering the effect-size results to be outcome variables in statistical models relating the outcome effects to variables describing the characteristics of the studies. This opened the door to a dramatic reconceptualization of statistical machinery and called for a rethinking of common practice. However, because the primary use of these techniques was to augment interpretive reviews of the literature, the meta-analytic methods suggested were all but segregated to that use alone, and seen only as a set of techniques to replace the review of the literature.

While this is certainly a valid use of the methods, we would like to reframe the discussion from the common question of "how to do a quantitative literature review" to the more fundamental statistical issues that Glass identified: How do we deal with the limitations of binary decisions obscuring effects, how do we measure effects across experiments, and how do we model effects in the long run, taking into account both random fluctuation and systematic variation due to individual experiment characteristics? In sum, we want to suggest that the logic of a modeling approach to meta-analysis serve as the broader framework within which all experimental research is conceptualized.

Remembering Random Fluctuation

To begin, consider the two distributions depicted in Figure 7.6 that consist of 10,000 observations each. The distribution shown in Figure 7.6A has a mean of zero with a standard deviation of 1. The distribution in Figure 7.6B has a mean of 0.25 and a standard deviation of 1 as well. We can think of these distributions as the control and experimental populations. Repeated samples drawn from these populations would represent samples that would be obtained from repeated experiments. Figure 7.7 shows a series of 20 95%

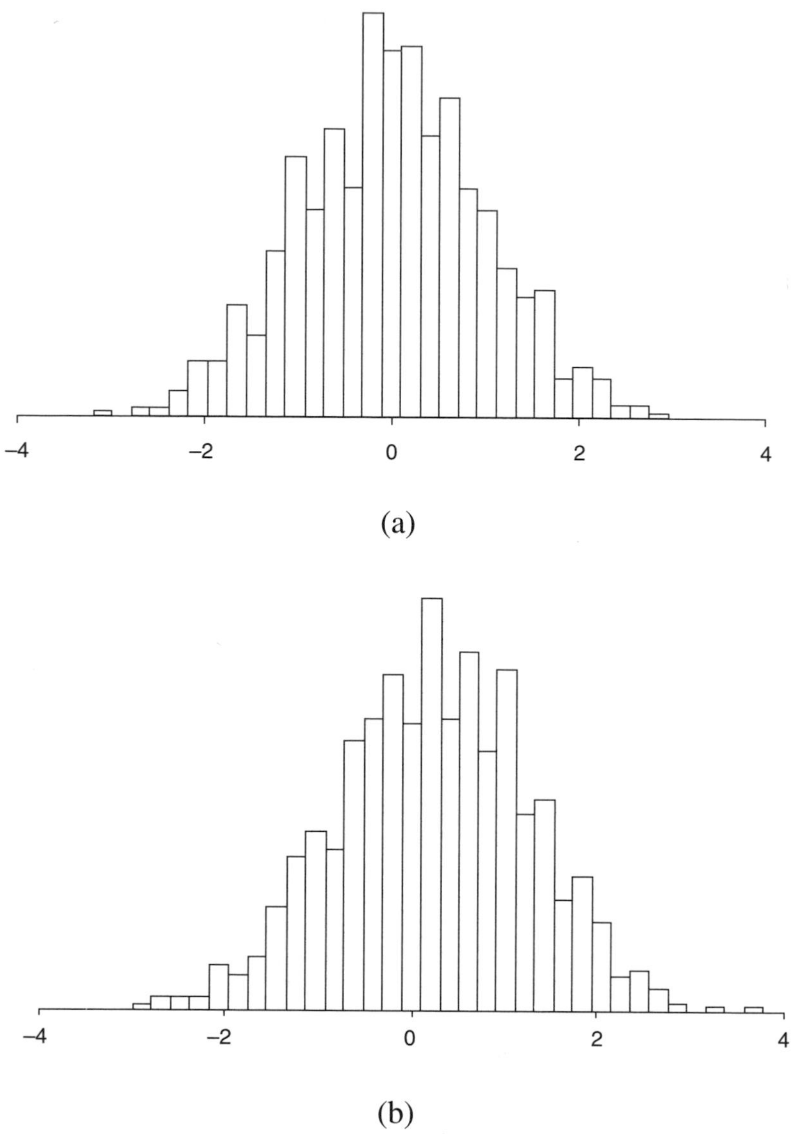

FIGURE 7.6A–B
Two distributions, both with N=10,000, with identical standard deviations differing only with regard to the means.

confidence intervals around mean difference effect sizes for samples of 25 drawn from each of these populations. While the true population effect size is 0.25, the sample-to-sample values range from moderate negative-effect sizes to large positive-effect sizes. There are several things to note from this figure. First, observe how 14 of the 20 confidence intervals contain the null hypothesis population effect size of zero. This means that for almost all of the study outcomes, the null hypothesis is not rejected, though a clear effect exists. Second, notice that for each individual sample, the confidence interval is quite wide, reflecting the low power and relative uncertainty.

Figure 7.8 shows a similar graphic with samples of size 40 depicted. Note the increased sample size leads to smaller confidence intervals and now only

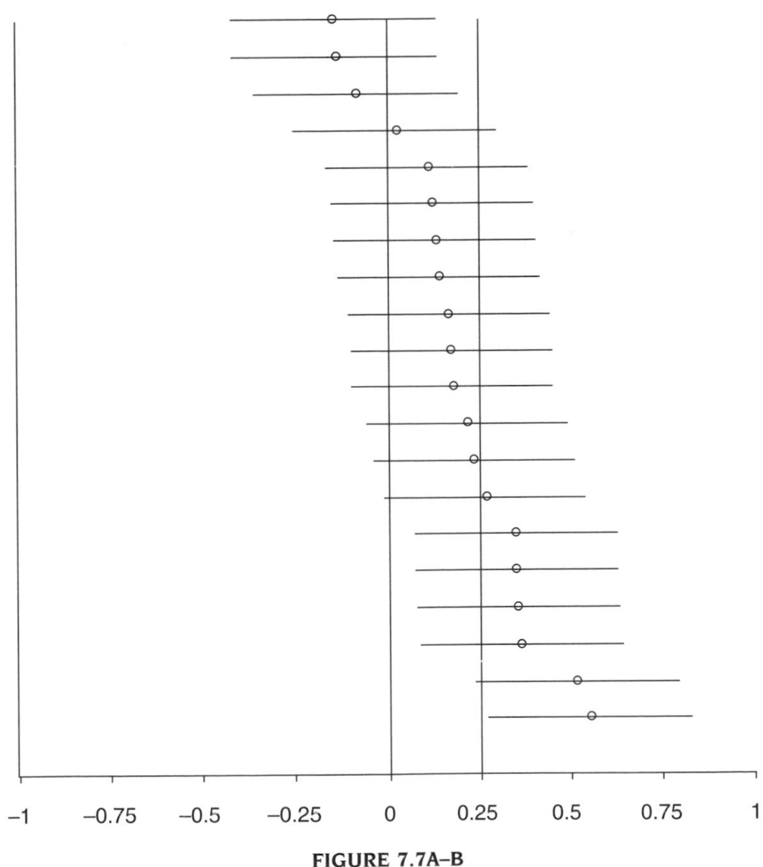

FIGURE 7.7A–B

A: Confidence intervals and effect sizes from population effect size of 0.25 with $n = 25$. **B:** Confidence intervals and effect sizes from population effect size of 0.25 with $n = 40$.

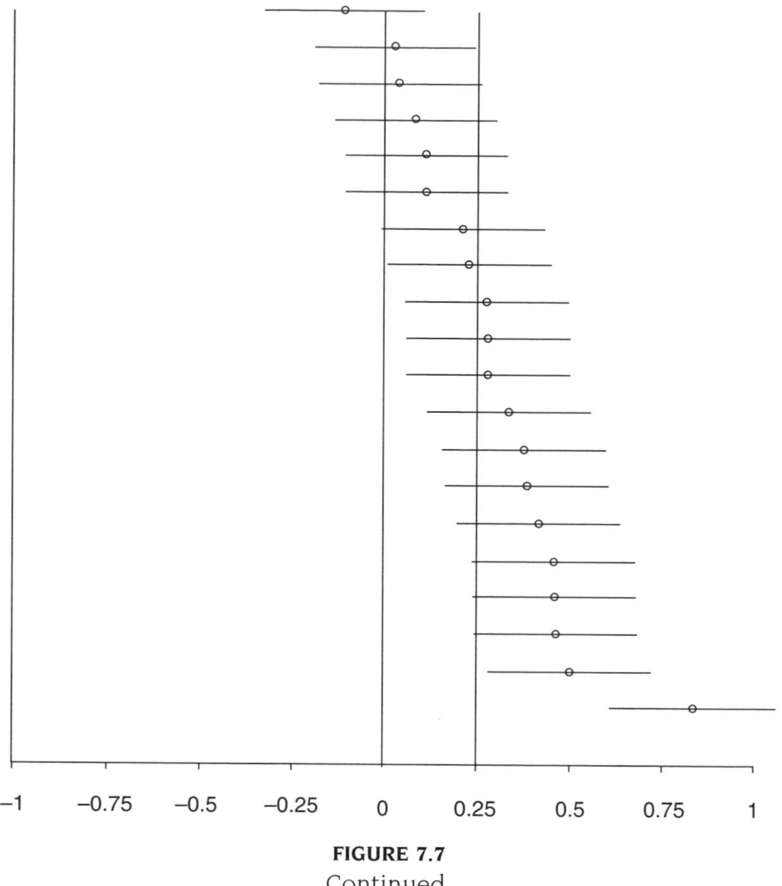

FIGURE 7.7
Continued.

7 of the 20 hypothetic studies lead to the erroneous failure to reject the null. In general, as the sample size increases, the variation from the population mean (0.25) decreases, as does the error rate on improperly rejecting the null. This process illustrates how things must be understood in the long run, and how individual focus on consistency with the null hypothesis alone misleads the researcher.

Figure 7.8 depicts confidence intervals from a meta-analysis reported by Behrens (1997b) regarding correlations between subscales of the White Racial Identity Attitude Scale (Helms, 1990). As the reader can see, here the intervals vary in size because they represent the results of empirical studies that varied in size; therefore, the precision of estimation varied. Interestingly, several of the wide intervals, which would lead to judgments of "nonsignificant" because they include the null value of zero, also cover the estimated population value as well. The very small interval in the lower panel repre-

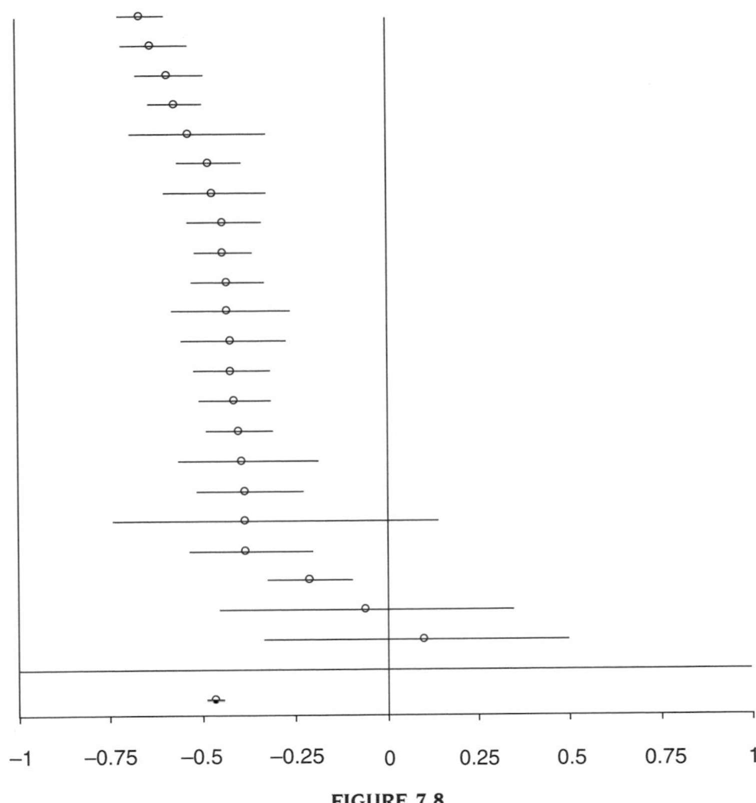

FIGURE 7.8
Results of empirical meta-analytic confidence intervals from data by Behrens 1997b.

sents the effect as estimated using meta-analytic summarization of all the information in each interval.

From this "God's eye view" of research over time, a clear pattern can be discerned, but from the vantage point of any single study, the results seem only to give a hint of things going in one direction or another. With relatively small sample sizes, we can easily fluctuate into negative effects when in fact the underlying process produces systematically positive effects. It is important that we always keep in mind this betrayal of data from random sampling of empirical data.

Remembering Nonrandom Fluctuation

In the real and simulated meta-analytic data presented in the previous section, there is only one dimension; no additional structure is suggested and a simple mean or median would suffice to summarize the effect. In most cases, however, the world itself is more complicated and our mind desires to understand not just the outcome itself, but its relationship to other study characteristics: Are the effects greater for boys than girls? Do longer class times lead to higher achievement? Do schools in the intervention program do better? In all these questions, the logic laid out by Glass (1976) and Glass, McGaw, and Smith (1981) is that the results of quantitative studies could, and should, serve as the primary data for subsequent statistical analyses of all sorts: regression, ANOVA, cluster analysis, and so forth.

Although there is some activity in this area and increasing statistical sophistication, a deeper opportunity for the research community has largely been missed. And, although the techniques for meta-analysis will be used primarily for specialists, the conceptualizations suggested by Glass (1976; Glass et al., 1981) can have a much more broad-range value by helping us conceptualize our results not only among a list of fluctuating effects around a population value, but also as a function of study characteristics.

Consider the graph of effect sizes shown in Figure 7.9 from Behrens and Yu (2003). This is a graphic depiction of the relationship between presentation speed, percentage size of stimulus target for a word recognition task, and the study effect size. The graph indicates that the average effect size at each level of target is constant across presentation speed. However, for any fixed presentation speed, the effect that will be found in the study is highly dependent on the target size.

Here again we are presented with a God's eye view of long-term research. Such multivariate graphics help to depict the fact that each individual study is not simply an effect in isolation but has a value because of its study characteristics. Variation in those characteristics will lead to variations in outcomes and conclusions. This points to a major contribution of Glass's modeling approach. In the same way that common regression of individual raw values helps us relate dependent variables to independent variables, and the outcomes of individuals will depend on where they fit in the regression space, the outcomes of individual experimental studies will often vary as a function of their study characteristics, and individual outcomes may depend on their location in such regression space as well. If one considers each study individually, the larger landscape is missed.

Consider, for example, the data from Kulik and Kulik (1988) presented in Figure 7.10. This bivariate histogram describes the study space that had occurred historically up to the time of Kulik and Kulik's review regarding the effect of delayed versus immediate feedback. As the reader can see, although there is some dispersion in number of days the participants practiced the tasks (duration), there is also some dispersion in the time to follow-up and feedback presentation (days). A large spike at 0 and 0 represents the fact that many studies had less than a 1-day delay and had immediate follow-up.

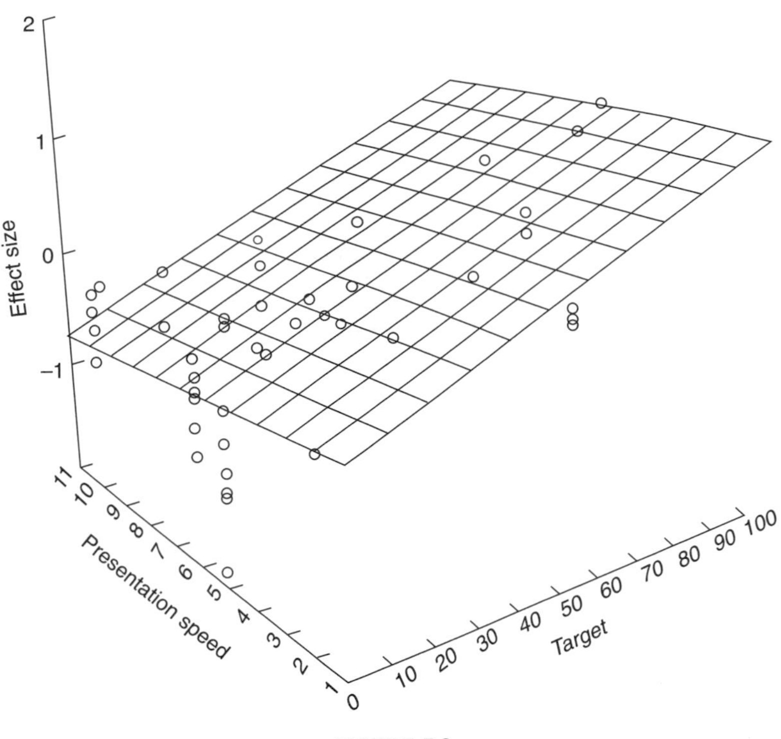

FIGURE 7.9

Linear model of experimental effect sizes. (From Behrens, J. T., & Yu, C. H. (2003). Exploratory data analysis. In J. A. Schinka & W. F. Velicer, (Eds.). *Handbook of psychology* II: *Research methods in psychology*, pp. 33–64. New York: Wiley & Sons.)

Interestingly, when this density graph is decomposed by study type (applied, laboratory list, or multiple choice), as shown in Figure 7.11, the choices for previous study characteristics that were taken across different traditions are made evident. All laboratory list-learning experiments provided immediate feedback and immediate follow-up.

Using graphics such as those suggested from the EDA literature and combining them with long-term meta-analytic data often provides a valuable description of the study profiles and outcomes of previous work. The plots in Figures 7.10 and 7.11 clearly lay out what has been done and what needs to be done to fill in the landscape of study characteristics in this area.

These statements, then, call for researchers to move away from their conceptualization of their work as one-time "shots" that may or may not be replicated later with an eye toward external validity. Rather, these patterns suggest that each study should be conceptualized as occurring in this mul-

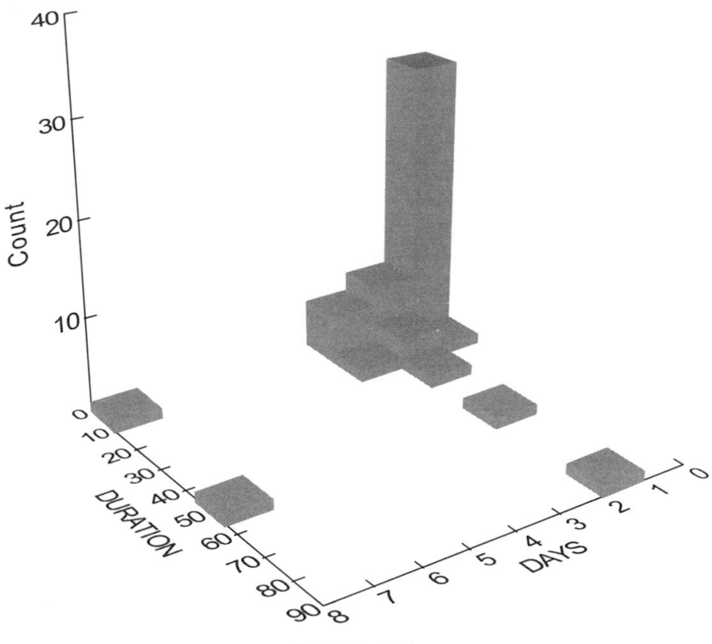

FIGURE 7.10

Plot of study characteristics from meta-analysis. (Data from Kulik, J. A., & Kulik, C. (1988). Timing of feedback and verbal learning. *Review of Educational Research*, 58, 79–97.)

tidimensional space of study features. Using such a view, researchers would try to imagine an effect-size landscape in which their current study was embedded. By trying to imagine the relevant variables to raise effects on that landscape, the researcher would be identifying sources of variation and possible causes for alternate explanations. By considering such issues proactively, the research can build in a measure for the effect *a priori* and communicate to other researchers about the value of the relevant study features that should be held constant or manipulated purposely.

META-ANALYSIS AND PROGRAMMATIC EXPERIMENTAL RESEARCH

While the meta-analytic methods described above deal forcefully with many of the most vexing problems of statistical inference, they have primarily been applied for retrospective summarization. However, this has helped summarize the past in gross generalities while failing to wed these rich descriptive techniques with a prescriptive approach that can inform programmatic

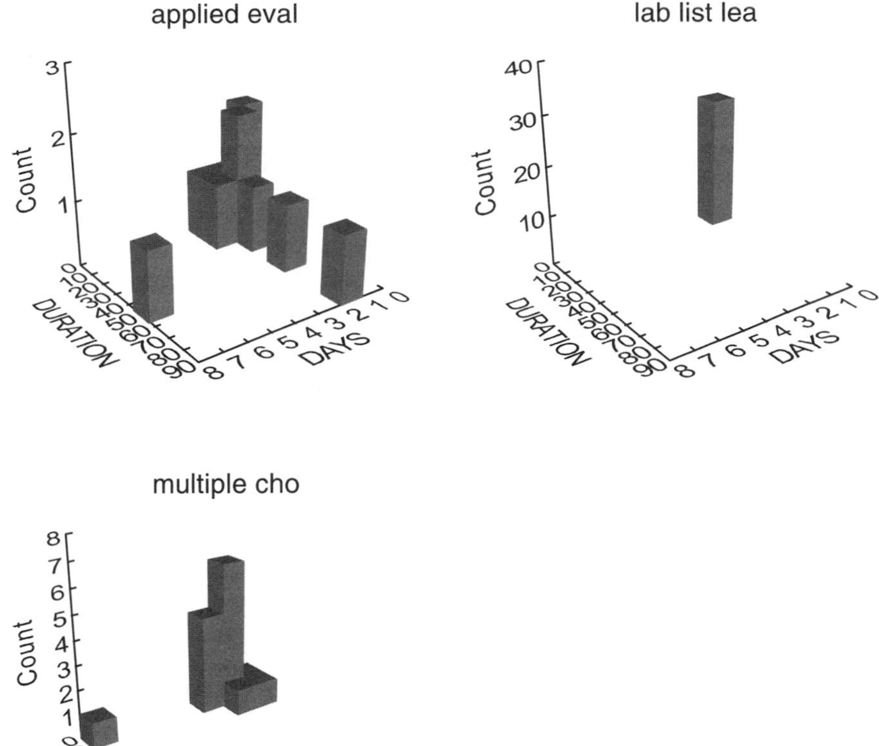

FIGURE 7.11
Data from the Kulik and Kulik (1988) review of immediate versus delayed feedback.

research. Rather than simply looking at the landscape in the rear-view mirror, we believe the meta-analytic approach emphasizing modeling and landscape description can be extremely useful for targeting future endeavors in programmatic research.

Thus far, we have discussed two data analysis approaches that educational researchers who conduct experiments would do well to more closely follow. Both involve taking a closer look at the data by graphing data landscapes at the individual- and multiple-study levels. Missing from the latter approach, involving meta-analysis, has been the Fisherian tradition of programmatic experimental research. Robinson (2004) has even argued that the rise of single-summary, review-only meta-analysis may be partly to blame for the decline of experimental methods in educational research (see also Hsieh et al., 2004). For many of these "meta-analysts," the goal is simply to reach a conclusion about whether a previously touted or criticized experimental effect is valid by pooling all the experiments and then averaging the effect sizes to see if they are positive or negative, minimal or considerable. Because there are several published experiments already in the educational literature, it is easy to see why some people are led to believe that we no longer need additional experiments. If we can simply meta-analyze the experiments that have been conducted so far, perhaps we can shed new light on the overall findings.

This line of thinking has been influential in fueling the controversy concerning whether statistical significance testing has a place in educational research. For meta-analysts, whether single studies are statistically significant is not a concern. Simply average the effect sizes and you will have an unbiased look at the effect. Thus, there has been an "effect-size movement" (Robinson, Whittaker, Williams, & Beretvas, 2003) over the past few years in which more journals are requiring authors to report effect sizes. As meta-analysts look at the wasteland of single-experiment studies out there, each dichotomously classifying their findings as significant or not, they rightfully become dismayed with significance testing (e.g., Cohen, 1990; 1994). Schmidt (1996) noted that "[a]s conclusions from research literature come more and more to be based on findings from meta-analysis, the significance test necessarily becomes less and less important" (p. 116).

The fact that experimental educational research is characterized more by single-experiment, piecemeal studies rather than investigations that involve a series of experiments may be the culprit. Moreover, where do educational researchers first learn that conducting and publishing single experiments as studies is the norm? Think of the first course in statistics. How are the research examples presented in introductory statistics textbooks? Because of space considerations/limitations, small-sample experiments are described and students are encouraged to interpret the outcome of such single-shot experiments as either significant or not. Eventually, students move on to the dissertation proposal. The dissertation is supposed to be a "study," and not just any study but a grandiose study—one that will not only impress the committee but will also get the student national recognition and hopefully a job. Thus, students begin to think in graduate school that to make it in this profession is to design successful studies.

Consistent with the recommendations presented in the previous section, Glass (2000) suggested that educational research would do well to move away from the notion that research is simply doing studies and instead think of contributing in terms of dosage–response curves (i.e., what interventions produce desirable results for what types of students, content, environments, and so forth?). We believe this will be best accomplished if educational researchers stop publishing single-shot experiments and instead begin publishing multiple experiments that are programmatic in nature. This idea is certainly not new and was promoted emphatically by Joel Levin (1991) when he served as editor of the *Journal of Educational Psychology*.

Calls for replication have been made by both Tukey (1969) and Cohen (1994), along with several others. Replication lowers type I and type II error rates. In the Fisherian tradition, true experiments are continuous, with each new experiment representing an attempt to build on the previous one. In Fisher's view, only after a treatment has been consistently shown to be reliable should we conclude that it works. Educational researchers would do well to view experiments as continuous, with the ultimate goal of strengthening internal and external validity.

Instead, the present culture is one of conducting the perfect study rather than viewing research as a process where one conducts several studies programmatically to determine an effect and reveal the extensions and limitations of a treatment. Most doctoral programs prohibit students from even beginning work on the dissertation until they apply for candidacy, usually after 2 years of coursework. Graduate students should be up to their elbows in their program of research by the time they finish their first 2 years. The dissertation should consist of a series of experiments students present at a point in time when they feel a contribution to science has been made. (This is indeed the format B. F. Skinner followed in graduate school at Harvard.) We agree with Glass that chasing the perfect study is silly: It does not exist. Rather, a series of studies that programmatically build on each other with replications and extensions better serves science.

A series of experiments can identify an intervention's effect and extend the effect to different learning environments and student characteristics (i.e., dosage–response curves). This is preferable to meta-analyzing a set of non-programmatic, single-shot studies that have little in common. In addition, once a series of investigations, examined as a series, provides convincing evidence to consider implementation in schools, should we then subject the studies to a meta-analysis where we simply look at effect sizes?

Let us assume that we have a set of five programmatic experiments. The first two experiments resulted in nonsignificant p values and small effects, prompting the researchers to make some changes in the design. The third through fifth experiments result in significant p values and consistently larger effects as the researchers simply increase the length of the intervention. Because each of the five experiments investigates the efficacy of using, say, some strategy training with fifth graders, the meta-analyst throws the results of all five experiments into the analysis and concludes that the strategy is essentially useless, providing an average effect size that is unimpressive. What has been revealed here as opposed to concealed?

Glass (Robinson, 2004) referred to this as something Lee Cronbach called the "Flat Earth Society." Averaging effect sizes is a gross misuse of meta-analysis. Dosage–response curves imply looking at more than just means–researchers should dig deeper. But remember that examining a set of nonprogrammatic studies using meta-analysis holds far less potential for revealing useful information concerning which interventions work best for which students in which learning environments than does a set of programmatic studies (Wainer & Robinson, 2003). For educational intervention research, meta-analytic techniques may serve us better when examining findings from randomized field trials (Boruch, de Moya, & Snyder, 2002).

SUMMARY

In this chapter, we have recommended a set of microanalytic positions and techniques largely following the work of John Tukey, along with a macroanalytic view and set of techniques from the meta-analytic work started by Gene Glass. We believe each of these approaches targets the very heart of the research endeavor for the quantitative researcher: understanding data and building models with great intimacy with the phenomenon and its realization in numeric values, and a long-term, big-picture view of inference as embedded in probabilistic and ongoing processes that must be conceptualized, interpreted, and planned in a comprehensive manner. In writing this chapter, we hope to help move these techniques from the specialty seminar to the foundational textbook and fundamental discussion for all students. These techniques have been greatly refined both computationally and conceptually, and there are many best practices available to move the field forward. However, as we said at the beginning, the change needed to advance research is not simply the addition of supplemental techniques, but a strong focus on the logical underpinnings of the research endeavor writ large. As researchers continue to integrate these methods into their conceptualizations and toolboxes, we improve the chances for appropriate and useful inferences.

References

Almond, R. G. (1995). *Graphical belief modeling*. London: Chapman & Hall.

Anscombe, F. J. (1973). Graphs in statistical analysis. *The American Statistician*, 27, 17–21.

Behrens, J. T. (1997a). Principles and procedures of exploratory data analysis. *Psychological Methods*, 2, 131–160.

Behrens, J. T. (1997b). Does the white racial identity attitude scale measure racial identity? *Journal of Counseling Psychology*, 1, 3–12.

Behrens, J. T., & Yu, C. H. (2003). Exploratory data analysis. In J. A. Schinka, & W. F. Velicer (Eds.). *Handbook of psychology*. II: *Research methods in psychology* (pp. 33–64). New York: Wiley & Sons.

Behrens, J. T., & Rowe, W. (1997). Measuring white racial identity: a reply to Helms. *Journal of Counseling Psychology*, 44, 17–19.

Behrens, J. T., & Smith, M. L. (1996). Data and data analysis. In D. C. Berliner & R. C. Calfee (Eds.). *Handbook of educational psychology* (pp. 949–989). New York: Macmillan.

Boruch, R., de Moya, D., & Snyder, B. (2002). The importance of randomized field trials in education and related areas. In F. Mosteller & R. Boruch (Eds.), *Evidence matters: randomized field trials in education research*. Washington DC: Brookings Institution Press.

Cohen, J. (1990). Things I have learned (so far). *American Psychologist*, 45, 1304–1312.

Cohen, J. (1994). The earth is round (p < .05). *American Psychologist*, 49, 997–1003.

Cook, T. D., & Campbell, D. T. (1979). *Quasi-experimentation: design and analysis issues for field settings*. Chicago: Rand McNally.

Edwards, D. (2000). *Introduction to graphical modeling* (2nd ed.). New York: Springer-Verlag.

Glass, G. V (1976). Primary, secondary, and meta-analysis of research. *Educational Researcher*, 5, 3–8.

Glass, G. V, McGaw, B., & Smith, M. L. (1981). *Meta-analysis in social research*. Beverly Hills, CA: Sage.

Griffin, M. M., Robinson, D. H., & Rittschof, K. A. (in press). Does spatial or visual information in maps facilitate text recall? Evidence against the conjoint retention hypothesis. *Educational Technology Research & Development*.

Helms, J. E. (1990). *Black and white racial identity attitudes: theory, research, and practice*. Westport, CT: Greenwood Press.

Hoaglin, D. C., Mosteller, F., & Tukey, J. W. (Eds.). (1983). *Understanding robust and exploratory data analysis*. Reading, MA: Addison Wesley.

Hoaglin, D. C., Mosteller, F., & Tukey, J. W. (Eds.). (1991). *Fundamentals of exploratory analysis of variance*. Reading, MA: Addison Wesley.

Hsieh, P., Hsieh, Y. P., Chung, W. H., Acee, T., Thomas, G. D., Kim, H. J., & Robinson, D. H. (2004). *Declining trends in experimental research published in educational psychology journals*. Manuscript submitted for publication.

Kirk, R. E. (1995). *Experimental design: procedures for the behavioral sciences* (3rd ed.). Pacific Grove, CA: Brooks/Cole.

Kulik, J. A., & Kulik, C. (1988). Timing of feedback and verbal learning. *Review of Educational Research*, 58, 79–97.

Leinhardt, G., & Leinhardt, S. (1980). Exploratory data analysis: new tools for the analysis of empirical data. *Review of Research in Education*, 8, 85–157.

Levin, J. R. (1991). Editorial. *Journal of Educational Psychology*, 83, 5–7.

Micceri, T. (1989). The unicorn, the normal curve, and other improbable creatures. *Psychological Bulletin*, 105, 156–166.

Robinson, D. H. (2004). An interview with Gene V Glass. *Educational Researcher*, 33(3), 26–30.

Robinson, D. H., & Funk, D. C. (in press). Changing attitudes toward corporal punishment: an intervention that increases knowledge about ineffectiveness to build more consistent feelings and beliefs. *Journal of Behavioral Education*.

Robinson, D. H., Whittaker, T., Williams, N., & Beretvas, S. N. (2003). It's not effect sizes so much as comments about their magnitude that mislead readers. *Journal of Experimental Education*, 72, 51–64.

Shadish, W. R., Cook, T. D., & Campbell, D. T. (2002). *Experimental and quasi-experimental designs for generalized causal inference*. Boston: Houghton Mifflin.

Schmidt, F. L. (1996). Statistical significance testing and cumulative knowledge in psychology: implications for training of researchers. *Psychological Methods*, 1, 115–129.

Tukey, J. W. (1969). Analyzing data: sanctification or detective work. *American Psychologist*, 24, 83–91.

Tukey, J. W. (1977). *Exploratory data analysis*. Reading, MA: Addison Wesley.

Wainer, H., & Robinson, D. H. (2003). Shaping up the practice of null hypothesis significance testing. *Educational Researcher*, 32, 23–31.

Wainer, H., & Velleman, P. (2001). Statistical graphs: mapping the pathways of science. *Annual Review of Psychology*, 52, 305–335.

Wilkinson, L. (1999). *The grammar of graphics*. New York: Springer.

PART III

Producing Credible Applied Educational Research

Beyond the Laboratory or Classroom: The Empirical Basis of Educational Policy[1]

ROBERT BORUCH[2]
University of Pennsylvania

INTRODUCTION

How can we reduce the rate at which children drop out of schools in low-income or high-income countries? We might diagnose the problem in low-income countries, as some people have, by arguing that the children's opportunities are in working in agricultural fields, for example. Moreover, we may suppose that the children's needs lie in supplementing their family's income.

The problem of school dropouts, the diagnosis, and the purportedly effective interventions is important in many countries. To Mexico's credit, the

[1] Research on this topic during 2001 to 2004 was supported by the Rockefeller Foundation, Knight Foundation, and the IES. Part of this chapter is based on an invited discussion at the World Bank Operations Evaluation Department's Fifth Annual Conference. This report does not necessarily accord with views of people in any of these organizations.

[2] Boruch is University Trustee Chair Professor at the University of Pennsylvania, with appointments in the Graduate School of Education, the Statistics Department of the Wharton School, and the Fels Institute of Government.

government transcended political regimes to test a conditional cash transfer program that involves paying mothers in families as long as the children stay in school and the family meets other conditions. Because Mexico recognized that the effects of such a program could differ from the economic forecasts of the program's effects, the country supported a randomized trial.

About 500 villages in seven Mexican states were randomly assigned to a conditional cash transfer program, called Progresa, or to a control condition in which village, family, and children activity went on as usual. The random assignment ensured a fair comparison, an unbiased estimate of the intervention's effect, and a scientifically sustainable statistical statement of one's confidence in results (see Chapter 1). The trial was deemed necessary because the forecasts of effects, though plausible, were debatable. Mothers in families were paid, because that is the way part of the world works (see Parker & Teruel [2002, 2003] and related references that follow).

Mexico's Progresa trial gets well beyond the laboratory and classroom. In this essay, I discuss such *randomized* trials mainly in the context of education. The frame of reference is international, but with attentiveness to in-country interests. The intent is to identify ways to move forward for organizations such as the World Bank, the Organization for Economic Cooperation and Development (OECD), and for the research and evaluation organizations of national governments, especially the United States, and for others at the state, province, village, and city levels.

DEFINITIONS

In microlevel randomized trials, a sample of individuals who are eligible for services are identified and then randomly assigned to two or more interventions that are purported to enhance the individual's well being. The random assignment ensures that there are no systematic differences, at the outset, among the groups so composed. When the trial is carried out properly, we can then develop a statistically unbiased estimate of the relative effects of the interventions and a defensible statistical statement of one's confidence in the results.

In macrolevel randomized trials, entire institutions, clusters, or groups of individuals, such as schools or classrooms, factories, geopolitical jurisdictions, or other entities, may be randomly assigned to different interventions. These are also known as "cluster-randomized trials" or "group-randomized trials," "macroexperiments," and "saturation trials" in various research literature. In these macroexperiments, one aim is the same as in microexperiments: unbiased estimates of the relative effects of intervention and a defensible statistical confidence in the results.

In what follows, randomized trials that involve larger entities are emphasized (i.e., the macrolevel trials). This emphasis is not intended to denigrate bench science, classroom-based research, or other microlevel trials. The products of the latter have been substantial in education sciences, as they have been elsewhere (randomized trials that involve individuals, as opposed to entities). In any event, microlevel randomized trials can be combined with macrolevel randomized trials, at least in principle. The intent is to discuss some important features of trials that are "scaled up."

The Progresa study is not the only example of large-scale trials being mounted in the interest of evidence-based policy in the developing world. I will give other illustrations here.

PLACE-RANDOMIZED TRIALS

For education policy, the schools, villages, and other entities are important. The import of place-randomized trials has been the focus of international and national attention.

Consider, for instance, the Fifth Biennial Conference of the World Bank's Operations Evaluation Department in 2003. The papers that were presented by Laura Rawlings (2005) and by Duflo & Kremer (2005) recognized that randomized trials are a scientifically important approach to producing statistically unbiased estimates of the relative effects of social and educational interventions, as indeed such trials are crucial in the health sector.

In Latin America, these examples include Mexico's Progresa, Nicaragua's Red de Proteccion Social, and Honduras' Programa de Asignacion Familiar. These tests of conditional cash transfer programs, and their effect on education and health-related outcomes, are ably described by Rawlings and Rubio (2003) and Newman et al. (2002). Martin Ravallion (2003) reiterated the import of such trials in reporting on Argentina's Proemplo Experiment, a wage subsidy and training program that was subjected to a randomized experiment.

From Duflo and Kremer (2003), we learn about randomized trials in Kenya to understand the effect of school meals on preschool children's achievement; trials on the effects of textbooks, uniforms, and construction; and studies on flip-chart effects and on other potentially important ways to enhance children's educational achievement. From these authors, we also learn about Indian trials on using second teachers in informal classrooms and on forms of remedial education and about Colombian trials on school vouchers.

For the aspiring trialist who appreciates precedents, Riecken et al. (1974) provided uniform abstracts on Nicaraguan place-randomized trials on radio-based mathematics education, the Cali (Colombia) sector randomized trials on educational and health programs, and a failed trial in El Salvador on education reform. In the United States, one of the early interesting efforts involved a trial to understand the impact of training programs for people who managed Good Will Industry Stores.

Researchers in OECD countries have undertaken micro- and macrolevel randomized trials. In Australia, for instance, school-based randomized trials have been undertaken to understand the effects of asthma education. Ireland mounted what we think is the only place-randomized trial on the effects of introducing standardized tests to children and teachers. In Japan, a microlevel trial was done to understand how real-world knowledge was taken into account by fifth graders who try to learn mathematics. New Zealand and The Netherlands have been unnervingly productive to some (this writer at least) in mounting fair randomized trials in reading, driver's education, job training, and other topics. For references at least, and abstracts at best, see the Campbell Collaboration's Social, Psychological, Educational, and Criminological Trials Register (C2-SPECTR).

In the more speculative vein that workshops invite, participants in the Operations Evaluation Department's International Program for Development and Evaluation Training seminars in 2003 in Ottawa produced interesting ideas about how randomized trials might be mounted to inform understanding of whether new tourist programs work in eastern Europe, what drilling programs might work in parts of Africa, and how one might configure trials on other programs that could be developed with World Bank loans.

Before 2004, the World Bank invested little in randomized trials to generate better evidence on the effects of Bank-supported interventions. The Bank's perspective is changing to judge from its investing in conferences in the United States in 2004 and elsewhere on evidential standards including randomized trials. Pitman, Feinstein, and Ingram (in press) demonstrate courage and stamina in this respect.

Until 2002, the United States government had not invested substantially, with the exception of Planning and Evaluation Service under Alan Ginsberg's direction, in randomized trials in education. The U.S. agencies had done so in the health arena, as other countries have. In a remarkable effort that depended on bipartisan support, the U.S. Congress created an Institute of Education Sciences (IES), a long-term effort that put randomized trials at a high priority (Whitehurst, 2002).

In what follows, I build on the World Bank's theme for the Fifth Biennial Operations Evaluation Department Conference: "Challenges and the way forward." Because some challenges are obvious, I stress the opportunities and attend to what the IES and other agencies have done in the United States.

FAIR COMPARISONS OF INTERVENTIONS: UNBIASED AND BIASED ESTIMATES

Randomized trials, when they are conducted well, produce statistically unbiased estimates of the relative effects of economic, medical, behavioral, and other social interventions. Nonetheless, some people declare that such trials are unnecessary because other methods can produce fair estimates of effect. Surveys and quasi-experiments can do as well, they say.

The counter-declaration is this: Analyses of data from passive surveys or from administrative records or quasi-experiments cannot similarly assure unbiased estimates of the interventions' relative effects. We cannot ensure unbiased estimates, in the narrow sense of a fair statistical comparison, even when the surveys are conducted well, the administrative records are accurate, and analyses of resultant data are based on thoughtful economic models. The risk of misspecified models, including unobserved differences among groups, is high in many social sectors, including economic, criminologic, and education research. For a fine technical review of the endogencity problem in nonrandomized trials in the human development arena, see Duncan, Magnuson, and Ludwig (2004).

Declarations and counter declarations of this sort raise an important empirical question. Do estimates of the effects of interventions based on nonrandomized trials (quasi-experiments) really differ from estimates that are based on randomized trials? Empirical studies that involve comparing the results of the different approaches are critical in answering the question. The study by Glazerman, Levy, and Myers (2003) was mounted under the auspices of the Campbell Collaboration as a test bed project supported by the Smith Richardson Foundation (*http://campbellcollaboration.org*). Its results should worry, if not dismay, those of us who build statistical models that are based on observational studies and quasi-experimental designs rather than on randomized trials. Using microrecords and performing reanalyses of 12 large-scale trials in the employment, training, and welfare sectors, the authors conclude that the absolute magnitudes of biases in estimated effects that are based on nonrandomized trials are often substantial. Moreover, the absolute magnitude of the bias usually cannot be predicted.

The results, put simplistically, are as follows. First, bias in nonrandomized trials is lower in absolute magnitude when the comparison group is local rather than taken from a national sample. Second, regression analysis and matching reduce bias, and both have a partially additive effect. Third, the matching technology matters: one-to-one propensity matching reduces but does not eliminate bias. Fourth, exploiting background (baseline) data is important, and preintervention outcome measures appear to reduce bias notably, but do not eliminate all bias. Shadish, Luellen, and Clark (in press) progressed beyond the reanalyses of existing work performed by Glazerman et al. (2003), in at least one important respect: They did not merely reanalyze data from existing studies. They randomly assigned people to either a full-blown randomized trial *or* to a quasi-experiment that depended on propensity scores to estimate the effects of intervention. The interventions, directed toward college students, were either mathematics training or vocabulary training. Roughly speaking, the results based on the randomized trial differed appreciably from the results of the quasi-experiments.

Nuance is important, however. Analyses based on propensity approaches to the quasi-experimental data produced estimates that were close to those based on the trial but only when closely coupled to the propensity score approach. They can perform badly too, under the conditions that Shadish et al. (in press) describe.

The results by Glazerman et al. (2003) and Shadish et al. (in press) are important and new in some respects, and old in others. The Salk vaccine trials of the 1950s, for instance, involved randomized trials and a parallel set of uniform nonrandomized trials. Estimates of the vaccine's effect on the incidence of poliomyelitis differed appreciably depending on whether one relied on the results from the randomized trials or from the quasi-experiments (Meier, 1972). That estimates based on each approach were in the same direction seems important. However, the reasons for differences in magnitude and similarity in direction are still being examined (Smith, 2002).

People who know the history of quantitative policy analysis, econometrics, and so on, know that useless compensatory education programs can be made to look as if they have harmful effects by using statistical methods that were common in the 1970s, if the analysts did not depend on randomization. This was understood by Campbell and Erlbacher (1970) and elaborated on by Campbell and Boruch (1975) on simple grounds. Unreliably measured covariates, omitted covariates, dependent variables that differ in the quality of their measurement across intervention and comparison groups, are now obvious and potentially important sources of biases in quasi-experiments.

Contributions to this topic in the health care field convey similarly disconcerting news. Kunz and Oxman (1998) examined 18 meta-analyses and found that estimates of the effects of interventions based on nonrandomized trials cannot be trusted unless there is some other evidence that the comparison is fair or one is willing to make substantial assumptions. The assumptions are often not testable.

The Petrosino, Turpin-Petrosino, and Buehler (2002, 2003) systematic review of Scared Straight programs for youth at risk of crime is no more encouraging. Numerous quasi-experiments, surveys, and anecdotes led to declarations that the Scared Straight's effects were positive. The randomized trials uncovered and examined critically by the authors provide dependable evidence that the effects are negative.

Lest we think that the physical sciences and engineering are free of such concerns, recall that one of the reasons for the Columbia space shuttle failure has been attributed to the *Crater Equation*. This equation was called "semiempirical" in some publications. It was used to estimate a projectile's damage to the Columbia shuttle's wing. The equation, or its application, was wrong, to judge from experiments carried out as part of the subsequent research on why the Columbia failed to enter earth's atmosphere safely (Chang, 2003).

In addition, lest we think that agricultural research is simpler than the education sector, consider the following. In the late 1940s, people in many countries needed to know how to increase potato crop yield for postwar European populations. Multiple regression analyses based on passive observational data suggested that farmyard manure had a negative and statistically significant effect on yield. Randomized trials, on the other hand, demonstrated that farmyard manure increased potato crops remarkably and did so beyond what one would expect on the basis of chance. The story is reported by Snedecor and Cochrane (1989).

Comparative empirical studies of the difference in results of randomized versus nonrandomized trials have been based on trials in which individuals, rather that entities, are the targets for random allocation and analysis. I am aware of no similar comparative studies on place-randomized trials (cluster, group) as opposed, say, to time-series estimates of the effects of interventions in homogenous populations such as Sweden or Norway.

An implication is this: One way forward for those interested in less equivocal evidence, including World Bank Group, OECD, and U.S. government agencies that sponsor applied research (on what interventions work), lies in encouraging empirical methodologic reviews. People who value scientific evidence as a basis for decisions need to know about potential biases in different approaches to estimating the effects of interventions, and more importantly, about the domains in which bias can be substantial.

At this writing, the medical, education, criminologic, and welfare sectors have trustworthy standards in randomized trials. The way forward then lies partly in using such methodologic studies to build capacity and incentives to do trials. It also lies in studies of when the estimates of effect from randomized trials accord with, or are discordant with, results of nonrandomized trials.

ECONOMIC FORECASTS, ASTRONOMY, AND PIGS

A member of the audience at the World Bank's Fifth Biennial meeting on evaluation offered an audacious and interesting opinion. He declared that economists ought to behave like astronomers. That is, economists ought to improve on their ability to predict, instead of doing randomized trials.

No one can disagree with an aspiration to predict better. However, asking economists, medical people, and engineers for that matter, to predict what happens in the absence of a new and untested intervention is akin to asking them to levitate.

More to the point, our ability to forecast is "domain specific." During the early 1970s, for instance, the effectiveness of bulletproof cloth (body armor) was under debate. Police officers had good reason to understand the effects of the intervention (i.e., the allegedly bulletproof cloth). To test the intervention's effect in at least one place, police researchers draped the cloth over a pig. They then fired a large-caliber pistol at the pig. The cops then determined whether there was any blood shed. The "intervention worked" in that the cloth prevented the bullet from penetrating the pig. That is, no blood was shed.[3]

How many control pigs were needed, do readers think, to ensure that this estimate of the intervention's effect was fair? That is, how many naked pigs had to face possible extinction to make the causal connection?

The answer in the early 1970s, as now, depends on earlier science and is domain specific. The consequences of firing a high-caliber weapon at a pig are predictable, if the aim is right, if the weapon functions properly, and if the pig is not equipped with body armor. Assume that the aim is right and that the device works properly, resulting in a nice big bang in the pig's direction.

This ability to predict what happens, however, is specific to the domain of ballistic equations. The origins of the equations date from the 17th century if we use Galileo and Newton as benchmarks. In any case, Galileo, as a good scientist, learned how to develop prediction models and how to experiment under controlled conditions (Coyne, Heller, & Zycinski, 1985). The World Bank, research organizations such as the IES in the United States, and the rest of us cannot wait 400 years for prediction equations to an answer to the question, "What is the relative effect of an intervention?" Randomized trials provide brisker answers.

LEARNING ABOUT RANDOMIZED TRIALS

From presentations at conferences on evidence-based policy and on research and evaluation, we learn occasionally about interesting randomized trials in different countries. In 2003, the World Bank Fifth Biennial meeting conference on evaluation presented a fine opportunity to do this (Pitman, Feinstein, and Ingram, in press). So too did the Campbell Collaboration's multidisciplinary conference on place randomized trials, convened in Italy and in the United States (*http://campbellcollaboration.org*). The National

[3] In the parlance of the U.S. Office of Management and Budget, this would be designated as a direct controlled experiment, as opposed to a randomized controlled trial (*www.whitehouse.gov/omb/part*).

Academy of Sciences' Committee on Research in Education provided in-country examples (Towne & Hilton, 2004).

But we in the education, social, and behavioral sciences, including criminology, and researchers and policy makers in government, must ask ourselves some strategic research policy questions: How can we make the learning more regular? Less episodic? How can the World Bank, the OECD, government agencies such as the U.S. Education Department, and members of research societies, learn routinely about randomized trials in all the sectors that are pertinent to their interests? Why did participants at the World Bank meeting in 2003 learn about the large-scale trials at the meeting, rather than easily through the Internet?

Until recently, there has been no reliable and readily accessible resource for locating randomized trials. The situation in health care research changed in 1993. The international Cochrane Collaboration (*http://www.cochrane.org*) was created to prepare, maintain, and make accessible systematic reviews of studies of effects of health interventions. Randomized trials have been the main ingredients for these systematic reviews. Cochrane's electronic library on trials contains more than 350,000 entries. Cochrane set a remarkable precedent for accumulating and building a knowledge base of this sort.

In 2000, the international Campbell Collaboration (*http://campbellcollaboration.org*) was created as Cochrane's younger sibling to prepare, maintain, and make accessible systematic reviews of studies of the effects of interventions in education, crime and justice, welfare, and other social arenas. Like Cochrane, the Campbell Collaboration depends heavily, but not exclusively, on randomized trials. The Collaboration's Web-accessible library, the C2-SPECTR, contains more than 13,000 entries on randomized and possibly randomized trials and more than 300 entries on place-randomized trials. It grows as reports on more trials are located and as resources permit their location and entry into the register.

For the World Bank Group, OECD, and the international community of researchers, a way forward lies in fostering and using Web-accessible registers of randomized trials, assuming that people want to know about fair trials. Building reliable, continuously improved, and comprehensive registers of this sort is a nontrivial challenge. In fact, the IES has taken a leadership role in developing a What Works Clearinghouse, which includes registers and reviews of trials in a variety of education sectors, to inform people about dependable evidence based on randomized trials and some types of quasi-experiments (see *http://w-w-c.org*).

Both Campbell and Cochrane recognize, for instance, that the results of trials are not always made public, especially if the results run contrary to a particular political view. Both organizations recognize that keeping abreast of new trials is important to ensuring that we can then recognize the suppression of reports and track new studies. For this reason, the Campbell Collaboration is creating a prospective register of trials as part of C2-SPECTR.

That is, grants and contracts for new trials are put into a register. Personal contacts and networks count heavily in this effort, of course. Surveys of organizations that sponsor or conduct such trials are also essential, partly because many of these do not produce reports in refereed academic journals (see Turner et al., 2003).

The Campbell and Cochrane Collaborations have discovered a further serious and general problem in identifying randomized trials: the coverage bias of electronic search engines. That is, the search engines on which the Web depends usually do not pick out many of the trials. Hand-searching academic journals, for instance, typically yields three times the number of trials that can be identified in a Web-based search (Turner et al., 2003).

LEARNING HOW LARGE-SCALE TRIALS ARE DONE

How are large-scale randomized trials designed? How do they get off the ground? What political–institutional problems were confronted and how were they resolved? How was the trial managed? How do we think about the ethics of place-randomized trials?

No one has all the answers, of course. Part of the answers and part of the future for the World Bank, OECD, and the international community of researchers lies in identifying such trials and in supporting the development of registers of trials. However, identifying trials and developing registers is hard work.

Learning about how the trials are designed and how they are run is harder work. Part of the future lies in bringing people together to share understanding of how place-randomized and other kinds of trials have been mounted. The Rockefeller Foundation, for example, sponsored a set of commissioned papers and meetings on this topic. Convened by the Campbell Collaboration's Secretariat, the aim was to build the knowledge base across disciplines–education, crime and justice, welfare, health and welfare (see *http://campbellcollaboration.org*). This effort helped to build the knowledge base across countries, inasmuch as it covered trials in Mexico, China, the United Kingdom, United States, Canada, and elsewhere. Organizations such as the World Bank Group, OECD, and national governments can do much more than a single private foundation.

The challenges to learning how to do large-scale randomized trials in education to enhance children's achievement, and the outcomes that are correlated with their achievement, are similar to those encountered in efforts to change other institutional environments. In particular, the challenges are similar to those encountered by colleagues who try to change the delivery of health care in medical units to reduce mortality rate, deploy programs throughout entire housing projects to improve residents' capacity to get jobs, and revise police approaches to reduce crime. All of these efforts involve entities that have been the units of random assignment and analysis in place-randomized trials (cluster randomized, group randomized). These trials are the scientific basis for estimating the relative effects of interventions deployed system-wide. In such trials, the challenges include the following:

- *Identifying entities that are ready to change and to participate in a trial that produces evidence on the effects of the change.* Readiness includes being educated about trials and ensuring that there are incentives to participate in them. The task also requires patience because learning what works better takes time.
- *Determining how to deploy the intervention in multiple schools, hospitals, villages, police jurisdictions, and so on.* The intervention, although it must be uniform in some respects, must be tailored to suit the setting. It includes developing systems to train people, such as teachers, physicians, nurses, and beat cops and their superior officers, who need to know what to do and be reinforced in the learning.
- *Learning how to monitor the deployment of the intervention and ensure its fidelity or integrity at a reasonable cost.* Combining numeric and narrative evaluation methods has been a major challenge because of intellectual provincialism in universities in North America and some of the western countries of Europe.
- *Trying to ensure that randomized trials are used where appropriate to estimate relative effects and to counter ignorant claims that randomized trials cannot be done or that nonrandomized approaches will produce unbiased estimates of effect.* These claims made about nonrandomized trials are sustainable only if one is willing to make assumptions. The assumptions cannot often be defended.
- *Learning how to design randomized trials at the macro- or microlevel so that the trials yield the most information at the least possible cost and produce useful information.* The challenge to build capacity was joined in 2004 by the W. T. Grant Foundation and the U.S. Department of Education's IES, among others. Under Robert Granger's direction, the foundation initiated technical seminars on the design of macrolevel trials (*http://wtgrantfdn.org*). Under Russ Whitehurst's direction, the IES entertained proposals for graduate fellowship programs in this arena and funded at least six major efforts that will help us learn more. The National Academy of Sciences has also assisted in capacity building (see Towne & Hilton, 2004).

ETHICAL CONDITIONS FOR RANDOMIZED TRIALS

When should a multinational organization such as the World Bank, the OECD, or a government research agency or anyone else consider supporting a randomized trial to understand the relative effects of an intervention? The future for such organizations lies in making explicit the conditions for considering a trial.

Deciding to mount a randomized trial should be based on affirmative answers to the following simple questions. This interrogatory approach, based on Boruch's report (1997), depends heavily on the Federal Judicial Center's (1981) analysis:

1. Is *the education problem serious*? If the answer is yes, consider a randomized trial. Otherwise, a trial is not worth the effort nor is it ethical.
2. Are *purported solutions to the education problem debatable*? If yes, consider doing a randomized trial. If the answer is no, adopt the purported solution if the evidence is sufficient to do so.
3. Will *randomized trials on the purported solution to the education problem yield more defensible (less equivocal and unbiased) estimates of the effects of an intervention than alternative approaches to estimating effects*? If the answer is yes, consider mounting a randomized trial. If the answer is no, rely on the alternative approach. Of course, one must have evidence that the alternatives produce unbiased estimates. The empirical methodologic studies identified earlier are important here as is the domain-specific ability to forecast.

So far, nobody in education research or in medical research or anywhere else has been able to produce a better way to make a fair comparison then relying on a randomized trial. At the national level, in the United States, the director of the IES, Russ Whitehurst (2002), has recognized this; in the United Kingdom, cabinet officer Philip Davies (2004) has also done so.

4. Will *the results of the randomized trial on an education innovation be used*? If the answer is yes, consider mounting a randomized trial. If the answer is no, be wary. Of course, one cannot be certain that any given trial's result will be used by a government to inform policy or practice. Recall that it takes 5 to 10 years for the results of medical trials to be incorporated into medical guidelines, for instance. It took more than 5 years for the results of a high-quality trial on class size in Tennessee to reach the attention of politicians, who then took action.
5. Will *human rights be protected*? If the answer is yes, consider a randomized trial. More important, design the randomized trial so that rights are indeed protected. The strategy and policy of a lottery-based "rollout" of interventions across regions of a country, or a lottery-based allocation of interventions to different grades in different schools, constitute a trial design that satisfies a social standard of ethics at times.

For example, the problem of keeping children in school and out of the agricultural fields has been important to Mexico. The purported solutions to the problem, including conditional income transfer programs, have been debatable partly because of equivocal evidence and our inability to make precise predictions about what would happen to children at the local and regional levels. The Progresa trial that Parker and Teruel (2002) describe is a case in point. Families and villages that clearly do not need conditional income transfers do not receive them–an ethical and political judgment. Families and villages at the margin and beyond are identified as eligible for a cash transfer on the basis of census and other data. Because the resources for conditional income transfers are scarce, a lottery allocation meets a reasonable standard for protecting one kind of right: equitable distribution of resources at a certain level to families/villages when the total resources are scarce and the level of resource is important (see Parker & Teruel, 2003).

Questions 1–5 are put plainly. They seem sensible in delimiting the conditions under which we may consider mounting randomized trials to estimate the relative effects of different interventions. They can be used by organizations such as the World Bank, OECD, or government research agencies to decide when a randomized trial can be justified.

Questions of this sort must be tailored, of course, to the ethical, social, and evidential standards of each country and each organization. They need to account for the interests and values of the countries that served by the organization. They are crude, but they are a beginning.

CONCLUDING REMARKS

Aiming to make fair comparisons about what works in education is important. It is not easy to achieve this aim. Societal values attached to an interest in fair comparison may or may not agree with the scientific value attached to such a comparison. These societal values may in turn differ from human rights values, which have to be taken into account in any attempt to mount a fair trial. And, of course, political values may take precedence, and will at times, over the scientific values.

By way of closing this discussion, let me depend for the *n*th time on Walter Lippman who, in the 1930s, said, "Unless we are honestly experimental, we will leave the great questions of society and its improvement to the ignorant opponents of change on the one hand, and to the ignorant advocates of change on the other." Going beyond the laboratory to engage in place-randomized field trials is a way of taking direct responsibility for honest answers to some of these questions in education as in medicine, welfare, employment, and other sectors.

References

Bootzin, R., & Smith, H. (Eds.) (2003). *Discussion of the Jerry Lee Invited Lecture: Second Annual Meeting of the Campbell Collaboration*. Philadelphia, PA: University of Pennsylvania.

Boruch, R. F. (1997). *Randomized experiments: a practical guide*. Thousand Oaks, CA: Sage Publications Inc.

Bryk, A. S., & Raudenbush, S. W. (1992). *Hierarchical linear models: application and data analysis methods*. Thousand Oaks, CA: Sage Publications Inc.

Campbell, D. T., & Erlebacher, A. (1970). How regression artifacts in quasi-experimental evaluations can mistakenly make compensatory education look harmful. In J. Hellmuth (Ed.). *Compensatory education: a national debate*, 3: *Disadvantaged child* (pp. 445–463). New York: Brunner-Mazel.

Campbell, D. T., & Boruch, R. F. (1975). Making the case for randomized assignment treatments by considering the alternatives: six ways in which quasi-experimental evaluations in compensatory education tend to underestimate effects. In C. A. Bennett & A. A. Lumsdaine (Eds.). *Central issues in social program evaluation* (pp. 195–296). New York: Academic Press.

Chang, K. (2003). Questions raised on equation NASA used on shuttle peril. *New York Times*. June 9, 2003; p. 38.

Coyne, G. V., Heller, M., & Zycinski, J. (1985). *The Galileo affair: a meeting of faith and science. Proceedings of the Cracow Conference, 24 to 27 May 1984*. Citta Del Vaticana: Specola Vaticana.

Donner, A., & Klar, N. (2000). *Design and analysis of cluster randomization trials in health care*. New York: Oxford University Press.

Duflo, E., & Kremer, M. (2005). The use of randomization in the evaluation of development effectiveness. Paper presented at: Fifth Biennial World Bank Operations Evaluation Department Conference on Evaluation and Development Effectiveness; July 15–16, 2003; Washington DC. In K. Pitman, O. Feinstein, & G. Ingram (Eds.), *Development effectiveness: World Bank series on evaluation and development* (pp. 205–231). New Brunswick, NJ: Transaction Publishers.

Duncan, G. J., Magnuson, K. A., Ludwig, J. (2004). The endogencity problem in development studies. *Research in Human Development*, 1, 59–80.

Federal Judicial Center. (1981). *Social experimentation and the law*. Washington, D.C: Federal Judicial Center.

Glazerman, S., Levy, D., & Myers, D. (2003). Nonexperimental versus experimental estimates of earnings impacts. *The Annals of the American Academy of Political and Social Sciences*, 589, 63–93.

Kunz, R., & Oxman, A. D. (1998). The unpredictability paradox: review of empirical comparisons of randomized and non-randomized clinical trials. *British Medical Journal*, 317, 1185–1190.

Meier, P. (1972). "The biggest public health experiment ever: the 1954 field trial of the Salk poliomyelitis vaccine." In J. Tanur, et al. (Eds.), *Statistics: a guide to the unknown* (pp. 2–13), San Francisco: Holden Day.

Newman, J., Menno P., Rawlings, L., Ridder, G., Coa, R., & Eviva, J. (2002). "An Impact Evaluation of Education, Health, and Water Supply Investments of the Bolivian Social Investment Fund." Revised *World Bank Economic Review* submission (March 2002). Authors: World Bank and other organizations.

Parker, J., & Teruel, G. (2002). The Progresa Trials in Mexico. Commissioned Paper presented at: Campbell Collaboration Conference on Place-Randomized Trials; November 21–25, 2002; Rockefeller Foundation Center, Bellagio, Italy and Rockefeller Foundation, New York, NY (December 18, 2003).

Petrosino, A., Turpin-Petrosino, C., & Buehler, J. (2002). Scared Straight: a Campbell Collaboration systematic review: Campbell Library. *http://campbellcollaboration.org*.

Petrosino, A., Turpin-Petrosino, C., & Buehler, J. (2003). Scared Straight and other juvenile awareness programs for preventing juvenile delinquency: a systematic review of the randomized experimental evidence. *Annals of the American Academy of Political and Social Sciences*, 589, 41–62.

Pitman, K., Feinstein, O., & Ingram, G. (Eds.). (2005). *Evaluating development effectiveness: World Bank series on evaluation and development*. New Brunswick, NJ: Transaction Publishers.

Ravillion, M. (2003). Randomized trials of development policies and projects: some comments. Presented at: World Bank OED Fifth Biennial Conference; July 15–16, 2003; Washington, DC.

Rawlings, L. (2005). Operational reflections on evaluating development programs. Paper presented at: Fifth Biennial World Bank Operations Evaluation Department Conference on

Evaluation and Development Effectiveness, Washington, DC (July 15–16, 2003). In K. Pitman, O. Feinstein, & G. Ingram (Eds.), *Evaluating development effectiveness: World Bank series on evaluation and development* (pp. 193–204). No. 7: New Brunswick, NJ: Transaction Publishers.

Rawlings, L., & Rubio, G. (2003). *Evaluating the impact of conditional cash transfer programs: lessons from Latin America*. Draft Manuscript (May 14). Authors: Latin American and Caribbean Human Development Department, World Bank.

Riecken, H. W., Boruch, R. F., Caplan, N., Campbell, D. T., Glennan, T. K., Rees, A., Pratt, J., & Williams, J. (1974). *Social experimentation: a method for planning and evaluating social programs*. New York: Academic Press.

Shadish, W. R., Luellen, J. K., & Clark, M. H. (in press). Propensity scores and quasi-experiments: a testimony to the practical side of Lee Sechrest. In *Festschrift-for Lee Sechrest*. Washington, D.C.: American Psychological Association.

Snedecor, G. W., & Cochrane, W. B. (1989). *Statistical methods* (8th ed.). Ames, IA: Iowa State University Press.

Towne, L., & Hilton, M. (Eds.). (2004). *Implementing randomized field trials in education: report of a workshop*. Washington, DC: National Academics Press.

Turner, H., Boruch, R., Petrosino, A., de Moya, D., Lavenberg, J., & Rothstein, H. (2003). Populating an international register of randomized trials. *Annals of the American Academy of Political and Social Sciences*, 589, 203–225.

Whitehurst, G. (2002). New wine in new bottles. American Educational Research Association Annual Meeting Chicago. *http://www.ed.gov/about/offices/list/ies*.

Academic Learning and Academic Achievement: Correspondence Issues

GARY D. PHYE
Iowa State University

The *view from Washington* D.C. that is offered by Reyna (see Chapter 2) contains the following statement:

> The main conclusion that emerges from this analysis is that if this legislation is to be successful, fundamental changes must be made in the kind of educational research that is conducted and in how colleges and universities prepare prospective researchers, practitioners, policy makers, and other educational decision makers.

This message is consistent with that provided by Whitehurst (2003) in an invited address at the annual meeting of the American Educational Research Association.

In this chapter, I provide a discussion of a fundamental addition to the between-group research designs that are used by many educational intervention researchers. The traditional between-group design has been extensively used to assess differences between or among groups of students receiving differing instructional activities. When these between-group designs are used to assess student achievement, the data are typically

Empirical Methods for Evaluating Educational Interventions

reported in terms of grade level averages in a subject (e.g., mathematics) for a particular school. Typically, this is a yearly assessment that reflects group differences between grade levels. The addition of a within-student design element provides the basis for also assessing educational *change* and *individual differences* in academic learning and academic achievement. This combining of a between-group comparison with a within-student comparison produces a mixed design with cross-sectional and longitudinal components.

The mixed design has great practical utility when determining the impact in schools of "scientifically based educational interventions." This utility stems from the fact that the *No Child Left Behind* (NCLB) Act mandates that schools track the academic development of individual students across their educational careers. Pragmatically, the development in student academic achievement must be monitored in two ways: (a) within a grade level during an academic year and (b) across grade levels during the academic career in that school. For purposes of this chapter, I am using the term *academic learning* to identify the change in academic knowledge constructed by individual students during an academic year. I am using the term *academic achievement* to denote changes in academic knowledge constructed by individual students during an academic career.

However, prior to an extended discussion of research design and alignment issues, I want to share my perspective on the NCLB legislation in terms of three roles that educational researchers may play as this legislation is rolled out and implemented. The following roles are defined by what I see as the three major scientifically based research dimensions that define NCLB: (a) the development of scientifically based pedagogical practices, (b) the determination of school system accountability as measured by adequate yearly progress of student achievement, and (c) the determination of the impact of scientifically based educational interventions on student achievement (defined in terms of causal relationships).

ROLES FOR EDUCATIONAL RESEARCHERS

The obvious role and the one most frequently addressed in this volume is the educational researcher as the developer of "scientifically based instructional practices." As has been articulated by several chapter authors, issues such as random assignment, control groups, and clinical trials are major topics that meet the "gold standard" when designing educational research studies.

The second role that educational researchers will play involves the issue of school accountability defined in terms of adequate yearly progress. These activities involve working directly with school districts and include such practical accountability issues as defining adequate yearly progress (AYP) in terms of learner outcome variables. Again, the crux of these efforts is the development of instruments that provide credible data (reliable and valid) that are collected within a data collection paradigm based on experimental methodology. Several of these issues are discussed by D'Agostino (see Chapter 6).

These psychometric efforts typically involve the determination and development of an acceptable benchmark that operationally defines "proficiency." The accountability effort is then directed at determining the proportion of a cohort (grade level) that meets or exceeds the benchmark every year with the benchmark for that grade being raised in future years. This is a major challenge for educational researchers in that NCLB calls for the "student" as the primary unit of analysis. In addition, these data must be aggregated to classroom, building, district, and state levels of analysis. Further, state-wide data must also be disaggregated by such student variables as socioeconomic status, gender, second language proficiency, and so forth. In other words, these requirements define a focus on individual differences and group differences tracked developmentally across grades. This is a stark contrast to past practices in many states where achievement data have traditionally been analyzed at the classroom level or district level with no tracking of students across grades.

This same point (unit of analysis) can also be made by raising our level of analysis to a comparison of adequate yearly progress of student achievement outcomes across states using National Assessment of Educational Progress (NAEP) data. For the first time ever, data from all 50 states are available. However, because each state has defined "proficiency" in its own unique manner, directly comparing yearly progress across states is difficult.

The third role that educational researchers may fill is providing evidence that scientifically based practices (role one) used as educational interventions actually affect student achievement. This is an issue of the alignment of learning assessment during the academic year and the end of the year achievement assessment. Here, the educational researcher will be involved with design development, instrument development, data collection, and data analysis that can determine if the observed adequate yearly progress in student achievement can be attributed (said to be caused) by the scientifically based practices that were implemented (as educational interventions) by the classroom teacher. The success of this endeavor will be predicated on the success of the educational researcher engaging in the two previously identified roles to deliver credible evidence about the effectiveness of educational interventions. Given credible evidence of effectiveness, program evaluators may then use experimental research designs to determine the effectiveness of the educational system. These program evaluation efforts will typically focus on the effectiveness of the educational system to impact a teacher's implementation of the "best practices" and their impact on student achievement when the unit of analysis is the school or district.

This is the scaling up process that has typically been ignored in educational research efforts devoted to systemic change efforts.

Several experimental designs can be developed to address research questions involving instructional impact on student achievement in reading, mathematics, and science within a grade and between grade levels. A central theme common to all such experimental designs using a longitudinal component is the repeated measurement of individual students across time. In effect, this defines a research design that provides the opportunity to assess student change. In the simplest sense, this amounts to viewing academic learning as process (formative assessment) and academic achievement as product (summative assessment) at various points in time.

These research roles provide a schema for identifying research questions that will dictate the development of data collection designs and methods. However, without defining what we mean by academic learning and academic achievement, the communication process that is critical for translating research findings into effective educational practice is hindered. Consequently, the first section of this chapter is devoted to defining academic learning and academic achievement within a theoretical context identified as *pragmatism and educational research* (Biesta & Burbules, 2003). The second section introduces the use of a mixed research design for data collection efforts that provide a basis for addressing not only achievement status but also individual differences and change in academic learning and achievement.

EDUCATIONAL RESEARCH: DEWEY AND PRAGMATISM

Philosophy of Science

"Educational research, one might say, is not so much research *about education* as it is research *for education*" (Biesta & Burbules, 2003, p. 1). I am couching the following discussions in the context of John Dewey's pragmatism that shares much in common with that of William James and gave rise to a school of thought frequently referred to in psychology as the "Chicago School of Functionalism" (Bredo, 1997). I subscribe to the position taken by Biesta and Burbules (2003, p. 3): ". . . we believe that many of Dewey's ideas are still relevant today—something that, despite the many books that have been written about Dewey over the past two decades, has not yet been sufficiently recognized, at least in the context of educational research." Accordingly, when the question arises about how educational researchers should use pragmatism, Biesta and Burbules offer the following advice:

> Pragmatism is not a recipe for educational research and educational researchers; it does not offer prescriptions. It is as we have presented it here, as much a way of

> unthinking certain false dichotomies, certain assumptions, certain traditional practices, and ways of doing things, and it can open up new possibilities for thought. It is, in short, a resource that can help educational researchers make their research activities more reflective and—to use one of Dewey's most favorite words a final time—more intelligent (p. 114).

Pragmatism in the United States has had a pervasive influence in social science research. In addition to John Dewey, early proponents in the United States included such luminaries as William James in psychology, Charles S. Pierce the philosopher–scientist, and the sociologist George H. Mead. Pragmatists argue that philosophy should take into account the methods and insights of modern science (Biesta & Burbules, 2003): "Dewey, for example, stressed the significance of the experimental method of modern science as a model for human problem solving and the acquisition of knowledge" (p. 5).

The main significance of Dewey's pragmatism for educational research lies in the fact that it provides a different account of knowledge and a different understanding of the way in which human beings can acquire knowledge. Dewey's approach is different in that he deals with questions of knowledge and the acquisition of knowledge within a framework of *action*, in fact, a philosophy that takes action as its *most basic* category. This connection between knowledge and action is especially relevant for those who approach questions about knowledge primarily from a practical angle—such as educators and educational researchers (Biesta & Burbules, 2003).

For both James and Dewey, the basic "function" for human organisms is adaptation to the world. Within this macroview focus (world view), a given is the constant state of change of both the organism and the material world we inhabit. This blooming, buzzing, constantly changing state of our existence as human beings is the norm, not the exception. At this macrolevel of analysis, human beings have the unique ability to cognitively construct alternative hypotheses about "best strategies" for adapting to our evolving world. This *knowledge* (constructed hypotheses) has no functional utility until action is taken to test the hypotheses. It is the means of testing the success or lack of success of our hypotheses at a macrolevel that characterizes a pragmatic approach to the practice of science in the social sciences.

This philosophical discussion provides a rationale for the use of the term *capturing* in the title of this chapter. Academic learning and academic achievement are not explanations for change. Rather, they are descriptions of the conditions under which change has been captured. Although this distinction may appear pedantic, "capturing" rather than "discovering" is what educational research is all about. In my opinion, this distinction is the key to successful implementation. Educators must understand that a successful educational intervention that produces positive change elsewhere will be successfully implemented to the extent that comparable conditions exist in their school.

Correspondingly, the microview focus of adaptability can be identified as a single student who is a member of a cooperative learning team or a student engaged in individual seatwork during class. Regardless, the basic tenets of Dewey's *action theory* also apply to the analysis of this situation. Students in classrooms are adapting to multiple demands from a constantly changing world. Consequently, their basic function as students is to adapt by constructing hypotheses or plans about the assignment being engaged. These "strategies" are simply ideas that involve symbolic process until they are tested by an action on the part of the student. This action provides the basis for confirmation or disconfirmation of the "plan to adapt." If successful, the assumption is that this idea would be constructed into personal academic knowledge to be drawn on at a later point in time when similar adaptation efforts are required. In educational circles, this level of analysis of the adaptive function is frequently called "problem solving" and the ability of a student to successfully adapt to successive educational demands to be "problem-solving transfer" (Phye, 2001).

The point is that Dewey's pragmatic action theory of knowledge construction is predicated on two principles that *current* experimental psychology as a discipline incorporates into the scientific approach describing, predicting, and explaining human behavior (including cognition). These principles are (a) the rejection of a dualistic approach to explaining psychological reality (e.g., mind/body dualism) and (b) the rejection of a reductionism approach to macro- and microlevels of analysis that insists on "cause–effect" relationships between or among levels with the ultimate explanation being located in the most basic level of analysis. Rather, a *correspondence* between levels of analysis (Stanovich, 2001) based on both credible and creditable research (see Chapter 1) provide the logical basis for articulating the necessary and sufficient conditions for describing, predicting, and explaining change in student behavior.

Philosophically, Dewey's pragmatism provides a functional philosophy of human behavior with powerful potential for promoting educational science. I make this statement in light of the continuing debates being waged by educational researchers who continue to resurrect "realism" and "logical positivism" as the straw person against which they rile. Nearly a century ago, Dewey initiated a pragmatic approach to the study of human behavior. These methods of science hypotheses have been tested by the actions of experimental psychology for the last century with remarkable success in promoting our understanding of human behavior. Can we as educational researchers make comparable claims?

The Educational Sciences View

Reyna's call for a reevaluation of educational research is not a call to "reinvent the wheel" of research methods in human learning and the assessment of academic achievement. Rather, it is an invitation to examine psychology's contribution to understanding human learning and achievement that has been accumulating at a rapid rate during the past 25 years. Many educational researchers have missed that part of the cognitive revolution in psychology where research methods and statistical tools that produce credible data have been applied in real-world settings. A few examples would include the subdisciplines of developmental psychology, cognitive-social psychology, cognitive-memory psychology, school psychology, and educational psychology. Each of these subdisciplines view the phenomena of learning and achievement through a "different lens." For the most part, however, when the behavior being investigated is academic learning and achievement, three common themes can be observed in the published research: (a) Dewey's theory of action, which amounts to a theory of experimental learning; (b) functional correspondence requiring the use of operational definitions to define actions; and (c) individual differences.

The first theme is the use of an organic model. This simply acknowledges that human behavior is the product of an interaction between a person's environment and his or her genetic makeup; in some respects, everyone is unique. This acknowledgment identifies individual differences as variables that must be considered when describing, predicting, or attempting to understand "how" someone learns or "what level" of achievement he or she has attained. In the research literature, these are commonly referred to as subject variables or abilities.

The second theme is the use of operational definitions when identifying the knowledge to be acquired and/or constructed and the conditions or situation in which this occurred. Is it a group setting or an individual setting? Is the academic material to be mastered math, science, or others? Operational definitions are a critical means of communicating *with precision* the situation in which a particular person demonstrates the desired learning outcome. In the research literature, these operational definitions of the task and environment are frequently the independent variables to be actively manipulated or passively recognized (field studies) and assessed. These independent variables or fixed variables are operationally defined with precision for a reason. If there has been an impact on the dependent variables (academic learning and academic achievement), strong or weak arguments can be made that the changes in learning or achievement are attributable to the influence of the independent or fixed variables. The utility of operational definitions is their ability to communicate with precision the conditions under which the behavior (action) was observed. In this regard, implementation at other sites (replication) and scaling up at differing levels (classroom, district, statewide, and so forth) becomes a possibility. If the primary focus of a research effort is the validation of best practices within content areas at varying grade levels, followed by classroom implementation by teachers in various settings (rural/urban), then precision in communication is critical.

The third theme that characterizes much of psychological research is a consideration of individual differences. I am including a consideration of research designs that provide the basis for a consideration of individual differences for two reasons. The first reason is practical. NCLB mandates require the tracking of individual students' academic progress across their academic careers. Further, group differences are also identified as disaggregated data within the larger data set. These groupings include gender, socioeconomic status, language status, developmental status, and so forth. The second reason is theoretical. Both Lee Cronbach (1957) and Benton Underwood (1975) have called for an integration of research design characteristics that would permit the study of both group differences and individual differences, including change across time. Within the context of NCLB research, this translates into designs that provide for the analysis of group and individual student change in the development of academic knowledge (reading, math, or science) within the same study.

Academic Learning

Learning has so many meanings that it is necessary to first add a qualifying adjective. In the environmental setting we call the classroom, there are different types of learning experiences. Some experiences involve motor learning that serves as the basis for motor skill development. In some cases, learning activities focus on behavior that serves as the basis for social skills development. On the other hand, academic learning involves primarily the processing, construction, and communication of cognitive information (symbolic) about the subject matter we teach in the classroom.

Having identified academic learning in terms of a "type of learning activity," scrutiny of a commonly accepted definition of academic learning serves as a means of considering what is frequently referred to as the "learning process." In the third edition of *Learning Theories: An Educational Perspective*, Dale Schunk offers this suggestion, "*Learning* is an enduring change in behavior, or in the capacity to behave in a given fashion, which results from practice or other forms of experience" (Shuell, 1986; as cited in Schunk, 2000, p. 2). This definition of learning is consistent with a cognitive focus and captures the criteria most educational professionals consider central to academic learning.

Three elements of Shuell's definition of academic learning (behavioral change, endurance, and practice) deserve further attention, because these elements help define the *level of analysis* involved in the present use of the term. Together these three elements stress the idea that academic learning engaged in by students is not typically a single instructional experience. It is a process of (a) the acquisition of new information, (b) the refinement and organization of what is already known, and (c) the successful testing and use of that knowledge. Academic learning is the product of practice (action) that provides the basis for relatively long-term change in one's personal knowledge. Ideally, this change will increase students' ability to successfully adapt as they move from grade to grade where the curriculum requires more complex and specialized forms of personal knowledge.

Academic Achievement

Many distinctive characteristics of achievement tests can be identified. For NCLB, I am mentioning only three characteristics that are salient to our discussion of student learning outcomes as measured by end of the academic year assessments. These assessments may take the form of a commercial standardized achievement test (Iowa Test of Basic Skills) or a state developed test, and so forth.

In either case, these instruments are developed to assess what students have learned from their exposure to classroom instruction (in contrast to aptitude tests). In other words, a primary characteristic of an achievement test is the assessment of prior academic knowledge. With respect to the use of an achievement test to capture academic learning at the end of the academic year, a second characteristic is the static measurement of the status at which a student is performing at a given point in time. Last, but certainly not least, there is no guarantee that the prior knowledge status captured in this single assessment was the product of learning during the academic year. These three characteristics of achievement assessment at the end of an academic year frequently provide the basis for the determination of adequate yearly progress and is typically referred to as a summative assessment (Nitko, 2004).

Used in this way, achievement tests provide an indication of students' status in subject content areas relative to end of the year grade placement norms or standards. Phrased differently, this is the target behavior at which instructional goals and objectives are directed. An assumption is made that effective instruction engaged in by the teacher during the academic year promotes student learning that will be assessed by the achievement test. When testing this assumption, accountability data will be collected that reflect teachers' implementation of scientifically based practices. However, these scientifically based practices must be demonstrated to impact the end of the year achievement performance. This is where the problem of correspondence (both theoretically and in practice) becomes a major issue. Stated simply, how does one go about collecting data during the academic year that takes into consideration the hypothesis that academic learning (assessed as process or change) can be demonstrated to "cause" improvement in students' achievement status measured at the end of the academic year?

EDUCATIONAL INTERVENTIONS AND EXPERIMENTAL DESIGNS

Classroom Example (Data Collection)

How are academic learning and academic achievement alike and how are they different? Pragmatically, one can make the argument that learning and achievement are alike qualitatively, because a researcher is simply capturing the process of adapting to the school environment at different points in time. For example, Figure 9.1 depicts an assessment cycle that might be observed in the classroom. Assume that this is a fourth-grade classroom and the knowledge being assessed is mathematic computation and problem solving. Common sense tells us that students' learning is assessed in some fashion that culminated in a status check at the end of a 9-week grading cycle when report cards are issued. Obviously, daily and weekly assessments have preceded the status check. Thus, from a data collection point of view, the weekly assessments are said to be formative, and the quarterly assessment is said to be summative.

Moreover, a typical academic year is divided into four quarters with quarterly assessment, with the end of the fourth quarter typically taking the form of a state-mandated achievement test (see Figure 9.2). The assessment scheme in Figure 9.2 is simply an extension of the evaluation scheme portrayed in Figure 9.1. What was identified as a summative assessment in Figure 9.1 becomes a formative assessment in Figure 9.2.

These examples identify the crux of one correspondence issue. Is the knowledge base (cognitive and motivational abilities) being constructed on a daily and weekly basis being reliably assessed at the end of each quarter (content/construct validity)? Further, when the quarterly assessments become predictors of end of the year performance, do they still reflect what is being learned on a daily and weekly basis? Are the cognitive and motivational abilities and skills being constructed by students to meet the demands of quarterly assessments being assessed on the end of the year achievement test?

If not, then one can make the claim that qualitative differences may exist when the summative evaluations from Figure 9.1 become formative

Quarterly (9 week) data collection cycle

Week	W-1	W-2	W-3	W-4	W-5	W-6	W-7	W-8	W-9
Data Collection	X_1	X_2	X_3	X_4	X_5	X_6	X_7	X_9	Y_1

X = Weekly formative assessment
Y = Quarterly comprehensive assessment

FIGURE 9.1
Quarterly classroom data collection scheme

Yearly data collection cycle

Academic Year	W_1W_2.........Qtr1	$W_{10}W_{11}$.........Qtr2	$W_{19}W_{20}$.........Qtr3	$W_{28}W_{29}$.........End of Year
Data Collection	X_1X_2.........Y_1	$X_{10}X_{11}$.........Y_2	$X_{19}X_{20}$.........Y_3	$X_{28}X_{29}$.........Z_1
X = Weekly assessment Y = Quarterly assessment Z = Annual assessment				

FIGURE 9.2

Yearly classroom data collection scheme

evaluations in Figure 9.2. In other words, is there a correspondence between the cognitive motivational abilities of individual students being assessed as formative and summative evaluations depicted in Figures 9.1 and 9.2? This correspondence is assumed in many educational settings where the focus is on the development of an aligned curriculum within a grade level. My point, "How do you know"? This qualitative alignment assumption can be tested by taking an individual differences approach to addressing the question. Simply determine the nature of the relationships (correlation coefficients) among the data points within a 9-week quarter (Figure 9.1) and across the four quarters (Figure 9.2).

Between-Group Data Collection for Adequate Yearly Progress

Annual achievement testing at most grade levels has become a reality in our public schools. Because this is a relatively new effort, many schools have simply collected achievement data and reported them by groups (grade level) and then compared group performance from one year to the next. Determining the effectiveness (impact) of educational interventions typically takes the form of comparing different groups of students at different points in time.

The following example (Figure 9.3) reflects a simplified between-group data collection procedure involving two groups of students, each assessed at two different times (e.g., this year's fourth graders assessed in 2004 compared to last year's fourth graders assessed in 2003). Many schools are using an extended version of this data collection procedure to assess adequate yearly progress as required by NCLB. This is essentially a between-group comparison without a control group (this design actually does have a "control" or "comparison" group, though not a randomized, simultaneous, or good one from an experimental point of view).

Because data are collected from two different groups at two different points in time, when differences are observed in achievement, one can only recognize that a difference was observed. Any observed difference can be attributed to any number of factors because there is no comparison

Grade 4

End of 2003 Academic Year	Baseline Data Collected (Group 1)
Beginning of 2004 Academic Year	Intervention Introduced
End of 2004 Academic Year	Intervention Data Collected (Group 2)

FIGURE 9.3
Common annual yearly progress data collection scheme

group (again, there is a comparison group, just not a good one). More important, change cannot be inferred because individual student achievement is not being assessed at two points in time. A typical data collection scheme I have encountered in the schools I work with involves the assessment of academic achievement or adequate yearly progress with a between-groups design that looks something like the data collection scheme shown in Figure 9.3.

For a single grade, the typical comparison is a difference comparison between group 1 (last year's fourth graders) and group 2 (this year's fourth graders). However, we have fourth-grade students serving in the baseline condition different from those who are in the fourth grade when the intervention in introduced. Consequently, any observed differences in achievement between 2003 and 2004 can be attributed to individual and group differences in students as well as to the impact of the educational intervention. Alternatively, as a researcher would comment, we have a confounding that precludes us from attributing observed differences solely to the educational intervention.

In most cases, the AYP assessment process involves determining the proportion of fourth-grade students who met or exceeded the proficiency benchmark in 2003 and the proportion of students who met or exceeded the proficiency benchmark in 2004. However, the standard for proficiency increases annually. Thus, the standard for proficiency is a moving target. This is the big concern of educators in the public schools. This is an immediate practical concern for educational researchers producing credible data upon which policy analysis and administrative decisions are based. From an educational sciences perspective, research designs and data collection procedures of the type described in the paragraph above do not provide the credible data driven evidence needed to change policy or determine the effectiveness of educational interventions (see Chapter 1).

This discussion of the comparison of academic achievement between different groups of students with data collected at different points in time (this year vs. last year) is an introduction to another alignment issue. This type of alignment issue confronts researchers who are trying to determine the success or failure of the NCLB initiatives when the effort is to determine achievement gains for groups of students within an academic year and across grade levels during successive years.

Designing a Classroom Experiment with a Mixed Design

This design or data collection refinement is accomplished by extending the traditional between-group design to include a longitudinal component (repeated measures). This would involve combining the repeated data collection from individual students as portrayed in the short term (Figure 9.1) or the long term (Figure 9.2) with a treatment group and a comparison group. This extension produces a mixed design for data collection by including a within-student factor (repeated measures for each individual). A simple mixed design would be a 2 (group) × 3 (repeated measures) factorial with random assignment of students to a treatment group and a comparison group as shown in Figure 9.4. With students as the units of analysis, the assessment of performance at three points in time (repeated measure) provides the basis for assessing change. For example, with a mixed design we could assess the impact of a supplemental instructional intervention with a group of fourth graders. The first factor, "grade level," is a between-students factor with two levels (treatment/no treatment) and the second factor, "assessment of the same individuals prior to, during, and following the educational intervention," is a within-students factor (repeated measure). Because we are tracking individual students across time, we have the basis for describing observed differences in pretest, midpoint, and posttest performance as "change." The issue here is that we can infer change only when we analyze data for students who have a minimum of two performance scores. Given student mobility, this requires a check for differential dropout rates and so forth. Data collection involving the assessment of academic learning with a mixed design would look something like that shown in Figure 9.4.

Educational Intervention

	Pretest		During		Posttest
Treatment (Group 1)	X	------------------------	X	---------------------------	X
Control (Group 2)	X	------------------------	X	---------------------------	X

X = data collection

FIGURE 9.4
Mixed-design classroom data collection scheme

Because this is a classroom learning study and the educational intervention is typically supplementary instruction in a specific subject (math, reading, science), the control group is given a task that requires study but is not from the same content domain as the educational intervention. Assuming regular instruction will promote some improvement in performance across time, the researcher is interested in isolating effects of the educational intervention (supplemental instruction).

Thus, the research hypothesis of interest is the two-way group by repeated-measure interaction. One form of a statistically significant two-way interaction might look something like that plotted in Figure 9.5. To the extent that the improvement in pretest–posttest performance favors group 1, the unique impact of the educational intervention has been determined. Without going into detail, the within-student's factor also increases the power (sensitivity) of the statistical test to detect an intervention effect. In a short-term study, ethical issues can be circumvented by flip-flopping the treatment and control groups following the posttest data collection so that both receive the educational intervention.

A design of this type would typically be carried out at the classroom level in a single school. The unit of analysis is the student not the teacher or type

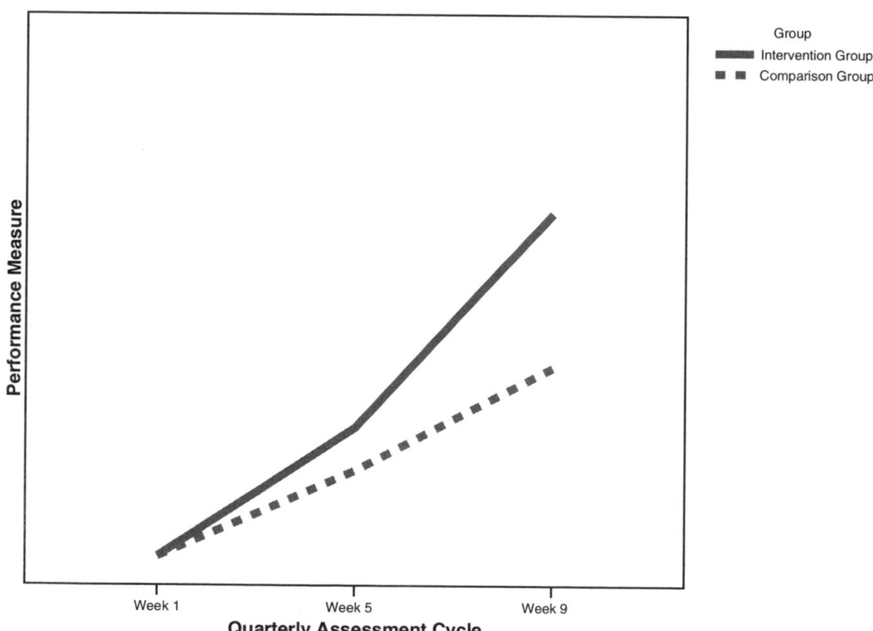

FIGURE 9.5

Anticipated two-way interaction for a successful educational intervention when using the mixed-design data collection scheme in Figure 9.4

of intervention. Rather, with random assignment (and the inclusion of multiple-classrooms—see Chapter 1), this design could be used to determine the effectiveness of a scientifically based educational intervention that positively impacts student performance. This would typically be a short-term experiment that would fit nicely within a quarterly reporting interval such as that described in Figure 9.1 and would typically be reported as an instructional-learning study.

Replication of Intervention

Now, let us assume that the supplemental mathematics intervention that was tested at the fourth grade in the example above proved to be effective. Consequently, the school administrators made the decision to extend the intervention for the entire academic year. This suggests a replication study with a data collection procedure similar to that in Figure 9.2. This data collection strategy in Figure 9.2 is simply an extension of the data collection strategy introduced in Figure 9.1 and creates the opportunity for a yearlong replication study. However, a constraint is that one cannot ethically withhold an educational intervention from half the class for an entire academic year. In this case, one frequently resorts to a clinical replication with no comparison group (classical one-group longitudinal study) or one develops a quasi-experimental design by creating a "matched classroom" comparison group. Although the development of a matched comparison group involves extra effort, any observed differences at the end of the year can more "possibly" be attributed to the educational intervention. Without the comparison group, one is still confronted with the question "compared to what?" when explaining observed change in achievement during the academic year. See Chapter 1 for alternative research designs for dealing with practical constraints.

Evaluating a School-Wide Intervention with a Mixed Methods Design

Further, assuming the intervention was successful at grade four, the efforts could be extended to include additional grades. In this way, the school would be assessing the effectiveness of the educational intervention across grade levels. Extending the math example to include grades four, five, and six would make sense from a curriculum perspective and would provide the basis for a mixed-design data collection example to be used in a program evaluation effort by a single school.

The basic research question is, "Can we take a scientifically based educational intervention that we have successfully demonstrated impacts fourth-grade student achievement and scale up the intervention effort (within the same school), to include grades five and six"? Our example theoretically could include grades kindergarten through 12. For purposes of simplicity here, only three grades are considered. In addition, the following example is basically an integration and extension of the data collection procedure in Figure 9.2 and the research design in Figure 9.4.

The following quasi-experimental design involves 3 years of data collection. The data being collected are end of the year achievement test performance for individual students. Data are collected for all students in grades four, five, and six at the end of the current academic year and for the next two academic years (2005 and 2006). At the end of 3 years, the data collected could be organized as shown in Figure 9.6. The Xs simply denote that the state-mandated achievement test was administered to all grades every year. In our example, these data collection procedures produce a data array from which data sets can be developed for testing various research hypotheses about student change (across grades), group differences in student performance (between grades), and teacher/curriculum influence (time-lag comparison).

It must be pointed out that these types of analysis are possible only to the extent that the state-mandated test has been scaled so that comparisons can be made across grade levels using a normalized or standardized score (see Chapter 6).

At the end of the 2004 academic year, research questions about grade level differences can be addressed by making cross-sectional comparisons in achievement scores among grades four, five, and six. This would involve a comparison among groups designated X1, X2, and X3 in Figure 9.6. The research questions addressed would deal with only group differences (developmental differences) because the comparisons involve different students in different grades at a single point in time.

At the end of the 2005 academic year, a between-groups analysis can again be performed to address research questions involving group differences. In essence, this is a cross-sectional replication of the 2004 study

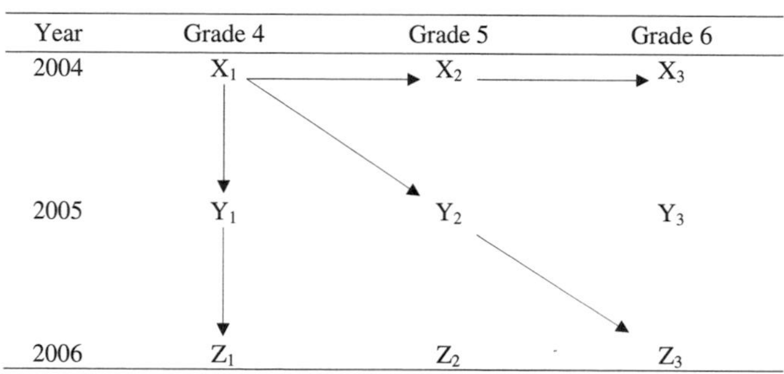

Year
Grade 4
Grade 5
Grade 6
2004
X1
X2
X3
2005
Y1
Y2
Y3
2006
Z1
Z2
Z3

FIGURE 9.6
Multimethod data collection scheme for scaling up for school-wide implementation

with different students in different grades. This involves a comparison among groups designated Y1, Y2, and Y3. However, we can now add a longitudinal component to the analysis to analyze for developmental change. This would involve a comparison of data sets X1 and Y2 for students who have taken both tests. Thus, the analysis involves the same students followed across two grades. This comparison is also possible for data sets X2 and Y3. These two longitudinal analyses provide information about developmental change from fourth to fifth grade and from fifth to sixth grade. Further, a comparison can now be made between data sets X1 and Y1 at the fourth grade, X2 and Y2 at the fifth grade, and X3 and Y3 at the sixth grade. These are time-lag comparisons because one is comparing different students at different times for the same grade. Any differences observed would raise questions about teacher or curriculum influences. This time-lag comparison is an extension of the between-groups design identified in Figure 9.3.

At the end of the 2006 academic year, the longitudinal analysis now includes data sets X1, Y2, and Z3. Developmental change can now be analyzed for students who completed grades four, five, and six. Also, the cross-sectional analysis for differences among grade levels can be performed on data sets Z1, Z2, and Z3 as a second replication of the original 2004 analysis to monitor group differences in grade-level performance. Further, the time-lag analysis can be continued by comparing Y1 and Z1 at the fourth grade, Y2 and Z2 at the fifth grade, and Y3 and Z3 at the sixth grade.

The data collection design in Figure 9.6 is a multiple-methods design (Friedrich, 1972; Nesselroade & Reese, 1973). This type of design is of value when research questions address a school's ability to implement a scientifically based educational intervention on a school-wide scale. Granted, this is a quasi-experimental design and there are problems with both the credibility and the generalizability of findings. However, the multiple-methods design is useful for scaling up efforts from a classroom level of analysis to a school-wide level of analysis and can provide useful data to drive administrative decision making and policy analysis at the local school-district level.

Scaling Up with Clinical Trials

Theoretically, it is possible to take our example from Figure 9.6 and move it to the next level of replication. However, as pointed out by Levin (see Chapter 1), the tradeoff is one of introducing potentially new problems pertaining to internal validity threats. However, if confronted with the task of scaling up educational interventions that involve a school-wide system, replication with random assignment and appropriate control groups is still the "gold standard." An example would be an educational intervention that takes the form of a new professional development delivery system. Assume the basic intervention model has been demonstrated to be effective based on an analysis of data collected from a single school (see Figure 9.6). Now, the question is whether or not the successful intervention results can be replicated in other schools.

Without going into detail, assume that the new professional development model that serves as the educational intervention is the pilot project for a statewide initiative. The pilot project data indicate that this new model is a "strong positive" based on 3 years of data collection and analysis. Consequently, a representative sample of schools from within the state are identified and randomly assigned to the treatment group of schools or the control group of schools. In this case, a power analysis was performed to determine the size of the school sample because the unit of analysis is schools (not classrooms or students). Furthermore, our data collection procedure could essentially be the same as that portrayed in Figure 9.6. Again, a 3-year cycle of data collection would be sufficient to provide credible as well as creditable data (see Chapter 1). These data could then serve as the basis for statewide policy analysis and administrative decision making by the state department of education.

SUMMARY

My efforts have been directed toward the reintroduction of Dewey's pragmatic approach to scientific research into the current discussion of educational science. This theoretical approach has a long history in education and has been successfully used by psychologists to describe, predict, and explain adaptive human behavior (including academic learning and achievement). An organic model of adaptability and change, this approach has a great deal of potential application for educational researchers. The storyline for our discussion of data collection efforts has been hierarchical in nature. The rationale for this organizational scheme is practical and theoretical. Practically speaking, the stakeholders vary as one moves from a consideration of scientifically based instructional practices in the classroom to systems operating at the level of a school district or a state initiative. Theoretically, two obvious issues are involved. The first point is the one for which examples have been given: Research design issues change as research questions change across these authentic levels of analysis. The second point is subtler. This relates to the correspondence principle, when a level of analysis approach is taken to the analysis and interpretation of hierarchical data.

As noted at several points in the chapter, a pragmatic approach to data interpretation can be located on a continuum that reflects the limitations of data interpretation based on the nature of the data collection and analysis. This is typically translated into the concept that data in the social sciences can be used to describe, predict, or explain the behavior under investigation. This basic theme runs through all chapters in this volume. However, a corollary assumption, the *correspondence principle*, is frequently ignored. The correspondence principle states that our continuum of data interpretation does not necessarily hold as we move from one level of analysis (classroom) to the next (school district) and design characteristics change. What may have been a data collection procedure that led to a causal explanation at one level of analysis, when used at a differing level of analysis may provide only prediction or description. Simply including random assignment and the addition of a control group to a data collection procedure is a necessary but not sufficient condition for ensuring a credible causal attribution across levels of analysis.

From a pragmatic perspective, scientific methods in educational research are pluralistic. To make significant advances in educational reform, we must ask better questions and use both experimental and quasi-experimental design elements in our data collection efforts. Continuing to view academic learning and achievement as static products of instructional manipulations contrasted between groups is only a first step. Educational researchers must include data collection procedures and data analysis procedures that provide an opportunity to determine who benefits from best practices (individual differences) and how these students develop academically (change) as a result. A limited research repertoire for an aspiring educational researcher is as self-defeating as a limited repertoire for an aspiring musician. As mentors of the next generation of educational researchers, we (graduate faculty in colleges of education) must do better.

References

Biesta, G. J. J., & Burbules, N. C. (2003). *Pragmatism and educational research*. Lanham MD: Rowman & Littlefield Publishing.

Bredo, E. (1997). The social construction of learning. In G. D. Phye (Ed.), *Handbook of academic learning: construction of knowledge* (pp. 1–45). San Diego: Academic Press.

Cronbach, L. J. (1957). The two disciplines of scientific psychology. *American Psychologist*, 12, 671–684.

Friedrich, D. (1972). A *primer for developmental methodology*. Minneapolis, MN: Burgess Publishing.

Nesselroade, J. R., & Reese, H. W. (1973). *Life-span developmental psychology: methodological issues*. New York: Academic Press.

Nitko, A. J. (2004). *Educational assessment for students* (4th ed.). Upper Saddle River, NJ: Pearson Education.

Phye, G. D. (2001). Problem-solving instruction and problem-solving transfer: the correspondence issue. *Journal of Educational Psychology*, 93, 571–578.

Schunk, D. H. (2000). *Learning theories: an educational perspective*. Upper Saddle River, NJ: Prentice Hall.

Stanovich, K. E. (2001). The rationality of educating for wisdom. *Educational Psychologist* 36, 247–251.

Underwood, B. J. (1975). Individual differences as a crucible in theory construction. *American Psychologist*, 30, 128–134.

Experimental Research in Classrooms

ANGELA M. O'DONNELL
Rutgers, The State University of New Jersey

The term "evidence-based research" has come to be something of a loaded term because of the political context surrounding discussions of what constitutes high-quality educational research. Discussions about the nature and quality of educational research go back a number of years but the passage of the *No Child Left Behind Act* (2002) and the *Education Sciences Reform Act* (2002) brought national attention to these discussions. In 1995, the National Academy of Education established a commission to provide guidelines that would assist in making judgments about the quality of research. Other groups (FINE Foundation [First in the Nation in Education: Ducharme, Licklider, Matthes, & Vannata, 1995]; U.S. Department of Education's National Center for Education Statistics [NCES, 1991]; National Science Foundation's Division of Research, Evaluation, and Communication [Suter, 1999]) also grappled with the issue of identifying standards for quality research in education. The concern about methodology was also increasingly reflected in solicitation for research proposals. For example, Kent McGuire, the assistant secretary of the Office of Educational Research and Improvement, alerted prospective grant writers to the importance of considerations of research quality and noted the continued debate about relevance and rigor

Empirical Methods for Evaluating Educational Interventions

of educational research (McGuire, 1999). The continued importance of the topic is shown in the recent publication of a number of books: *Evidence-Based Educational Methods* (Moran & Malott, 2004), *Evidence Matters: Randomized Trials in Education Research* (Mosteller & Boruch, 2002), and *Scientific Research in Education* (Shavelson & Towne, 2002).

The National Academy of Science's Committee on Scientific Principles for Education Research (Shavelson & Towne, 2002) concluded that educational research is subject to the same scientific methods as other fields. Like Levin and O'Donnell (1999), they suggested that the methods should fit the questions posed in the research. Consistent with recent trends, the program announcement from the Institute of Education Sciences (2004) for an interdisciplinary research training program noted, "The dominance of qualitative methods in research reports in leading education research journals and the dominance of what works questions among practitioners is a clear sign of the mismatch between the focus of the practice community and the current research community" (p. 3). Different methodologies are needed to answer different kinds of questions. Levin and O'Donnell (1999) noted the importance of preliminary research (both laboratory-based and classroom-based research) in developing an understanding of the phenomena influencing classroom practice. However, further efforts beyond preliminary research are needed to determine if there are generalizable practices that will work in a variety of contexts. As the program announcement for the predoctoral training program in the Institute of Education Sciences notes, the question of what works is best addressed by experimental research.

Bullock (2004) notes that in some of the debates about what it means to have evidence-based decision making, random assignment and experimental control are "held as the gold standard" (p. 1). This view of experimentation as the "gold standard" of methodology is not well received in some quarters. Bullock indicates that there is widespread concern about a single methodology being reified as the only kind of methodology that can yield scientific evidence. However, Bullock also comments that although fields such as epidemiology or astronomy have yielded findings that are believed to be incontrovertible, the effects of interventions can best be understood using an experiment.

THE NATURE OF EXPERIMENTS

An experiment typically involves a comparison of an experimental treatment and a control group or other comparison group. The goal of experimentation is to determine if differences between groups can be attributed to the treatment provided to one group and the absence of that treatment in the other group. The researcher attempts to attribute causality for observed effects to the presence/absence of a treatment. Every effort is made to rule out alternative explanations for results. Random selection of participants for inclusion in an experiment can be an important aspect of experimentation as it limits the possibility of selection bias. It is not, however, a necessary or even important component of an experiment (Levin, 2004). Random assignment of comparable units to treatment or control conditions is a necessary part of experimentation in order to preclude alternative interpretations. Diffusion of treatment between experimental and control groups is a concern.

Efforts to rule out alternative interpretations of results reflect concern about the internal validity of an experiment. Shadish, Cook, and Campbell (2002) describe internal validity as follows: "The validity of inferences about whether the observed covariation between A (the presumed treatment) and B (the presumed outcome) reflects a causal relationship from A to B as those variables are manipulated or measured" (p. 38). Threats to internal validity weaken causal inferences about relationships among variables as they allow for alternative explanations of results. They describe a number of threats to internal validity. For example, problems with selection of participants can constitute biases that pose a threat to internal validity. Thus, one might observe that students who were taught using cooperative learning methods perform better than students who are taught using more teacher-centered methods, resulting in individualized learning. The comparison of cooperative learning classrooms and individualized classrooms may be confounded by a selection problem. The observed differences in performance on some academic outcome measure may be due to differences between the kinds of students who were in classes in which cooperative learning was used as an instructional strategy and those that used individualized learning. Many of these internal validity problems can be eliminated through the random assignment process. Until such threats to the internal validity of an experiment are ruled out, conclusions cannot be drawn about the causes of particular outcomes.

Levin (1997: cited in Levin & O'Donnell, 1999) and Derry, Levin, Osana, Jones, and Peterson (2000) identified four components of research that can produce credible evidence. These four components together are referred to as CAREful intervention research: Comparison, Again and again, Relationship, and Eliminate. According to Levin and O'Donnell (1999), evidence of an intervention is credible if the intervention is compared with an appropriate comparison group, the outcomes produced by the intervention can be replicated, a direct relationship exists between the intervention and the outcome (i.e., the intervention actually produces the effect), and alternative explanations can be ruled out. This latter concern is a concern about internal validity as previously described. Comparisons with appropriate control groups are important in that they allow us to see what the unique contribution of a particular intervention is to outcomes of interest. Replication of results also strengthens the credibility of evidence. Because of the complex nature of educational research and low levels of available funding for such research, few replications of particular findings are ever conducted. The research conducted in the 1980s on cooperative learning comes close to having a substantial body of work in which consistent findings for the effect of a particular instructional strategy have been found. If a direct relationship between a putative cause and an effect cannot be demonstrated, it is difficult to implement interventions with any confidence about effects. Finally, it is critically important to eliminate alternative interpretations of the results of an experiment. Threats to internal validity such as selection biases in recruitment of students, teachers, and schools as participants to research on educational interventions are important to control.

An important strategy for protecting the internal validity of an experiment is the use of random assignment of participants to conditions (experimental or control). Random assignment is intended to ensure that the two (or more) groups being compared are equivalent with respect to key variables except for the treatment. Cook and Payne (2002) note the well-publicized objections to the use of random assignment in education (see also Chapter 1). Among the objections to the use of randomized experiments they list are objections to such experiments because they represent a simplified theory of causation, an oversimplified epistemology unsuited to the complexity of American schools, and entail tradeoffs that are not worth making. Cook and Payne argue against each of these objections and point out the limitations of the arguments made in support of a position that devalues the role of random assignment. They conclude that random assignment

> (1) Provides a logically more valid causal counterfactual[1] than any of its plausible alternatives; (2) it almost certainly provides a more efficient counterfactual in that the few studies conducted to date show that where randomized experiments and their experiments converge on the same answer, randomized experiments do so more quickly, and (3) it provides a counterfactual that is more credible in nearly all academic circles and increasingly more so in educational policy ones (Cook & Payne, 2002. p. 17)

Because of the need to attend to issues of internal validity in an experiment, many researchers have assumed that experiments are necessarily laboratory-based, are artificial, and have little implication for natural contexts. All of these considerations reflect concerns related to external validity. Specifically, many people believe that research findings that are generated in contexts that are not natural, or in which efforts are made to control variables, will not be applicable to other contexts. In contrast, many assume that research in classrooms can never be experimental as such research fails to address issues of context, focuses on single variables, and is inauthentic. The recent popularity of design research (Kelly, 2003, 2004) reflects this

[1] A counterfactual is information that contradicts the fact under consideration, a falsification of information at hand.

set of assumptions about the kind of research that can be legitimately done in classrooms.

Levin (1994) describes the creation of a false dichotomy that is used to distinguish between laboratory-based research and school-based research with the former being considered as well controlled and the latter as weakly controlled. As Levin and O'Donnell (1999) point out, the methodological rigor associated with particular venues for research is not an inevitable consequence of the venue itself. Methodologically weak research can be conducted in laboratories and rigorous research can be conducted in complex contexts. In the pages that follow, I will provide an overview of design research and how it contrasts with experimental classroom research.

DESIGN RESEARCH

The pervasiveness of the dichotomy observed by Levin (1994) can be seen in recent writings on design research (e.g., Collins, 1999; Collins, Joseph, & Bielaczyc, 2004; Kelly, 2003; Kelly, 2004). The term *design experiment* was first introduced by Ann Brown (1992) and Allan Collins (1992). Brown (1992) described the transitions she made from conducting research in laboratory contexts to conducting research in schools. Trained as an experimental psychologist, this transition was not easy. The realities of classroom and school life make control of extraneous variables difficult (although not impossible). In introducing the concept of design experiments, Brown (1992) was very alert to the methodological challenges that this research provoked.

Collins (1992) provided the following example of a hypothetical design experiment:

> Our first step would be to observe a number of teachers, and to choose two who are interested in trying out technology to teach students about the seasons, and who are comparably effective, but use different styles of teaching; for example, one might work with activity centers in the classroom and the other with the entire class at one time. Ideally, the teachers should have comparable populations of students . . . Assuming both teachers teach a number of classes, we would help the teacher design her own unit on the seasons using these various technologies, one that is carefully crafted to fit with her normal teaching style (p. 19).

This example seems to suggest an experiment as typically understood. A number of problems related to internal validity surface almost immediately. The small sample of teachers is a problem because they may vary enormously in skill, experience, motivation, and creativity. Researchers would need to know how students are assigned to classes and use this and other information to determine if the students were comparable. If the researcher were conducting design research, many variables would continue to change in the course of the research. In the example above, the teacher's design of his or her own unit on seasons might change during implementation as a result of interactions with other teachers, professional development activities, or other events. In the context of design research, the continued adjustment is permissible. However, it would be very difficult to interpret differences in the outcomes from these contexts. Because changes on many variables occur throughout the course of the research, and many variables are not controlled, attributions of effects to particular variables or constellations of variables cannot be done. The term *experiment* has more recently given way to *design research* or *design-based research*, a change that removed some of the confusion associated with the methodology.

Special issues of a number of journals have been devoted to design research: *Educational Research* (2003, Vol. 32), *The Journal of the Learning Sciences* (2004, Vol. 13), and *Educational Psychologist* (2004, Vol 39[4]). Examples of projects that illustrate the kinds of characteristics delineated by Collins et al. (2004) can be found in these special issues.

Collins et al. (2004) compared experimental laboratory studies of learning and design research in terms of seven contrasting aspects of their methodology. In their analysis, experimental studies were laboratory-based, involved a single dependent measure, sought to control variables, used fixed procedures, and involved social isolation of participants and the testing of hypotheses, and the researcher made all the decisions. In contrast, design experiments involved messy situations that were difficult to characterize. Multiple dependent measures were involved and researchers attempted to characterize the situation while acting in the role of coparticipants. The participants in design research are usually engaged in social interaction and the goal of the researcher is to develop a profile of the design in operation. The process of design research is iterative and researchers continue to improve elements of the design as they proceed with their research. The primary goal of design research is to "investigate how different learning environment designs affect dependent variables in teaching and learning" (Collins et al., 2004).

A number of key problems exist with the contrast invoked by Collins et al. (2004). Although there are fewer experiments conducted in classroom contexts than are conducted in laboratory settings, the contrast drawn by Collins et al. between experimental research and design research is exaggerated. There is an extensive literature, for example, of experimental research in cooperative learning that was conducted in schools (Johnson, Maruyama, Johnson, Nelson, & Skon, 1981). Furthermore, the very nature of the treatments involved in the studies reported in the Johnson et al. meta-analysis involved students working in groups; thus, the characterization of experimental research as involving students working in social isolation is not always accurate.

The explicit recognition of the complexity of learning contexts and the need for multiple dependent measures in classroom research by proponents of design research are appealing. There are many reasons why some members of the research community are uncomfortable with the idea of conducting experiments in classrooms. First, the word "experiment" is often linked to negative affect, invoking notions of "manipulation" and potential misuse of participants. Boruch (see Chapter 8) chose to use the word "trials" in his discussion of randomized field experiments because of the negative connotations associated with the word "experiment." Concerns about the ethical treatment of children who might be denied access to effective interventions are important considerations also (see, for example, Chapter 1).

The characterization of laboratory-based research as involving single dependent measures is an interesting illustration of the belief that complex conditions cannot be understood with the context of experimental research. Collins et al. (2004) note that experimental research tends to rely on single variables such as some measure of learning outcomes. The characterization of the kinds of research done in laboratory experiments has little relationship to the nature of classroom experiments. For example, much of the research on cooperative learning has concerned itself with both cognitive outcomes (student performance on assessments of learning) and social outcomes (students' acceptance of other students). Students are not isolated in their participation in the experiment and studies on cooperative learning are typically conducted using materials that are appropriate to the normal curriculum of the schools. Thus, these experiments are conducted in authentic contexts and with authentic tasks.

Design research is less well controlled than typical experimental research. The efforts at objectivity that typically characterize experimental research are no longer possible in design research. Researchers are coparticipants in the design of curricula, instructional strategies and materials, and other aspects of the work along with teachers and others who are involved in the classrooms. The inevitable trade-off between internal and external validity is not an all-or-none phenomenon. Eisner (1999) described a true experiment as follows:

> A true experiment requires both random selection[2] and random assignment, it requires conditions that preclude contamination among experimental and control group, and if the consequences of the treatment are to be explainable from the theory from which it was derived, the treatment needs to be prescriptive—that is, its features cannot depend on the idiosyncratic judgments of individual teachers. These conditions confer upon the true experiment a high degree of internal validity, but these are precisely the conditions that are so difficult to replicate in other "natural" settings (p. 20).

Recent critiques of design research (Dede, 2004; Kelly, 2004) are particularly critical of the lack of standards for what constitutes successful design research. Both Dede (2004) and Kelly (2004) note the lack of agreement among design researchers about purposes, procedures, and standards for

[2] Note, random selection is not a requirement for experimentation (see Levin, in press).

success and failure of a research project. Design research might involve the development of a particular software program, the implementation of instructional strategies, or the introduction of other kinds of artifacts into the learning environment. The purposes of such projects can vary enormously. When is a "design" ready to be implemented? When should efforts at implementation be terminated? The possibility for endless revision of designs has important implications for classrooms, curricula, and students' time. Engaged academic time is a precious resource in schools, particularly for children in poorer districts who may not have the resources in their homes or communities to supplement or extend the work that occurs during school hours. The use of classroom time for the purposes of research (either experimental or alternative types of research) must be used with great care and criteria for identifying promising instructional interventions or interventions that are unworkable should be clearly in place. This caution is true for both experimental and design research, although the latter tends to require more time and the exit point is uncertain. Although some reject the notion of conducting experiments in classrooms as a valid way to investigate what kinds of interventions work, alternative research methodologies have not provided better solutions to date. This is not to say, however, that the *only* useful kind of research methodology is an experiment. Levin and O'Donnell (1999) argue for matching the research methodology to the research question at hand.

Experimental researchers must be careful about selectivity in data collection. This difficulty is exacerbated in design research. Dede (2004) described it as underconceptualized and overmethodologized. He criticized design research as underconceptualized because in his view, the theoretical basis for much of the design work was conceptually weak. His reason for describing many design research projects as overmethodologized is that only 5% of the huge amounts of data collected were needed to induce the findings. Brown (1992) raised concerns about what she termed the *Bartlett* effect or a tendency to be selectively attentive to data that conform to the researchers' expectations. According to Brown, this is "particularly acute when portions of edited transcripts or clinical interviews are selected to illustrate a theoretical point, or when descriptions of planning sessions, peer tutoring, or teacher coaching are culled from a vast array of potential examples" (p. 162). The problem is how to avoid misrepresenting the data. Collins et al. (2004) also recognized the problems presented by an inordinate amount of data. Brown (1992) noted that she did not have room to store all her data, let alone score it.

Issues related to external validity of research are very important. Researchers typically wish their work to be relevant and useful outside of the specific context in which a particular research study was conducted. Design research might be considered to focus more on external than internal validity in that authentic contexts, complex instruction, and social interaction are key features of design research. Design research, however, has not solved the problems of studying complex phenomena in complex settings. There are problems with generalization because there are typically a small number of participants involved in the kind of in-depth analyses that are characteristic of design research. It is also difficult (if not impossible) to rule out alternative explanations for outcomes. The very nature of design research in which adjustments can continually be made in the implementation of an instructional intervention make it very difficult to know what combination of features of the intervention actually contribute to its success. It is difficult to make generalizations across contexts because of the complexities involved in implementation and the associated confounds in identifying contributors to success. The context itself is not "natural" as it represents the joint efforts of researchers, teachers, students, and others who in the normal life of a school do not typically work so closely. To the extent that the researchers become integrally involved in the design, implementation, and revision of the intervention, their subsequent withdrawal from this involvement changes the context again. Ironically, design research may be less authentic in some key characteristics than laboratory research. Having released a grip on issues of internal validity, design research has not sufficiently addressed issues of external validity.

RESEARCH QUESTIONS AND EXPERIMENTS

As Bullock (2004) commented, questions about what works are best addressed by experiments. The fact that experiments can be difficult to conduct does not detract from their methodological utility in answering particular kinds of questions. An example of a simple question that might be answered by conducting an experiment is as follows: Is learning strategy A more effective than learning strategy B? This question can be best answered by comparing the performance of two groups of participants, one group that uses strategy A and the other uses strategy B. Random assignments to strategy training group would be done to evaluate the answer to this question. Variables that might influence the outcomes, such as students' motivation or ability, will be randomly distributed to strategy training groups as a result of such random assignment. Outcome measures might include immediate and delayed recall of targeted materials. This kind of question is not difficult to address. The question is simple, the comparison that is needed is straightforward, and the outcomes measured are clearly linked to the research question.

Other questions are more complicated. For example, is reading program A more effective than reading program B? This question is more complicated than the previous one because a new group of participants are involved, that is, teachers. Answering this question requires us to be concerned about the fidelity of the implementation of a reading program by particular teachers as well as attention to issues of internal validity (see Chapter 6). Outcome measures that might be used in an experiment designed to answer this question might include measures of reading fluency or reading comprehension. An experiment to determine the relative effectiveness of these two reading programs would require random assignment of classes to one or the other reading program (see Chapter 1; Levin & O'Donnell, 1999). This would certainly not be trivial to arrange. Researchers would also need to ensure that the outcome measures they selected to address this question had appropriate psychometric properties of reliability and validity (see Chapter 6). The strong tradition of reading research would be helpful to such researchers in guiding their selection of appropriate measures.

Other questions that ask about the effects of complex interventions are much more difficult. For example, "Do students in charter schools have higher achievement than students in regular public schools?" With this kind of question, it becomes much more difficult to rule out threats to internal validity. Selection of students for charter schools may reflect a selection bias. The task of the researcher in conducting an experiment to evaluate the relative effectiveness of public schools and charter schools is much more difficult than answering a question about what learning strategy works best.

The fact that some questions are more difficult to answer than others does not necessarily mean that an experiment is inappropriate or uninformative. It does mean that great care must be taken in conducting such an experiment and more complex questions will be more expensive to answer. The relative difficulty of answering some questions and ease of answering others has generated arguments about what constitutes a worthwhile question and debates over what kinds of research are valued and credible.

There are many examples of research topics that have a substantial knowledge base, the cumulative nature of which has developed from the contributions of different kinds of research (e.g., descriptive studies, experiments, protocol-analysis studies, and so forth). Frequently, the most credible knowledge has been accumulated through a series of experiments. Among the instructional strategies for which there is solid evidence of effectiveness are reciprocal teaching (Rosenshine & Meister, 1994), tutoring (Cohen, Kulik, & Kulik, 1982), teaching children to generate questions to improve reading comprehension (Rosenshine, 1996), and cooperative learning (Johnson & Johnson, 1989).

RESEARCH ON COOPERATIVE LEARNING

Cooperative learning as an instructional/learning strategy has been the subject of a great deal of research, including experimentation. The value (and perils) of experiments in classroom research will be illustrated here by reference to some examples of research on cooperative learning. Meta-analyses by Johnson and colleagues (Johnson & Johnson, 1989; Johnson, Maruyama, Johnson, Nelson, & Skon, 1981) consistently show that cooperative learning is effective in improving student achievement in comparison with instructional strategies that either are individualistic or depend on competition.

Research on cooperative learning has in large part followed Levin's (Levin, 1997; Levin & O'Donnell, 1999) CAREful intervention research: Comparison, Again and again, Relationship, and Eliminate. Large numbers of studies have compared the effects of cooperative learning contexts with competitive or individualistic learning environments (Johnson & Johnson, 1989). The findings from these studies are quite consistent and show that cooperative learning environments generally producing better effects on achievement. Slavin (1996) described the research on cooperative learning as "one of the greatest success stories in the history of educational research" (p. 43). *Comparisons* with appropriate control groups were made and they were made *Again and again* as recommended by Levin and O'Donnell (1999). The research on cooperative learning is not without its flaws. However, the consistency of the findings related to the success of cooperative learning over a period of 25 years dating from the 1970s is hard to ignore.

The work on cooperative learning also illustrates another key component of Levin's (1997; Levin & O'Donnell, 1999) CAREful intervention research by demonstrating that a direct relationship exists between the intervention and the outcome (i.e., the intervention actually produces the effect). Many alternative theories of *how* cooperative learning achieves its effects on student learning have been proposed (O'Donnell & O'Kelly, 1994; Slavin, 1996). Cooperative learning may be a successful instructional/learning strategy for a variety of reasons. Students may be more motivated when working together (Slavin, 1992); they may engage in deeper processing of content through their explanations (Webb, 1992); interaction among mutually influential peers may activate equilibration processes (De Lisi & Golbeck, 1999); or peers may be able to scaffold one another's learning by operating in one another's zone of proximal development (Hogan & Tudge, 1999).

Research on cooperative learning during the 1970s and 1980s largely focused on examining the effects of various kinds of cooperative learning techniques on variables such as students' achievement, attitudes to school and their peers, acceptance of others, and other prosocial outcomes. These studies compared the effects of cooperative learning with those of competitive learning or individualistic learning environments. These research studies did not include a lot of process data. The lack of such data has resulted in some sharp criticisms of the "black box" approach to research in classrooms. The kinds of criticisms articulated by Collins et al. (2004) tend to equate experiments with the necessary absence of these kinds of data.

However, there is nothing inherent in experimental classroom research that makes it impossible to collect data that are more complex.

Clear effects of cooperative learning were demonstrated in many contexts, across different age groups, with different kinds of learners, and in many different subject matter domains (Johnson & Johnson, 1989). Research on cooperative learning in the 1990s and subsequent years has focused on understanding why and how the positive effects of cooperative learning occur. More recent work on cooperative learning uses comparison groups that allow inferences to be made about the mechanisms underlying effective cooperative learning. Slavin (1996) reports, for example, that the median effect size for methods of cooperative learning that included group goals and individual accountability across 52 studies was 0.32. In comparison, in 25 studies that did not include group goals and individual accountability, the median effect size for cooperative learning methods was only 0.07.

CLASSROOM-BASED EXPERIMENTS

Can good experiments be conducted in classrooms? The answer is "yes" and "no." Classroom-based experimental research is difficult and in many published articles, there is insufficient detail in the description of the methods and procedures that could inform and educate other researchers. There are many problems associated with implementation of an adequate research design in schools. Maintaining the internal validity of an experiment by ensuring random assignment of participants to experimental conditions is difficult, but not impossible. Changes in the operation and regulation of institutional review boards that supervise the ethical conduct of research have made classroom-based research increasingly challenging. The increased emphasis on high-stakes testing in many grade levels may also increase the reluctance of school districts to allocate classroom time to research activities, particularly those that might extend over an extended period of time. Many factors can contribute to the emergence of a selection bias when recruiting schools, classrooms, teachers, and parents for cooperation in conducting classroom-based research, in general, and experiments in particular.

Conducting classroom research can be very expensive and it may be very difficult to marshal the personnel and other resources needed to conduct the research in a large number of classrooms. Consequently, researchers may use small samples of classrooms, resulting in low power in their research. The issue of small samples also affects the unit of analysis in data analysis strategies. Are intact groups or classes to be used as the unit of analysis? When the sample size of available classrooms is very small, researchers often use the individual student as the unit of analysis, a decision that may not be appropriate (see Chapter 1).

Even when access is possible, there are ongoing problems of implementation. It is with good reason that Collins et al. (2004) described classrooms as "messy." Classrooms are characterized by frequent interruptions. Weather conditions, illnesses that affect teachers or children, and other events can change the classroom context a great deal. Instructor effects and researcher effects on student performance and attitudes can also occur. The kind of problems described here are considerations in conducting any kind of experiments in classrooms. However, two of the main problems in conducting good experiments in classrooms are problems of concept and problems of implementation.

PROBLEMS OF CONCEPT AND PROBLEMS OF IMPLEMENTATION

Experiments in classrooms are often constrained by difficulties in recruiting sufficient numbers of classrooms and teachers. Some experiments are weakened by insufficient attention to the research questions that frame the work. In the two examples that follow, I illustrate both of these kinds of problems.

Johnson, Johnson, Roy, and Zaidman (1985) conducted a classroom-based experiment in which they compared individualistic and cooperative learning situations. The intent of the study was to examine some of the social interaction and cognitive processes that may influence academic achievement in cooperative groups. In particular, the researchers sought to examine the quality and quantity of verbal interaction among group members. The cooperative group consisted of 24 students (13 girls, 11 boys) and the individualistic learning condition consisted of 24 students (14 girls, 10 boys). Each condition contained six high-, 11 medium-, and 7 low-achieving children. Children's achievement levels were defined on the basis of their reading scores on the fourth-grade Scholastic Aptitude Test. High achievers were defined as those with scores between 48 and 78 (a 30-point spread). Medium achievers were defined as those with scores between 20 and 40 (a 20-point spread). Low achievers scored between 10 and 19, a 9-point spread. No rationale for the differing bandwidths used to categorize children was provided. It was surprising that each of the two classes had the same number of high-, medium-, and low-achieving students. It would have been useful to know how students were assigned to classes in the particular school in which the study was conducted.

There were many carefully considered elements of the experiment. For example, to avoid teacher effects on outcome measures, the two teachers involved switched classrooms in the middle of the experiment. Both teachers were extensively trained in the use of cooperative learning. Using a larger sample of classrooms and teachers would have been a more effective way to control for teacher effects. Little information is provided about the "normal" instruction provided by the teachers. Given that they were both experienced practitioners of cooperative learning, it would have been useful to know if the use of cooperative learning in one of the classrooms represented a continuation of previous practices for the children in that classroom and whether the use of individualistic learning in the other classroom represented a continuation of past practice or a deviation from typical classroom instruction.

Six research assistants observed the students' verbal interactions in both conditions. This was done on a daily basis. The researchers followed a clear schedule of observation during which they observed a group for 3 minutes using one observation measure and 2 minutes with a second measure. Inter-rater reliability of the observers was high. The protocols for observation were based on prior research.

The authors analyzed differences between the two conditions in terms of the amount and kind of oral interaction. In one condition, the cooperative condition, students were assigned to four-person groups and directed to work with one another to help one another learn. In the other condition, the individualistic learning condition, students were directed to work on their own, avoiding interaction with one another. It is hardly surprising that in evaluating the differences in the kind and quality of verbal interaction among students in the two classes, the researchers found that students in the cooperative group talked more. This hardly warranted analysis. It may have been useful to verify the lack of interaction in the individualistic learning condition as a manipulation check of the conditions in the experiment but the analysis itself is not meaningful. One might reasonably expect that if one encouraged some students to talk with one another and praised and rewarded them for doing so that they would in fact talk with one another. On the other hand, it is hardly surprising that students who were asked to avoid talking with one another and were praised for individual work would not talk with one another.

The researchers in this study attempted to answer too many questions with a very small sample of students. The primary focus of the study was to examine the kind of interactions among students in cooperative groups that might be associated with achievement. Rather than focusing only on this question, the authors complicated their study by the addition of a control group of students who were in an individualistic learning situation. In this situation, the effort to actually conduct an experiment detracted from the main purpose of the research. This kind of experiment is flawed conceptually as the research strategy does not map onto the research questions being addressed very well.

Problems of implementation occur more often. The current research on cooperative learning has gone beyond the comparison of cooperative learning and individualized learning. Much of the current research examines the kinds of interactions that promote achievement and other outcomes or investigates the effects of various kinds of structures or supports for promoting effective interaction. Gillies and Ashman (1998) conducted one such study. This particular study is a good example of the complexity of conducting experimental research in classrooms. It differs in fundamental ways from the characterization of experimental research provided by Collins et al. (2004) described as typical of experimentation.

Collins et al. (2004) partially justify the development of design research by drawing a comparison between it and laboratory studies of learning. As was noted earlier, however, Levin (1994) pointed to the false dichotomy drawn between laboratory research and school-based research. The study conducted by Gillies and Ashman (1998) is illustrative of how such a dichotomy can be misleading. The implication of some of the writings on design research is that experiments cannot be conducted in classrooms. Gillies and Ashman (1998), however, succeeded in implementing a rigorous experiment in 25 classrooms.

The research was conducted over a 9-month period and involved groups of children working on a 6-week social studies activity for each of three school terms. The purposes of the research were to examine whether the behaviors and interactions of children were influenced by whether they worked in structured or unstructured groups, whether these behaviors and interactions changed over time, and what effects the cooperative group experiences had on achievement. The research questions were grounded in an appropriate analysis of the literature. "Structured" cooperation was defined as including specific training on the social skills needed for cooperation and procedures necessary to facilitate participation by members such as breaking the task down into smaller tasks. The researchers were very careful about the selection of participants and the measures used in the study.

Two hundred twelve grade 1 students and 184 grade 3 students participated. Data were available for 152 of the grade 1 students and 152 of grade 3 students. The attrition rates for the two groups of students were 28% and 18% for grades 1 and 3, respectively. The attrition rates did not differ significantly as a function of grade level. The attrition rates were high because when individual children were not available, data for their entire group were lost. The children were drawn from 25 classes in 11 schools in Brisbane. The number of schools and classrooms involved in this study is larger than is typical of classroom studies. The duration of the students' participation is also extensive and somewhat atypical for this kind of research. The experiment was conducted in a natural context with authentic tasks that were part of the general school curriculum. The duration of the research ameliorated any potential difficulties with novelty effects related to the experience or researcher effects.

Stratified random assignment was used to create groups that were gender balanced. Students were assigned to structured or unstructured four-person groups based on their scores on the Otis–Lennon School Ability Test (Otis & Lennon, 1993). Each group comprised one student from the upper quartile on this test (high ability), two from quartiles 2 and 3 (medium ability), and one from the lowest quartile (low ability). Classes were then randomly assigned to either the structured or unstructured cooperative conditions. The use of stratified random assignment of students to groups and the use of random assignment of classes to conditions is noteworthy. However, the authors do not describe any difficulties in assignment. For example, in using the various quartiles of performance on the Otis–Lennon test, the authors do not describe whether they used the norms associated with the test itself or the local norms generated in this sample. It is hard to imagine that any single classroom of students broke down neatly into four person groups that were gender balanced and had the 1-2-1 combination of high-, medium-, and low-achieving students. The authors also do not describe how students are assigned to classes in the 11 schools that participated in this research, nor do they provide information about how many teachers *opted* not to participate. Teachers who agreed to participate needed to allow the experiment to continue all year. Students in their classes worked in cooperative groups for three 1-hour periods each week. Furthermore, teachers had to agree to the random assignment of their classes to the structured or unstructured condition. Although strategies such as random assignment to experimental conditions are helpful, selection biases cannot entirely be ruled out without further information being available.

Unlike the characterization of laboratory research on learning that uses only a single dependent measure (Collins et al., 2004), a variety of measures were used in the Gillies and Ashman (1998) study. Interactions among group members were observed and the behavior and verbal interactions of students were observed and coded. The coding schemes used to code the behavior, verbal interactions, and cognitive language strategies were strongly grounded in previous work by other researchers. Thus, the coding systems had a theoretical foundation in addition to an empirical base that justified their use. Interrater reliability in judging the occurrence of particular behaviors was very high.

Collins et al. (2004) criticize studies of learning that use "narrow measures" of learning outcomes. Gillies and Ashman (1998) use a measure of learning based on Bloom's taxonomy (Bloom, 1976). Individual teachers constructed six-item assessments of students' learning. These assessments consisted of questions that were designed to sample differing levels in Bloom's taxonomy. Students could earn a maximum score of six that indicated that they were able to answer a question of the highest levels of the taxonomy. It is unusual for each teacher in an experimental study to develop their own assessments, even when the design was constrained by the provision of generic question stems informed by Bloom's taxonomy. Five experienced teachers who were unaware of the research questions related to the project examined the assessments and deemed them appropriate to the content and accurately represented the content of Bloom's taxonomy. A second measure of learning outcome used was a word recognition test. The rationale for using this outcome measure was based on previous findings that documented increases in reading skill as a result of cooperation.

The research reported by Gillies and Ashman (1998) is unlike the sterile characterization of experiments on learning that one may encounter when reading about alternatives to experimental research. Such experiments are often criticized for their lack of external validity. The work was conducted in a large number of classrooms with two different age groups. A great deal of care was taken by the researchers in the selection of instruments, the training of teachers, and the commitment to a long-term project. The researchers hoped to link the students' cooperative behaviors to their subsequent achievement. Their ability to do this for the grade 1 students was utterly compromised by the manner in which teachers administered the learning outcomes questionnaire. In grade 1 classes, teachers allowed students to discuss the questions in small groups and develop a group response, thereby compromising the test of instructional effects on individual students. In addition, instructional effects of groups of children in different grades could not be assessed because of the different ways in which tests were conducted. Teachers compromised the testing of the children. It was unfortunate that after all the time and effort invested in the study, a key outcome variable was not available to the researchers. The researchers chose to use the individual student as the unit of analysis and the absence of individual level data for the grade 1 students made it impossible to conduct an analysis linking the quality of the cooperative experience in the structured and unstructured cooperative conditions to the learning outcomes. Likewise, the absence of a group response in the grade 3 classes made it difficult to use the group as the unit of analysis in a comparison with grade 1 classes.

The researchers provide no explanation of why the teachers in the grade 1 classrooms gave the learning outcome questionnaire as a group activity. Collins et al. (2004) note that in laboratory experiments the researchers are in control, making all the decisions about the design and implementation of the research, and determining the kinds of analyses to be conducted. Regrettably, in the Gillies and Ashman (1998) study, the researchers lost control over a vital part of their research design and in so doing, compromised their own work and efforts.

Advocates of design research (e.g., Collins, 2004) describe the importance of efforts to involve different participants in the design of research to capitalize on the expertise that such participants may bring to developing a research design. There is something for researchers who conduct classroom experiments to be learned from the ways in which design researchers involve and collaborate with the constituents of their research. There are many complexities involved in getting adequate numbers of schools and classrooms to participate in an experiment. Teachers vary in terms of experience, quality, and commitment. It is critical for a classroom researcher to get the full cooperation of the teachers when they are the individuals responsible for implementing the actual experimental conditions. The teachers need to fully understand why it is important to implement the research as designed even though there will be disruptions to implementation in the normal course of a school year.

If the teachers in the Gillies and Ashman study (1998) had understood the intended use of the learning outcomes questionnaire, it is unlikely they would have administered it as they did. If the researchers had involved the teachers in more substantive discussions of the research design (and it is not at all certain that they did not), perhaps the teachers and researchers would have opted for a different unit of analysis and had groups complete the questionnaire in each of the classes. In some ways, teachers had a lot of autonomy within the context of this particular study, designing a learning outcomes questionnaire to fit their own particular curriculum. Setting some boundaries on which things can be changed in the context of conducting an experiment and which things cannot be changed is an important feature of conducting classroom research. There are clear problems for the internal validity of a study when various agents in the research process make autonomous independent decisions and key issues of implementation. Graduate programs that train education researchers need to include the consideration of such practical issues of implementation and how to work with school personnel among the kinds of skills in which they train students.

Design research, which permits the continued change of various aspects of the research, has little chance of internal validity. Dede (2004) criticizes the lack of standards by which such research can be judged and the absence of criteria by which a failed design can be identified rather than continuously altered. As noted earlier, this issue is a key issue for research in schools, particularly schools in poorer socioeconomic groups.

WHAT WE KNOW ABOUT COOPERATIVE LEARNING

The research on cooperative learning is an example of what we can learn from classroom experiments. Current research on cooperative and collaborative learning draws upon an extensive literature accumulated over time to frame expectations, hypotheses, and choose research questions wisely. The principles that emerge from this literature are consistently supported by research evidence that is credible as defined by Levin (1997). Examples of such principles are "giving explanations promotes learning" or "gender balanced groups are more effective than gender imbalanced groups." Instructional interventions are developed through theorizing, description, experimentation, and replication. Perhaps the most important component of Levin's (1997) CAREful research is the component "Again and again." Consistency of findings lends important credibility to research.

Concerns about external validity remain important. An instructional intervention that is not usable in many contexts is not particularly useful. Some would argue that it is not possible to have an instructional intervention that is not context-specific. Such a viewpoint seems to argue for a view of human cognition that is utterly contextualized. However, research on such topics as working memory show that there are known limits to certain kinds of cognitive functioning that are pertinent across contexts (Miyake & Shah, 1999). The essential question asked about instructional interventions in terms of external validity is "Can my fish swim in your pond?" In other words, will the intervention developed and used in context A produce similar effects in context B? Before this question can be answered, we also need to ask the question "Is it a fish?" Can we describe the intervention in explicit terms so that it can be implemented? Do we know which elements of the intervention are particularly important and require faithful implementation and which elements can vary more?

References

Bloom, B. (1976). *Human characteristics and school learning*. New York: McGraw-Hill.

Brown, A. L. (1992). Design experiments: theoretical and methodological challenges in creating complex interventions in classroom settings. *Journal of the Learning Sciences*, 2, 141–178.

Bullock, M. (2004). What is evidence and what is the problem? Available at: *http://www.apa.org/science/psa/mar4edcolumn.html* Accessed March 15, 2004.

Collins, A. (1992). Towards a design science of education. In E. Scanlon & T. O'Shea (Eds.), *New directions in educational technology* (pp. 15–22). New York: Springer-Verlag.

Collins, A. (1999). The changing infrastructure of education research. In E. C. Lagemann & L. S. Shulman (Eds.), *Issues in education research: problems and possibilities* (pp. 289–298). San Francisco: Jossey-Bass.

Collins, A., Joseph, D., & Bielaczyc, K. (2004). Design research: theoretical and methodological issues. *The Journal of the Learning Sciences*, 13(1), 15–42.

Cohen, P. A., Kulik, J. A., & Kulik, C. C. (1982). Educational outcomes from tutoring: a meta-analysis of findings. *American Educational Research Journal*, 19, 237–248.

Cook, T. D., & Payne, M. R. (2002). Objecting to the objections to using random assignment in educational research. In F. Mosteller & R. Boruch (Eds.), *Evidence matters: randomized trials in education research* (pp. 150–178). Washington, DC: Brookings Institute Press.

De Lisi, R., & Golbeck, S. L. (1999). Implications of Piagetian theory for peer learning. In A. M. O'Donnell & A. King (Eds.), *Cognitive perspectives on peer learning* (pp. 3–37). Mahwah, NJ: Erlbaum.

Dede, C. (2004). If design-based research is the answer, what is the question? A commentary on Collins, Joseph, & Bielaczyc; DiSessa & Cobb; & Fishman, Marx, Blumenthal, Krajcik, & Soloway in the JLS special issue on design-based research. *The Journal of the Learning Sciences*, 13(1), 105–114.

Derry, S. J., Levin, J. R., Jones, M. S., Osana, H. P., & Peterson, M. (2000). Fostering students' statistical and scientific thinking: lessons learned from an innovative college course. *American Educational Research Journal*, 37, 747–773.

Ducharme, M. K., Licklider, B., Matthes, W. A., & Vannata, R. A. (1995). *Conceptual and analysis criteria: a process for identifying quality educational research*. Des Moines, IA: Fine Foundation.

Eisner, E. (1999). Rejoinder: a response to Tom Knapp. *Educational Researcher*, 28(1), 19–20.

The Elementary and Secondary Education Act as Reauthorized by the *No Child Left Behind Act of* 2001; Public Law 107–110, Passed January 8, 2002.

Education Sciences Reform Act, Public Law 107–279, Passed November 5, 2002.

Gillies, R. M., & Ashman, A. F. (1998). Behavior and interactions of children in cooperative groups in lower and middle elementary grades. *Journal of Educational Psychology*, 90, 746–757.

Hogan, D. M., & Tudge, J. R. H. (1999). Implications of Vygotsky's theory for peer learning. In A. M. O'Donnell & A. King (Eds.), *Cognitive perspectives on peer learning* (pp. 39–65). Mahwah, NJ: Erlbaum.

Johnson, D. W., & Johnson, R. (1989). *Cooperation and competition: theory and research*. Edina, MN: Interaction Book Company.

Johnson, D. W., Maruyama, G., Johnson, R., Nelson, D., & Skon, L. (1981). Effects of cooperative, competitive, and individualistic goal structures on achievement: a meta-analysis. *Psychological Bulletin*, 89, 47–62.

Johnson, D. W., Johnson, R. T., Roy, P., & Zaidman, B. (1985). Oral interaction in cooperative learning groups: speaking, listening, and the nature of statements made by high-, medium-, and low-achieving students. *The Journal of Psychology*, 119, 303–321.

Kelly, A. E. (2003). Research as design: the role of design in educational research. *Educational Researcher*, 3, (theme issue): 3–4.

Kelly, A. E. (2004). Design research in education: yes, but is it methodological? *The Journal of the Learning Sciences*, 13(1), 115–128.

Levin, J. R. (1994). Crafting educational intervention research that's both credible and creditable. *Educational Psychology Review*, 6, 231–243.

Levin, J. R. (1997, March). Statistics in research and the real world. Colloquium presentation at: Department of Psychology, University of California, San Diego.

Levin, J. R. (2004). Random thoughts on the (in)credibility of educational-psychological intervention research. *Educational Psychologist*, 39, 173–184.

Levin, J. R., & O'Donnell, A. M. (1999). What to do about educational research's credibility gaps? *Issues in Education*, 5(2), 177–229.

McGuire, K. (1999). *Request for proposals*. Washington, DC: U.S. Department of Education.

Miyake, A., & Shah, P. (1999). *Models of working memory: mechanisms of active maintenance and executive control*. New York: Cambridge University Press.

Moran, D. J., & Malott, R. W. (2004). *Evidence-based educational methods*. St. Louis, MO: Elsevier.

Mosteller, F., & Boruch, R. (Eds.). (2002). *Evidence matters: randomized trials in education research*. Washington, DC: Brookings Institute Press.

National Council for Educational Statistics (1991). SEDCAR (*Standards for Educational Data Collection and Reporting*). Washington, DC: U.S. Department of Education.

O'Donnell, A. M., & O'Kelly, J. (1994). Learning from peers: beyond the rhetoric of positive results. *Educational Psychology Review*, 6, 321–349.

Otis, A., & Lennon, R. (1993). *Otis-Lennon school ability test* (6th ed.). San Antonio, TX: Harcourt Brace.

Rosenshine, B. (1996). Teaching students to generate questions: a review of the intervention studies. *Review of Educational Research*, 66, 181–221.

Rosenshine, B., & Meister, C. (1994). Reciprocal teaching: a review of the research. *Review of Educational Research*, 64, 479–530.

Shadish, W. R., Cook, T. D., & Campbell, D. T. (2002). *Experimental and quasi-experimental designs for generalized causal inference*. New York: Houghton Mifflin.

Shavelson, R. J., & Towne, L. (Eds.). (2002). *Scientific research in education*. Washington, DC: National Academy Press.

Slavin, R. E. (1992). When and why does cooperative learning increase achievement? Theoretical and empirical perspectives. In R. Hertz-Lazarowitz & N. Miller (Eds.), *Interaction in cooperative groups: the theoretical anatomy of group learning* (pp. 145–173). New York: Cambridge University Press.

Slavin, R. E. (1996). Research on cooperative learning and achievement: what we know, what we need to know. *Contemporary Educational Psychology*, 21(1), 43–69.

Suter, L. (1999, April 20). Research methods in mathematics and science research. Paper presented at: American Educational Research Association, Montreal, Canada.

Webb, N. M. (1992). Testing a theoretical model of student interaction and learning in small groups. In R. Hertz-Lazarowitz & N. Miller (Eds.), *Interaction in cooperative groups: the theoretical anatomy of group learning* (pp. 102–119). New York: Cambridge University Press.

Promoting Internal and External Validity: A Synergism of Laboratory-Like Experiments and Classroom-Based Self-Regulated Strategy Development Research

STEVEN GRAHAM
KAREN H. HARRIS
Vanderbilt University
JENNIFER ZITO
University of Maryland

In the fall of 2000, we began a series of studies to test the effectiveness of writing strategy instruction with primary-grade children who were experiencing difficulty learning to write. This research was part of a larger effort involving three universities (Vanderbilt, Maryland, and Columbia) funded as the Center to Accelerate Student Learning (CASL) by the Office of Special Education Programs in the U. S. Department of Education. CASL was funded to identify effective instructional practices in the areas of writing, reading, and mathematics for young children with special needs and students at risk for academic difficulties. Our work at the University of Maryland has focused primarily on writing and included the four investigations described here (Graham, Harris, & Mason, in press; Harris, Graham, & Mason, in press; Harris, Graham, & Adkins, 2004; Saddler, Moran, Graham, & Harris, 2004), studies examining the effectiveness of supplemental instruction in handwriting and spelling (Graham, Harris, & Fink, 2000; Graham, Harris, & Fink-Chorzempa, 2002), and surveys of classroom practices and teachers' beliefs about writing instruction (Graham, Harris, Fink, & MacArthur, 2001, 2002; Graham, Harris, MacArthur, & Fink-Chorzempa, 2003).

Our approach to testing the effectiveness of writing strategy instruction with young struggling writers was consistent with a stage model of educational intervention research purposed by Levin and O'Donnell (1999). This model involves four stages. In stage 1, researchers carry out observations, develop preliminary ideas and hypotheses, and conduct pilot work pertinent to the development of their intervention. During stage 2, the researchers test the effectiveness of their intervention via controlled laboratory experiments or through classroom-based demonstration and design experiments. According to Levin and O'Donnell, stage 2 experiments are crucial to developing an understanding of how a treatment can inform classroom practices (the fourth stage in their model), but must be viewed as "preliminary." Controlled laboratory experiments are preliminary in that their careful scrutiny of a treatment lacks a classroom-implementation component. Classroom-based demonstration and design experiments, in contrast, are preliminary in that their treatment prescriptions are not usually based on scientifically credible evidence. For instance, the experimental treatment is not compared with an appropriate alternative or nonintervention condition and random assignment to conditions does not occur.

As a result, Levin and O'Donnell indicated that the testing and validation of an educational treatment must go beyond stages 1 and 2 to studies involving randomized classroom trials (stage 3). This consists of examining the effectiveness of the intervention under realistic and carefully controlled conditions. Realistic refers to administering the treatment in the classroom as intended as well as delivering it long enough for the intervention to take effect. It also involves assessing both desired and unwanted side effects. Carefully controlled conditions refer to testing the treatment using experimental procedures that control threats to internal validity and are based on random assignment of multiple students or teachers to alternative treatment/intervention conditions.

In the studies described here, we systematically tested the effectiveness of a treatment designed to teach young struggling writers strategies for planning their compositions. Our assessment of this intervention was not only compatible with Levin and O'Donnell's (1999) stage model of educational research, but was also consistent with what Derry, Levin, Osana, Jones, and

Peterson (1998) referred to as "CAREful" intervention research. They argued that evidence linking an intervention to particular educational outcomes is convincing if (a) the evidence involves Comparing the experimental treatment with an appropriate alternative or nonintervention condition; (b) expected outcomes are produced by the treatment Again and again; (c) a direct Relationship or connection exists between the treatment and the specified results; and (d) any reasonable competing explanations for the obtained outcomes are Eliminated (usually through methodologic care and randomization). In other words, intervention research yields scientifically convincing evidence, if appropriate Comparisons demonstrate Again and again a Direct relationship between the treatment and specified outcomes when other competing explanations for the outcomes are Eliminated. Thus, we conducted multiple studies, where randomization to treatment/control and other methodologic safeguards were instituted to eliminate competing explanations, so that direct relationships between strategy instruction in planning and predicted outcomes in young students' writing, writing knowledge, and motivations were assessed. The remainder of this chapter describes this program of research, using Levin and O'Donnell's (1999) four-stage model as a framework.

STAGE 1: OBSERVATIONS, PRELIMINARY IDEAS, HYPOTHESES, AND PILOT WORK

An effective line of intervention research does not begin in a vacuum, but is preceded by a thorough review of theories and research, careful observations, the development of preliminary ideas and hypotheses, and pilot work to test the feasibility of the intervention or proposed assessments. Researchers may also be guided and informed by other investigations they or others have conducted, including experimental tests of the proposed treatment (or a close variant) conducted under different circumstances (e.g., with older students, in different settings, and so forth). Of course, these are not the only factors that operate during stage 1 of Levin and O'Donnell's model (1999), and they do not generally occur in a linear manner.

Contextual Factors

One factor that influenced the line of intervention research described here involved a long-standing educational and political concern that too many children in the United States do not learn to write well (National Commission on Writing, 2003; National Council of Educational Progress, 1975; Riley, 1996). This problem is reflected in the last two writing evaluations conducted by the National Assessment of Educational Progress. In 1998, slightly more than 60% of fourth graders were classified as "basic" writers, demonstrating only partial mastery of the writing skills and knowledge needed at that grade level, whereas another 16% of students scored below this basic level (Greenwald, Persky, Campbell, & Mazzeo, 1998). Although some improvement occurred during the next 4 years, two thirds of fourth grade students were still classified as basic or below-basic writers in 2002 (Persky, Daane, & Jin, 2003). These findings show that writing progress in the early elementary grades is not what it should be for many children in America's schools.

Consequently, we decided to focus our attention on designing effective interventions for children in the primary grades (1–3) who were experiencing difficulty learning to write. We decided this was important for two reasons. One, providing effective instruction to these children right from the start should help to ameliorate their writing problems (Graham & Harris, 2002). Two, waiting until later grades to address literacy problems that originate in the primary grades has not been particularly successful (Slavin, Madden, & Karweit, 1989). We further decided to focus our research efforts on identifying instructional procedures that would be effective with diverse struggling writers in relatively poor urban settings. Although the writing scores of fourth grade students who typically attended such schools improved from 1998 to 2002 on the National Assessment of Educational Progress, the gap between Black and Hispanic students and white and Asian students remained substantial (Persky et al., 2003).

Our Previous Work on an Instructional Model for Teaching Writing Strategies

The instructional approach used to teach planning strategies in the four studies described in this chapter was based on our evolving work with children in fourth grade or above. This included students with learning disabilities (LDs) as well as other struggling writers. Harris and Graham's first strategy instruction study for children with LD in the upper-elementary grades was published in 1985. Arising from Harris's early research on cognitive-behavioral interventions for children (Harris, 1980, 1982) and Graham's early work on children's writing (1982), and their shared concern for children with LD who struggle with writing, we designed a strategy instructional model that was initially referred to as self-control strategy training. Over the past two decades, Graham, Harris, and their colleagues have further developed and evaluated this strategy instruction approach for developing writing and self-regulation strategies among students with significant writing problems, now referred to as Self-Regulated Strategy Development (SRSD).

In the area of writing, the major goals of SRSD are threefold (Harris, Schmidt, & Graham, 1998): (a) assist students in developing knowledge about writing and powerful skills and strategies involved in the writing process, including planning, writing, revising, and editing; (b) support students in the ongoing development of the abilities needed to monitor and manage their own writing; and (c) promote children's development of positive attitudes about writing and themselves as writers. Since 1985, more than 30 studies using the SRSD model of instruction have been reported in the area of writing, involving students from the upper elementary grades through high school (Graham & Harris, 2003; Wong, Harris, Graham, & Butler, 2003). Although most SRSD research has involved writing, reading, and math strategies, instruction has also been researched using SRSD, and one group of elementary through high school teachers has applied SRSD to homework completion and organization for classes and the school day (Bednarczyk, 1991; Case, Harris, & Graham, 1992; Harris et al., 1992; Johnson, Graham, & Harris, 1997; Mason, 2002).

SRSD research in writing has resulted in the development of composing strategies, typically with the assistance of teachers and their students, for a variety of genres; these include personal narratives, story writing, persuasive essays, report writing, expository essays, and state writing tests. SRSD has resulted in significant and meaningful improvements in children's development of planning and revising strategies, including brainstorming, self-monitoring, reading for information and semantic webbing, generating and organizing writing content, advanced planning and dictation, revising with peers, and revising for both substance and mechanics (Harris & Graham, 1996).

SRSD has resulted in improvements in four main aspects of students' performance: quality of writing, knowledge of writing, approach to writing, and self-efficacy (Graham et al., 1991; Harris & Graham, 1999). Across a variety of strategies and genres, the quality, length, and structure of students' compositions have improved. Depending on the strategy taught, improvements have been documented in planning, revising, content, and mechanics. These improvements have been consistently maintained for most students over time, with some students needing booster sessions for long-term maintenance, and students have shown generalization across settings, persons, and writing media. Improvements have been found with normally achieving students as well as students with LD, making this approach a good fit for inclusive classrooms (cf. Danoff et al., 1993; De La Paz, 1999; De La Paz, Owen, Harris, & Graham, 2000; MacArthur et al., 1996). In some studies, improvements for students with LD have resulted in performance similar to that of their normally achieving peers (Danoff et al., 1993; De La Paz, 1999; Sawyer, Graham, & Harris, 1992). Despite these impressive gains, we had not directed any of our efforts to examining the effectiveness of SRSD with children in the primary grades.

Theoretical Forces

It is important to note that the intervention research program we describe in this chapter was, and continues to be, guided by multiple theoretical perspectives, including theories of self-regulation (Bandura, 1986; Zimmerman & Riesemberg, 1997), early development of models of strategies instruction and self-controlled learning (Brown, Campione, & Day, 1981; Deshler & Schumaker, 1986; Meichenbaum, 1977), and models of writing and writing development (Hayes & Flower, 1986; Scardamalia & Bereiter, 1986). It has been further influenced by current thinking about the development of competence and expertise in a subject-matter domain (see Alexander, 1992, 1997; Pintrich & Schunk, 1996). These conceptualizations emphasize that learning is a complex process that depends, in large part, on changes that occur in the learner's strategic knowledge, domain-specific knowledge, and motivation (Alexander, Graham, & Harris, 1996). We reasoned that the effectiveness of an intervention for young struggling writers in poor urban settings would be maximized if the treatment was designed to address and enhance each of these variables.

For the SRSD intervention research described in this chapter, treatment focused on teaching students strategic processes for planning different types of compositions and the knowledge and self-regulatory processes needed to apply the planning strategies and better understand the writing tasks. The intervention also included procedures designed to foster aspects of motivation. The SRSD model provided an excellent instructional vehicle for our purposes for three reasons. One, it is compatible with current conceptualizations of competency development in subject-matter domains, as it includes instructional procedures for enhancing strategic behavior, writing knowledge, and motivation for writing (Graham, Harris, & Troia, 1998). Two, it is responsive to the characteristics of students who experience difficulty with learning, as it addresses the multiple cognitive, behavioral, and affective challenges often faced by these students (Harris & Graham, 1996). Three, SRSD has proven to be an effective approach for teaching writing strategies to slightly older, elementary-aged students (grades 4–6), including children with special needs and other struggling writers in urban schools (see Graham & Harris, 2003).

Observations and Preliminary Ideas: Why Was Planning the Focal Point of our Intervention?

Our decision to focus on strategies instruction in planning was based on our own observations and experiences as well as the research conducted by other scholars interested in writing development. In a number of studies involving struggling writers, we have observed these students write with little or no forethought, spending less than a minute of time thinking about their paper before they start to write it (e.g., Graham, 1990; MacArthur & Graham, 1987). Instead, they generate ideas on the fly, as they compose, quickly telling whatever comes to mind, and often ending their response abruptly.

Similar observations have been made by other researchers (McCutchen, 1988; Scardamalia & Bereiter, 1986; Thomas, Englert, & Gregg, 1987).

According to McCutchen (1988), this approach to composing is best described as writing from memory. Any information that is somewhat appropriate to the topic at hand is retrieved from memory and written down, with each new phrase or sentence stimulating the generation of the next idea. Little attention is directed at the constraints imposed by the topic or genre, the development of rhetorical goals, the organization of text, or the needs of the reader. The roles of planning and other self-regulatory processes are minimized, as this retrieve-and-write approach functions like an automated and encapsulated program, operating largely without metacognitive control.

In contrast, skilled writers spend a considerable amount of time planning what they will do and say (Graham & Harris, 2000). For instance, Kellogg (1987) reported that college students devoted about one fourth of their composing time to planning, whereas Gould (1980) found that business executives spend about two thirds of their writing time planning. Similarly, Hayes and Flower (1980) observed that, when adult writers were asked to "think aloud" while composing, almost 80% of their content statements focused on planning. Consequently, the approach to writing used by skilled writers is more deliberate, thoughtful, and reflective than the one used by struggling writers.

These differences between skilled and struggling writers led us and other researchers to examine if the writing performance of less skilled writers can be improved by teaching them strategies for how to plan their papers (e.g., De La Paz, 1998; De La Paz & Graham, 2002; Englert, Raphael, Anderson, Anthony, Stevens, & Fear, 1991; Graham & Harris, 1989a; Sawyer, Graham, & Harris, 1992; Wong, 1997). Typically, this has involved teaching struggling writers to use planning strategies that are similar (but less complex and more developmentally appropriate) to the ones used by more skilled writers. From fourth grade all the way through high school, instruction in planning strategies has proven to be profitable for these students, as it has resulted in large improvements in their writing across a number of different genres (see, for example, the meta-analysis conducted by Graham & Harris, 2003).

It was not clear, however, if strategy instruction in how to plan would have a beneficial effect on the writing performance of younger children who were experiencing difficulty learning to write. First, we were unable to locate any studies that specifically tested this proposition with primary-grade children. Second, McCutchen (1988) argued that one reason why many young struggling and novice writers use a retrieve-and-write approach is because the processes involved in transcribing ideas into written text (e.g., handwriting and spelling) are so demanding for these children that they minimize planning and other self-regulatory processes because they exert considerable demands as well. Thus, bootstrapping planning strategies into a system that may already be heavily taxed by other processing demands may not be successful.

Why then did we decide to examine the effectiveness of planning strategy instruction with young struggling writers? One reason is because there is a reasonable amount of anecdotal evidence that even primary-grade children can plan more when they learn to compose under favorable conditions, such as a classroom environment where self-regulatory processes such as planning are encouraged and supported (Cameron, Hunt, & Linton, 1996). A second reason is that planning has the potential to reduce some of the process demands involved in writing. A plan, especially a written plan developed in advance, provides an external memory, where a child can store ideas without the risk of losing them; this helps young writers overcome one of the difficulties associated with the processing demands of handwriting and spelling, as these children lose ideas and plans they are trying to hold in working memory because their transcription skills are so slow (Graham & Harris, 2000). Such a plan may further reduce the need to plan while writing, freeing resources to engage in other writing taxing processes, such as translating ideas into words and transcribing words into printed text (Kellogg, 1987, 1986).

Other Research/Pilot Work that Set the Stage for the Current Line of Inquiry

In evaluating the effectiveness of SRSD planning instruction with struggling writers in the primary grade, we drew upon the same types of planning strategies that proved to be successful with fourth through sixth grade students in our previous studies (Danoff, Harris, & Graham, 1993; Graham & Harris, 1989a, 1989b; Sexton, Harris, & Graham, 1998; Sawyer et al., 1992). This involved teaching students genre specific strategies for generating and organizing possible ideas in advance of writing, using the elements of the specific genre (e.g., story grammar elements) as a prompt to help focus students' attention as they carried out these processes. Existing strategies and instructional procedures were modified for younger students through consultation with primary-grade teachers and pilot work.

One of the genre-specific strategies was designed to help students generate possible ideas for a story. It involved answering a series of questions prior to writing; each question focused on a common story element (Stein & Glenn, 1979), such as "Who are the main characters?" and "What do they want to do?" The second genre-specific strategy that was taught provided a mechanism for generating possible ideas for a persuasive essay. It involved responding to a series of questions or prompts that focused on basic elements of persuasion (Scardamalia, Bereiter, & Goleman, 1982), such as "Tell what you believe!" and "Why do I believe this?" Students were taught how to use these genre-specific strategies as part of a more comprehensive strategy for planning and writing a paper. This comprehensive strategy reminded students to carry out three basic processes: pick a topic to write about, organize possible ideas into a writing plan (the appropriate genre-specific strategy was applied here), and use and upgrade this plan while writing. This basic approach to planning and writing is commonly used by skilled writers.

When students were taught to use one of the genre-specific strategies, they also learned about the importance of using words that make a paper more interesting, self-talk that facilitates performance, and the basic elements commonly included in that genre. This provided them with knowledge critical to using each genre-specific planning strategy, as students used these elements as a springboard for generating possible ideas for their papers. Students further learned about the purpose and characteristics of a well-constructed paper in each respective genre. This helped to ensure that they had a mental model of what constituted quality writing for each type of paper. Finally, students set goals to write complete papers (i.e., ones that included all of the basic elements), monitored and graphed their success in achieving this goal, compared their preinstructional performance with their performance during instruction, and credited their success to the use of the target strategies. Goal-setting and self-reflective practices, such as monitoring and evaluating performance, not only enhance motivation and effort, but also provide students with information about their capabilities (Schunk & Zimmerman, 1998).

Other Preliminary Ideas

Learning how to apply a strategy does not guarantee that students will use it when the opportunity arises or be able to adapt it to new, but appropriate, situations. As Salomon and Globerson (1987) noted, people often do not make good use of what they have mastered. This is especially true for children who have trouble with learning (Wong, 1994).

One reason why students may fail to use or transfer a learned strategy is that they do not recognize when to use it or how to adapt it to new situations. They may be reluctant to use a new strategy because it requires more effort or work than the procedures they routinely use. Students may also not realize that the strategy is worth applying or may underestimate its potency. Even students' efforts to use it in new situations may undermine strategy maintenance and transfer, as incorrect or ineffective application may mar perceptions of value, leading to a decline or even cessation in its use (Salomon & Globerson, 1987).

In designing the SRSD model, we assumed that maintenance and transfer would be problematic for many of the students we worked with (Harris & Graham, 1996). We tackled this problem head on by integrating a number of procedures into the model that were designed to promote these two aspects of learning. These included continuing instruction until students are able to use the strategy correctly and efficiently, helping them understand how the strategy works and provides an improvement over their current routine, asking them to monitor the impact of the strategy on their performance, working with them to identify when and where the strategy can be used as well as how to modify it for these situations, encouraging them to set goals to use the strategy, teaching them to use self-statements as a means to reinforce strategy use and cope with difficulties, and discussing with them how their application efforts fared.

Analysis of effect sizes for SRSD writing studies (Graham & Harris, 2003) suggests that our efforts to facilitate maintenance and generalization have been relatively successful. Effect sizes for SRSD-instructed students have ranged from moderate to large when children's performance has been tested over time, in new settings, or across genres. Nevertheless, some children continue to experience difficulty maintaining and transferring what they have learned (Graham et al., 1998), and we are constantly looking for new ways to enhance these abilities. As a result, we were interested in tweaking the SRSD model in order to make it even more robust. To do so, we drew on a concept that is quite common in clinical psychology (Brownell & Jeffrey, 1987; Jacobson, 1989); namely, peers helping each other to maintain and generalize the gains they have realized.

Thus, during the next stage of our investigations (i.e., stage 2: controlled laboratory experiments), we examined if SRSD effects would be augmented by adding an instructional component where peers worked together to support strategy use, maintenance, and generalization. More specifically, the peer-support component involved two students working together to promote strategy use. Periodically throughout instruction, the children and their teachers identified other places or instances where they could use all or part of the strategies they were learning and how they might need to modify a strategy or strategies for an identified situation. They were then encouraged to apply what they were learning to these situations, with the added provision that they remind and help each other as necessary. In subsequent SRSD instructional sessions, they were asked to identify when, where, and how they applied the strategies, indicating how the strategy helped them do better as well as detailing any problems they encountered. The children also identified any instance where they helped their partner.

Predictions

We expected that SRSD planning instruction would have a positive impact on the writing performance of young struggling writers. More specifically, we anticipated that students' compositions would become longer, more complete, and qualitatively better following instruction. This instruction was designed to help students sustain their thinking, generate ideas, include basic genre-specific elements, and write a complete and well-thought-out story or persuasive essay. Moreover, students received explicit, intensive, and scaffolded instruction designed to assist mastery of the strategies for carrying out these processes. As Brown and Campione (1990) indicated, students who experience learning difficulties often do not acquire cognitive strategies unless detailed and explicit instruction is provided.

We not only expected that SRSD-instructed children would write better stories and persuasive papers (the focus of the two genre-specific strategies students were taught), but that the length and quality of their papers in one or more uninstructed genres (i.e., personal narratives and/or informative writing) would improve as well. We also expected that students would incorporate additional story elements into their personal narratives following instruction, as these elements are relevant to narratives, and a small data base existed showing that the impact of SRSD can extend beyond a single instructed genre (Graham & Harris, 2003).

Although we did not test the impact of SRSD on students' knowledge and motivation in every study conducted in stages 2 and 3, we anticipated that this instruction would have a positive impact on both of these variables. It was expected that SRSD-instructed students would become more knowledgeable about how to plan a paper and better able to describe the elements of a good story and persuasive essay. These predictions were straightforward, as SRSD provided explicit instruction on these topics.

In terms of motivation, we expected that SRSD instruction would boost at least three aspects of motivation: self-efficacy, effort, and intrinsic motivation. These predictions were based on previous research, demonstrating that strategy instruction can enhance motivational attributes (Harris, Graham, & Freeman, 1988; Graham et al., in press; Pintrich & Schunk, 1996), as well as the deliberate inclusion of instructional components within the SRSD model designed to promote each of these attributes. For example, the model includes mechanisms for making children's writing gains evident, providing information that should influence their self-efficacy (Schunk & Zimmerman, 1998). Likewise, the model contains a number of practices to enhance intrinsic motivation, including treating students as active collaborators in the learning process; recognizing and rewarding effort; adjusting the pace of instruction to meet each student's needs; teaching students the tools they need to be successful; and emphasizing the evaluation of progress and mastery, not just outcomes (Wentzel & Wigfield, 1998).

Finally, we predicted that the addition of a peer-support component to SRSD instruction could lead to incremental gains in writing, knowledge, and motivation. The peer-support component included student discussion on when, where, and how to use the target strategies and opportunities to apply, monitor, discuss, and evaluate their use beyond the instructional setting. We anticipated that this would not only increase the likelihood that treatment effects would transfer to uninstructed genres, but that it would enhance writing performance for the instructed genres too, as students would have a more fully developed understanding of the intricacies involved in using the inculcated strategies. Likewise, children's knowledge of writing should show even greater shifts in the predicted directions, as they are asked to think about and discuss with their partner the application of substantive procedures involving planning as well as the application of story and persuasive writing knowledge to other literacy tasks. Further, the peer-support component provided students with additional opportunities to monitor and evaluate their successes and failures; such experiences yield information critical to shaping beliefs about competence and motivation (Schunk & Zimmerman, 1998).

STAGE 2: SCHOOL-BASED RESEARCHER DELIVERED EXPERIMENTS (EXPERIMENTS 1–3)

During stage 2, we conducted three experiments to test the effectiveness of the intervention with young struggling writers. However, in contrast to traditional laboratory experiments, which are often removed from the actual educational setting, instruction was delivered in each child's school. However, it was not delivered by the child's actual teacher. Rather, it was provided by graduate assistants majoring in education with prior teaching experience. In addition, the studies differed from design experiments in that they were true experiments involving careful controls for competing explanations. Thus, we have labeled these experiments "school-based researcher delivered experiments." These studies allowed us to rigorously test and fine-tune the intervention and assessments before conducting an even more stringent test, involving randomized field trials with teachers (stage 3).

As noted in the section of Preliminary Observations and Ideas, our prior work demonstrated that SRSD instruction in planning, using the two genre-specific strategies emphasized here, improved the writing of children in fourth through sixth grades (Danoff et al., 1993; Graham & Harris, 1989a, 1989b; Sexton et al., 1998; Sawyer et al., 1992). To assess the impact of such instruction (as well as the augmental effects of peer support) with younger students, we started with third grade children and then systematically moved instruction to second grade in two follow-up experiments. The first study conducted with second grade children used a single-subject design. This allowed us to first test the effectiveness of SRSD planning instruction with a small sample of second graders (N = 6), before conducting a larger study involving randomization. Rigorous single-subject design with proper controls in place can allow researchers to draw valid inferences, while at the same time carefully monitor each individual's response to an intervention (Kratochwill & Levin, 1992).

Before describing more fully the participants, treatment, and outcomes of these three studies, we specify ten of the more prominent tactics used across stages 2 and 3 to help ensure that valid inferences were drawn. One, in all but the single-subject design study (Saddler et al., in press), students were randomly assigned to all conditions. Two, previously validated measures for assessing writing, knowledge, and motivation were applied, and reliability of measures was established in each study. Three, evaluators who scored the dependent measures were unfamiliar with the design and purpose of the study and all test protocols were blinded. Four, writing prompts for each genre were field tested in advance to ensure that they were appropriate for young children. Assessments were counterbalanced within and across pretest, posttest, and maintenance. Five, a number of mechanisms were put into place to ensure that treatments were delivered as intended, including stringent training of instructors and teachers as well as repeated independent verification that treatment was delivered as planned. Six, instructors or teachers taught an equivalent number of groups from each condition (with the exception of the single-subject design study where participants served as their own controls). Seven, the SRSD-only and SRSD plus peer-support conditions were "yoked" so that each received an equivalent amount of instructional time. Eight, SRSD instruction was provided for a long enough time for treatment effects to manifest (if in fact they did exist). Nine, the normality of the data was examined and appropriate parametric and nonparametric analyses were used accordingly. Ten, the unit of analysis, in all but the single subject–design study, was the mean for each group taught by an instructor or teacher. Table 11.1 presents a list of the characteristics of the large-group studies we used in the line of research described in this chapter, highlighting differences between stage 2 and 3 studies.

With the exception of the single-subject design study, effect sizes were computed for all statistically significant findings. Effect sizes were calculated as the mean differences between treatments divided by the pooled standard deviations for the two treatments.

The criteria used to select study participants were the same across all stage 2 and 3 studies. We secured permission to conduct our studies in a large school district in the Washington, D.C. metropolitan area that served a high percentage of children from low-income families. Across these studies, 85% or more of the participants were Black or Hispanic and more than one half received free or reduced-fee lunch. Boys outnumbered girls by a three-to-two ratio.

Participants were selected using a three-step procedure. First, the writing of all students in the appropriate grade at each participating school was assessed with the Story Construction Subtest from the *Test of Written Language-3* (Hammill & Larsen, 1996), which measures a child's ability to write a complete and interesting story. If a child's score fell two thirds or more of a standard deviation below the mean for the test's normative sample, the child was identified as at risk in writing. Second, each child's

TABLE 11.1
Characteristics of experimental treatments SRSD studies in Stage 2 and 3

Participants

Struggling writers are identified by screening all students in the target grade in the participating schools.

Participants are described on multiple dimensions (including gender, race, SES, chronological age, disability status, writing achievement, and primary language).

Design

Students are randomly assigned to experimental and control conditions.

Measures and Assessment

The effects of treatment conditions on multiple aspects of performance are collected.

Previously validated measures are used to assess the effects of treatments.

Writing prompts are field tested in advance.

Reliability is established for each measure.

Maintenance and generalization are assessed.

Measures are counterbalanced within and across time of testing (i.e., pretest, posttest, and maintenance).

All identifying information is removed from test protocols before scoring.

Evaluators are unfamiliar with the design and purpose of the study.

Treatment

Treatments are field tested before the start of the study.

Treatments are provided for long enough time to allow possible treatment effects to occur.

Teachers or instructors teach an equivalent number of students in each condition.

Teachers or instructors receive intensive training in how to deliver each treatment.

Each treatment is scripted to help insure that it is delivered as intended.

Data is collected to assess if treatments were actually delivered as intended.

Time of instruction is held equivalent for each treatment condition.

Analysis

The unit of analysis appropriate to the design of the study is used in all statistical analyses.

Data are analyzed to determine if they are normally distributed.

Assumptions underlying each statistical procedure are tested.

Effect sizes are provided for all statistically significant findings.

Teachers are asked to provide feedback on the acceptability of treatments (Stage 3 only).

teacher confirmed or disconfirmed that the child was experiencing difficulty with writing. In more than 95% of the cases, teachers corroborated the test findings. Third, parents were asked to provide consent. Permission was granted 84% or more of the time across studies.

The general planning and writing strategy as well as the two genre-specific strategies students were taught are presented in Table 11.2. The more general strategy included three steps, represented by the mnemonic POW: Pick my ideas (i.e., decide what to write about), Organize my notes (i.e., organize possible writing ideas into a writing plan), and Write and say more (i.e., continue to modify and upgrade the plan while writing). Depending on which type of writing (story or persuasion) was being emphasized, students

TABLE 11.2
Planning Strategies

Planning and Writing a Story		
P	Pick my idea	
O	Organize my notes	
	W	Who are the main characters?
	W	When does the story take place?
	W	Where does the story take place?
	What = 2	What do the main characters want to do?
		What happens when the main characters try to do it?
	How = 2	How does the story end?
		How do the main characters feel?
W	Write and Say More	
Planning and Writing a Persuasive Essay		
P	Pick my idea	
O	Organize my notes	
	T	Topic Sentence (Tell what you believe)
	R	Reasons (Three or more)
		Why do you believe this?
		Will my readers believe this?
	E	Explain Reasons (Say more about each reason)
	E	Ending (Wrap it up right!)
W	Write and Say More	

were taught to use a genre-specific strategy to help them generate appropriate writing content for the second step of POW (Organize my notes). For story writing, this consisted of a series of planning questions about ideas for basic story parts, whereas for persuasive writing it involved both questions and prompts for generating relevant ideas. Students learned mnemonics to help them remember each step of the two genre-specific strategies (WWW, What = 2, How = 2 for story writing, and TREE for persuasive writing).

To illustrate how SRSD was used to teach students to use POW and the one of the genre-specific strategies conjointly, Table 11.3 provides a description of instruction when it focused on story writing. Instructional procedures were identical for persuasive writing except that TREE replaced the story-part strategy, students learned about the characteristics and parts of a persuasive essay instead of stories, students discussed why they should not use the story-part strategy to write essays, the graphic organizer and rocket sheet were changed so that they fit the TREE strategy, and students did not develop a new self-statement chart (instead they added additional self-statements to this chart).

Furthermore, when the SRSD condition included peer support, the following cycle was repeated once a week. First, students set a goal to use part or all of POW and/or the genre-specific strategies in another situation or class and to help each other. The students developed a list (with help from the instructor or teacher) of places and situations where they could apply

TABLE 11.3
Stages of Instruction for SRSD Planning Instruction for Story Writing

Develop Background Knowledge

Students were first taught the knowledge and skills needed to apply POW and the story parts strategy (i.e., the genre-specific strategy for story writing). The POW strategy was introduced, and teacher and students discussed what it stood for and why each step was important. Students worked together until they could explain what POW meant and its importance. Next, the characteristics of a good story were discussed, including that stories are fun to read and write, make sense, include several parts, and contain exciting, colorful, and descriptive words (referred to as million dollar words). The teacher then introduced the mnemonic—WWW, What = 2, How = 2—as a "trick" for remembering the seven basic parts of a story (these were the parts included in the story parts strategy). After the teacher provided examples of each part, students listened as a story was read; and as they identified a story part, the teacher wrote it in the appropriate place on a story part reminder chart. This continued with other stories until students were able to identify all of the parts accurately. Students also spent a few minutes during each succeeding lesson rehearsing POW and the story part mnemonic as well as what each meant (**Memorize It**). This continued throughout instruction until both were memorized.

Discuss It

Students reviewed what POW and the story parts strategy stood for and why they were important. They again practiced finding story parts, but this time they used a graphic organizer where they made notes for each part of the story. Next, self-monitoring and graphing were introduced. Students were asked to analyze their pretest story and determine how many basic story elements were in their paper. They graphed the number of elements included in the story by coloring the corresponding number of segments on the first rocket ship contained on a page with a series of rocket ships standing next to each other. Students then discussed which parts were and were not included. The teacher emphasized that even if a story part was included, it could be improved (e.g., fleshed out). Teacher and students also discussed how using POW and the story parts strategy could help them write better stories with all of the parts. Students were reminded that they could actually see how these strategies helped them by looking at their progress in coloring parts on the rocket ship graph. The teacher then introduced the concept of goal setting, indicating that their goal was to write a story that included all 7 parts, each part was well done, the story made sense, and it was fun to read. Finally, additional stories were read together; and students received more practice identifying story parts.

Model It

The teacher modeled, while "talking out loud," how to plan and write a story using POW and the story parts strategy. The teacher started by setting a goal to include all of the parts and emphasized the importance of using both of these strategies. Students helped the teacher write the story by generating ideas for the parts of the story. They recorded their notes for the story on a graphic organizer that included a prompt for each of the seven story parts. While applying the strategy, the teacher used a variety of self-statements to assist with problem definition (e.g., What do I have do here?), planning (e.g., What comes next?), self-evaluation (e.g., Does that make sense?), self-reinforcement (e.g., I really like that part!), and coping (e.g., I'm almost finished!). As the teacher wrote the story, students continued to help the teacher plan by suggesting new ideas as well as recommending modifications in the planning ideas initially recorded on the graphic organizer. Once the story was finished, the teacher and students discussed the importance of what we say to ourselves and the types of self-statements used by the teacher during modeling were identified. Students then identified a few personal self-statements that they would use while writing and recorded them on a small chart. The teacher and students then

TABLE 11.3
Continued

examined if the completed story had all 7 parts and graphed the results, reinforcing themselves verbally for a job well done.

Support It

This stage of instruction began with a collaborative writing experience. The teacher and students set a goal to include all 7 elements in their story and crafted a story together using POW, the story parts strategy, the graphic organizer, and their self-instructions chart. This time, however, students directed the process and the teacher only provided help when needed. From the plan they generated together, each student wrote his or her own story. Once they were finished, they read their papers to each other and graphed the parts, looking to see if they met their goal and how much improvement had occurred since pretest. They also discussed how the strategy helped them write better. After this collaborative experience, students then used POW, the story part reminder, and their self-statements to write additional stories (in response to pictures).The teacher provided students with as much assistance as needed to insure that they were successful in using the strategies. Scaffolding included teacher or peer support in using the strategies or accompanying materials (e.g., graphic organizer or self-statement chart). These supports were temporary, however, and were withdrawn as soon as possible. For each story, students set a goal to include all 7 parts, shared their completed story with a peer, graphed their performance, determined if they met their goal, and examined progress on the rocket ship graph.

Independent Performance

Students reached this stage when they could use POW and the story part strategy to write a story without using any props (e.g., chart with strategy steps, graphic organizer, or self-statement chart) or receiving any aid from the teacher or a peer. At this point, students wrote a story in response to a different stimulus (i.e., a sentence that briefly described a character). This insured that they could independently apply the strategies, knowledge, and skills they learned to a new situation. They did, however, continue to set a goal to include all 7 parts and graphed their performance.

Note: The Memorize It stage was integrated throughout instruction, starting with the first lesson.

these procedures. They further considered how the strategies might need to be modified for particular tasks (e.g., changing part of it). Second, during a subsequent lesson, students recorded how they used the strategies and helped their partner on an "I transferred my strategies/I helped my partner" chart. The instructor or teacher placed a star next to each instance and verbally reinforced students for meeting or exceeding the goals they had established in the previous lesson. They further considered how the strategies helped them and discussed difficulties they encountered. Students also identified other situations or classes where they could apply the strategies, again thinking about how to modify them as necessary.

For students randomly assigned to the control condition in studies conducted during stages 2 and 3, writing instruction followed the Writers' Workshop model (Calkins, 1986; Graves, 1983). This instruction was delivered by the classroom teacher. Writers' Workshop is the most popular approach to writing instruction in the primary grades (Pritchard, 1987), and teachers and principals at the participating schools were committed to this approach and were positive about its impact on students.

Interviews and observations conducted during the course of each study revealed that all of the teachers established a routine where students were expected to plan their composition, write a first draft, revise and edit this draft, and publish the completed paper. Teachers also held individual conferences with children about their current writing project, encouraged them to share completed or in progress work with their peers, and (at times) allowed children to work at their own pace and choose their own writing topics. There was variability among teachers, however, in how often personal pace, choice, conferencing, and sharing occurred. Some teachers, for example, held daily conferences and encouraged sharing each day, whereas others held conferences only once a week and limited sharing to a couple of times a month. All of the teachers taught basic writing skills, such as spelling and grammar, primarily relying on mini-lessons that were provided several times a week. There was little congruence across teachers in terms of what skills were taught when, as the content of mini-lessons was mainly based on teachers' judgments about student needs at that point in time.

Some of the mini-lessons did involve the teaching of planning strategies. This included brainstorming, outlining, webbing, sequence chains, generating a main idea, Venn diagrams, and F-TAP (a strategy for a statewide writing assessment test that asked students to identify the form of their writing, topic, audience, and purpose). Although teachers did not teach the same strategies, their approach to instruction was basically the same, and it differed greatly from SRSD. A strategy was typically taught in a single mini-lesson, with the teacher briefly describing it, showing students how to use it, and then asking them to apply it. Teachers were inconsistent in providing children with reminders to use these strategies at appropriate times. At no time did teachers provide instruction about POW, the story-part reminder, or TREE to control students (they agreed not to do so before the start of the study). During the course of each study, story and persuasive writing were emphasized in each teacher's classroom. Students also occasionally completed book reports, constructed poems, crafted personal narratives, kept a journal, and wrote descriptions.

Experiment 1

Our first study was designed to answer two questions (Graham et al., in press). One, is SRSD planning instruction effective with young struggling writers attending schools in a poor urban community when instruction is delivered by research assistants? Two, what is the incremental impact of adding peer support to SRSD? To answer these questions, 73 third grade children from four schools were randomly assigned to the following three conditions: SRSD planning instruction (referred to as SRSD only), SRSD planning instruction plus peer support (referred to as SRSD plus peer support), and control (Writers' Workshop). Over the course of this 5-month investigation, one student moved to another school, leaving us with 24 children in each condition. These students were taught by six instructors, all graduate students in the College of Education at the University of Maryland.

Before instruction began, students wrote papers for four different genres: story, persuasive, personal narrative, and informative writing. They also completed measures assessing their knowledge of writing and writing self-efficacy. Following these assessments, children in the two SRSD conditions learned how to plan and write a story, whereas students in the control condition received their regular writing program (i.e., Writers' Workshop). SRSD instruction in story writing took approximately 6 hours to complete (students worked in pairs with an instructor three times a week for 20 minutes a period in a quiet place in the school). Once instruction ended, students again wrote a story and personal narrative. This allowed us to examine if the two SRSD treatments had a positive and differential impact on children's story writing skills and determine if treatment effects transferred to a similar but different genre, personal narratives.

Next, students in the two SRSD conditions learned how to plan and write a persuasive essay (control students continued with Writers' Workshop). With this second genre, instruction was slightly more efficient, as students needed only about 5 hours of instructional time. After treatment, students wrote a story, persuasive essay, and informative paper. The story served as a maintenance measure, whereas the other two papers allowed us to examine once again the impact of the SRSD treatments on an instructed genre (persuasive writing) as well as transfer effects to an uninstructed one (writing to inform). At this point, knowledge of writing and self-efficacy were reassessed too.

As expected, SRSD instruction in how to plan and write stories and persuasive essays had a positive influence on students' writing, knowledge, and motivation. Following instruction, students in both SRSD conditions spent more time writing and produced stories and persuasive essays that were longer, more complete, and qualitatively better than those produced by their counterparts in the control condition (effect sizes were large, ranging from 1.46 to 3.23). The impact of SRSD instruction also appeared to be quite durable, at least for story writing, as these positive effects were maintained over a 10-week period of time for both treatment conditions (again effect sizes were large ranging from 0.81 to 1.60). The only exception involved story length, as the maintenance papers produced by SRSD plus peer-support students did not differ statistically from those written by controls.

Although SRSD-only instruction enhanced story writing, it did not have a correspondingly positive effect on the uninstructed, but closely related, genre of personal narratives. These students and controls produced narratives that were similar in length and quality, and their papers did not differ in terms of the inclusion of the story parts emphasized during SRSD instruction. One possible reason for the disappointing transfer effects to narrative writing for the SRSD-only students centered on our decision at the start of the study to remove two components from this condition. This included overt encouragement by the instructor for students to use the strategies outside the treatment setting as well as discussion about when, where, and how to use the learned strategies. This was done to eliminate overlap between the two SRSD conditions. Even though both components are typically included in SRSD studies, they were essential features of the peer-support procedures tested in this investigation. Their removal may have weakened the impact of the SRSD-only condition, especially in terms of transfer. This may also have restricted these students' opportunities to acquire new knowledge about writing through discussion. While SRSD-only students were able to identify more features of a good persuasive essay following instruction (effect size = 1.00), they were not more knowledgeable than controls about the parts of a good story or how to plan a paper.

Even with the removal of these two components, however, the SRSD-only condition was still powerful enough to facilitate transfer to informative writing once students had practiced applying the learned strategies and knowledge with a second genre (i.e., persuasive writing). The informative papers of SRSD-only students were longer and qualitatively better than those produced by their counterparts in the control condition (both effect sizes were large: 1.57 for words and 1.08 for quality). Not surprisingly, children in the SRSD plus peer-support condition evidenced these same advantages over controls. They were more knowledgeable than controls about the features of a good persuasive essay (effect size = 1.46) and their informative papers were longer and qualitatively better (both effect sizes were large: 1.58 for words and 1.15 for quality).

To return to our first question (Is SRSD effective?), the findings summarized so far show that this form of instruction provides a viable means for enhancing the performance of young struggling writers in poor urban schools. When delivered by graduate students, such instruction improved children's writing in two instructed genres, transferred to at least one uninstructed genre, increased knowledge about writing, and enhanced motivation in terms of time spent composing (it should be noted that SRSD instruction did not enhance students' self-efficacy for writing).

However, what about our second question, the incremental impact of adding peer support to SRSD? The addition of peer support was advantageous, but its effects were not as extensive as predicted. First, we expected that peer support would enhance transfer to narrative and informative writing. This happened to a limited degree for both genres. Students in the

SRSD plus peer-support condition included more story elements in their narratives (effect size = 1.28) and spent more time planning their informative papers (effect size = 1.20) than did controls. SRSD-only students did not outperform controls on either of these measures. Second, we anticipated that peer support would enhance students' knowledge about writing, as it provided children with additional opportunities to think about, discuss, and evaluate what they had learned. This did occur for planning, as students in the SRSD plus peer-support condition were able to better describe how to plan a paper than students in both the SRSD-only and control conditions (both effect sizes exceeded 1.78). SRSD-only students did not outperform controls on this measure.

Thus, this initial experiment provided a positive incentive for continuing our work in this area. Our next step was to perform a small-scale test of the effectiveness of SRSD planning instruction with even younger students—struggling writers in second grade. As in the third grade study, instruction was delivered by project staff, providing us with considerable control over the instructional environment during our stage 2 experiments.

Experiment 2

In contrast to the other stage 2 experiments, this investigation involved students in one urban school (Saddler et al., 2004). The six participating second grade children were from two classrooms, and they were divided into pairs for the purpose of instruction. Each pair of students was taught how to plan and write a story using SRSD plus peer support. Instruction was delivered by a doctoral student majoring in special education. He met with each pair of students three times a week for 20 minutes at a time (for a total of 4 to 5 hours of instruction, depending upon the pair).

The effects of the SRSD planning instruction in story writing were assessed through a multiple baseline–across-subjects design with multiple probes during baseline (Kratochwill & Levin, 1992). With this design, treatment was systematically and sequentially introduced to one pair of students at a time. Before the introduction of treatment, each student's story writing performance was measured over time to establish a baseline of typical performance. A functional relationship between the independent variable (SRSD plus peer support) and student's progress was established if the target behavior (story writing) improved only after treatment was concluded and if the noninstructed students stayed at or near preintervention levels across baseline at this point.

Maintenance data were obtained for two of the student pairs. The first pair of instructed students wrote two maintenance stories (at 3 and 6 weeks), whereas the second pair of instructed students wrote just one (at 3 weeks). The end of the school year prevented collection of a maintenance story from the third pair. To assess generalization to a related genre, students wrote personal narratives during baseline and after the administration of post-treatment story probes.

As expected, the SRSD treatment had a positive impact on students' story writing.

Following instruction, stories became more complete, longer, and qualitatively better. The only exceptions involved one child whose posttest stories became shorter, even though they were more complete and qualitatively better after instruction, and a second student (Lizbeth) whose stories became more complete, but evidenced a slight decline in quality and a 26% reduction in length. At maintenance, these two students continued to produce stories that contained most of the basic elements of a story, but the resulting papers were qualitatively better than those generated during baseline and posttreatment. Lizbeth's maintenance story was longer as well. For the other two students who wrote maintenance stories, similar effects were noted. Their maintenance stories were longer and qualitatively better than baseline and posttreatment papers.

In contrast to the experiment with third grade students, the effects of the SRSD treatment in story writing transferred to students' personal narrative writing. Following instruction, students' narratives were qualitatively better and contained more story elements than the papers they wrote during baseline. In addition, all but one of these students produced posttreatment narratives that were longer than their baseline papers. The only exception involved Lizbeth who evidenced no transfer effects to narrative writing.

This study provided confirmation, at least on a small scale, that SRSD planning instruction can enhance the writing performance of struggling writers in poor urban schools, even when these children are only in second grade. As a result, our final study during stage 2 was a larger-scale investigation, similar to experiment 1, where we again examined the effectiveness of SRSD and the incremental effects of peer support when instruction was delivered by research assistants, but this time with second grade struggling writers.

Experiment 3

In this study, 66 second grade students were randomly assigned to three conditions: SRSD only, SRSD plus peer support, and control (Harris et al., in press). Over the course of this 6-month investigation, three students moved: two children in the control condition and one student in the SRSD plus peer support. Instruction was delivered by six graduate students majoring in education, and students worked in pairs with an instructor three times a week for 20 minutes a period in a quiet place in the school.

As in experiment 1 (Graham et al., in press), students wrote papers in four different genres (story, persuasive, narrative, and informative writing) and answered questions designed to assess their knowledge of writing. Students in the two SRSD conditions were then taught how to plan and write a story (approximately 6.3 hours of instructional time), whereas students in the control condition received their regular writing program (Writers' Workshop). Following this instruction, students again wrote a story and personal narrative, allowing us to assess the impact of the treatments on the instructed genre and transfer to an uninstructed genre. Students in the two SRSD conditions next learned how to plan and write a persuasive essay (approximately 4 hours of instructional time), and Writers' Workshop continued for their counterparts in the control condition. After this treatment, students wrote a story (maintenance), informative (transfer), and persuasive paper. At this point, knowledge of writing was reassessed.

Based on experiments 1 and 2, we made several changes in the assessments and treatments. First, the third grade struggling writers in experiment 1 (Graham et al., in press) were generally positive about their writing capabilities. This mismatch between actual performance and perceived capabilities has been observed in older struggling writers as well (Graham & Harris, 1989a; Sawyer et al., 1992). As others have noted, primary-grade children may not be able to accurately assess their own capabilities (Gaskill & Murphy, in press), raising the issue of whether self-efficacy is a viable construct for such young children. Consequently, we did not administer a measure of self-efficacy in this study, but shifted our attention to estimates of student effort (MacIver, Stipek, & Daniels, 1991) and intrinsic motivation (Gottfried, 1990) completed by students' regular classroom teachers.

Second, we added two additional writing probes to the study that assessed generalization of instructional effects to a different setting. Students wrote a story and a persuasive essay in their regular classroom following SRSD planning instruction in story and persuasive writing, respectively. Unfortunately, some of the teachers provided children from their class with extra help when writing the story and we were unable to analyze the classroom data for story writing (this was not the case for persuasive writing, however).

Third, many of the instructors had told us that children in experiments 1 and 2 (Graham et al., in press; Saddler et al., 2004) experienced considerable difficulty explaining and saying more about their reasons when writing a persuasive paper (The first E in the TREE strategy; see Table 11.2). This led us to change TREE so that the first E stood for Ending (Wrap it up right!), and the second E reminded children to Examine if they included all of the parts in both their notes and the subsequent paper and to determine if their reasons were powerful. Instructors had further noted that students' compositions often lacked needed transition words. Thus, children in the two SRSD conditions were taught how to use appropriate transition words when writing their stories and persuasive essays.

Fourth, in an effort to strengthen the peer-support component, we inserted a functional mediator (see Stokes & Osnes, 1989), the instructor, into one of the possible generalization settings (i.e., the child's classroom). This occurred twice: at the end of story instruction and again at the end of persuasive writing instruction. During these planned events, the instructor came into the regular classroom and met just with the pair of students in the SRSD plus peer-support condition. She asked these students to write either a story or persuasive essay (depending on where students were at in the instructional sequence). This provided an additional stimulus for using the learned strategies in a different setting, but even more important, it provided a more controlled generalization situation, where students were able to identify, discuss, and evaluate strategy use with the instructor during the peer-support component.

As with the previous two experiments (Graham et al., in press; Saddler et al., 2004), SRSD instruction had a positive impact on students' writing and knowledge of writing. Following instruction in story writing and then persuasive writing, SRSD-only students wrote more complete stories (effect sizes were large, exceeding 1.51) as well as longer, more complete, and qualitatively better essays (all effect sizes were large, exceeding 1.30) than did their peers in the control condition. Furthermore, they were more knowledgeable than controls about how to plan a paper as well as the features of a good essay and persuasive paper (all effect sizes were large, exceeding 0.96).

In contrast to the third grade students in Graham et al. (2003), SRSD-only second graders in experiment 3 did not write posttest stories that were longer and qualitatively better than those produced by controls. By the time the story maintenance measure was administered, however, SRSD-only students' stories were not only more complete than control students' compositions, but they were longer and qualitatively better as well (effect sizes were moderate to large, ranging in size from 0.47 to 1.46). Possibly, younger students in this study did not do as well on the posttest story as the third grade children in experiment 1 (Graham et al., in press) because they were not ready academically or cognitively to take full advantage of the relatively sophisticated set of processes for planning and writing a composition that they were taught. This argument is weakened, however, by the findings that the second grade SRSD-only students in this study made as strong and impressive improvements as their third grade counterparts in the previous study when they learned to apply these procedures to persuasive writing. Perhaps a better explanation for this anomaly is that the younger students in this study needed more practice in applying the basic strategic actions (i.e., selecting topics, generating and organizing notes, and writing and saying more) and self-regulatory procedures (e.g., self-instruction, goal setting, and self-monitoring) they were learning before they could take full advantage of these processes. If this argument is valid, this should be reflected in their writing performance on the maintenance story probe, as SRSD-instructed students received additional practice in applying these processes to a second genre (i.e., persuasive writing) during the posttest/maintenance story interval. The maintenance data were consistent with this explanation.

SRSD-only students did generalize what they were learning to their regular classroom, as the persuasive essay they wrote in this setting was qualitatively better than the one produced by children in the control condition (effect size = 1.16). Even more impressively, transfer to narrative writing occurred, as they included more story parts than did controls when writing personal narratives (effect size = 1.15). This did not occur for the older third grade children in experiment 1 (Graham et al., in press). Unfortunately, there were no statistically significant differences between SRSD-only and control students in the length or quality of their informative papers (such effects were found in experiment 1). It is possible that broader transfer effects were not obtained for SRSD-only students in experiment 3 because of our decision to remove two typical SRSD components (encouragement to generalize and discussion about when, where, and how to do this) from this condition, so that we could more cleanly test the incremental effects of adding the peer-support procedures.

As in experiment 1 (Graham et al., in press), adding peer support to the SRSD condition was advantageous for the students in this study. Not only did SRSD plus peer-support students evidence all of the advantages over controls that SRSD-only students did (all effect sizes on these variables were large and exceeded 0.87), but these students' posttest stories were longer and qualitatively better, their classroom generalization persuasive papers were more complete, and their informative stories were qualitatively better (all effect sizes were large, exceeding 0.86). In addition, SRSD plus peer-support students wrote more complete persuasive essays following instruction than did SRSD-only students (effect size = 0.83) and their narrative papers contained more story elements (effect size = 0.85).

Experiment 3 confirmed again that SRSD planning instruction was an effective method for enhancing the writing performance of young struggling writers in urban schools. This study also provided additional support for including the peer component as part of SRSD regime. It was now time for us to move to stage 3 and test the effectiveness of SRSD plus peer support in a randomized field trial with the students' teachers providing instruction (i.e., experiment 4). There was no reason to test the SRSD-only condition, as it was less successful than SRSD plus peer support in experiments 1 and 3.

Before moving to the next section, we would like to point out that the two SRSD treatments did not influence teachers' judgments of students' effort or intrinsic motivation in experiment 3. Because these teachers did not deliver either of the experimental treatments, their opportunities for observing possible motivational changes were limited. Therefore, these measures were again administered in the study conducted during stage 3.

We also preserved the change in the TREE strategy and the addition of instruction on using transition words implemented in experiment 3. We did not need either the classroom generalization probe, as all writing probes were now administered by the students' teachers, or a functional mediator, as instruction occurred in the setting where students were expected to use what they were learning. We did not include the measures assessing students' knowledge of writing. In addition, the randomized field trial with teachers focused on SRSD plus peer support with story writing, examining the generalizability of such instruction to personal narratives.

STAGE 3: RANDOMIZED CLASSROOM TRIALS WITH TEACHERS (EXPERIMENT 4)

Eleven teachers delivered SRSD plus peer support as well as the control condition to struggling writers in their inclusive classrooms (Harris, Graham, & Adkins, 2004). Nine of the teachers were general educators; the other two were special education teachers. As in the previous studies, SRSD plus peer support was delivered to small groups of students (ranging in size from two to four students), 3 days a week for 20 minutes a period. Students in the control condition participated in Writers' Workshop. Thus, all teachers delivered both treatments, controlling for possible differences due to teacher effects. Each of the teachers had used the Writers' Workshop approach for several years and, in interviews with project staff, indicated their commitment to this approach and their belief that it was an effective method for teaching writing.

In this study, 53 children were randomly assigned by teachers to the two treatment conditions. Over the course of this 5-month investigation, two students in the control condition moved, leaving us with 27 SRSD plus peer-support students and 24 controls. Before the start of the study, teachers received thorough training in how to implement the SRSD treatment and assessment measures. Moreover, graduate students observed teachers' administration of both treatments throughout the course of the study. These observations confirmed that instruction was delivered as intended and that the experimental treatment procedures did not "bleed" into Writers' Workshop.

Prior to the start of instruction, students wrote a story and personal narrative (pretests), and teachers made judgments about each child's effort and intrinsic motivation for writing. Immediately after instruction, teachers completed the motivational measures again, and students wrote another story and personal narrative (posttests). A third story was written 1 month later (maintenance).

Consistent with the previous experiments, students in the SRSD plus peer-support condition wrote more complete and qualitatively better stories at posttest than did their peers in the control condition, and these gains were maintained 1 month later (all effects sizes were large, exceeding 0.88). Equally important, the effects of instruction transferred to an uninstructed genre, as SRSD plus peer-support students' personal narratives were qualitatively better and contained more story elements than those written by controls (both effect sizes were large, exceeding 0.87). Finally, the SRSD condition had a positive impact on teachers' judgments about students' motivation. They believed that SRSD-instructed students evidenced more effort and intrinsic motivation for writing than did controls (both effect sizes were large, exceeding 1.06).

The three experiments conducted during stage 2 demonstrated that SRSD plus peer-support planning instruction enhanced the performance of young struggling writers in poor urban schools when these procedures were administered under carefully controlled conditions. These studies, however, were not conducted under realistic conditions, as research assistants, not teachers, delivered this treatment. Experiment 4 addressed this situation and showed that this approach is effective with the target population under both realistic and carefully controlled conditions. When considered together, these studies also meet the "CAREful" intervention criteria established by Derry et al. (1998). SRSD plus peer-support planning instruction was Compared with an appropriate alternative (Writers' Workshop), and the findings from multiple studies demonstrated Again and again a Direct relationship between the treatment and improvements in students' performance when other competing explanations were Eliminated through careful controls for threats to internal validity, including random assignment to conditions.

STAGE 4: INFORMED CLASSROOM PRACTICE

The final stage of Levin and O'Donnell's (1999) stage model of educational research is the application of research-validated practices by classroom teachers. This involves at least three steps. First, teachers must become knowledgeable of these practices. Second, they must decide if their classroom and students are an appropriate match to the treatment and validating data. Third, they must implement and evaluate the effects of the treatment with their own students. In this final section of this chapter, we briefly consider all three of these.

Because many teachers do not read research articles or books like this one, other venues are needed to make evidenced-based practices like SRSD available to practitioners. We have used four different strategies to accomplish this goal. This includes writing articles and books (see for example Harris & Graham, 1996; Harris, Graham, & Mason, 2002, in press, 2004) specifically for teachers, providing a detailed account of the intervention, how to implement it (and modify it), who benefits from its application, and the types of gains obtained during testing (in teacher-friendly terms). We also developed a videotape in conjunction with the Association for Supervision and Curriculum Development (2002), providing a visible model of what the intervention looks like in a real classroom setting. We also placed lesson plans for the intervention on the Web and mailed hard copies of them upon request. Furthermore, our colleagues, our students, and we have conducted numerous workshops and in-services on how to apply SRSD, including working with a consortium of teachers to implement this model in their classes.

Before implementing a particular research-based practice, we encourage teachers to carefully consider how likely the treatment is to have the same impact on their students as it did in the studies where it was validated. In our view, a research-based treatment is more likely to be successful if the correspondence among student, teacher, and contextual variables in the teacher's classroom and the intervention test sites is high. A low correspondence does not necessarily mean that the intervention will be ineffective if implemented in the new setting, but it does increase the need for teachers to evaluate its impact with her or his students. Even when the match is high, such assessment is needed, as there is no guarantee that the treatment will yield the same results in all similar situations.

Finally, when assessing the impact of a research-validated practice in their classroom, it is not only important to evaluate changes in students' progress following instruction, but also to assess instruction while it is ongoing (Harris et al., 2003b). In addition to tracking changes in students' performance during instruction, we encourage teachers to monitor if they are implementing the treatment appropriately. This includes evaluating how well and how correctly they executed each aspect of the treatment. The potential impact of a validated procedure is likely to be weakened if it is not delivered as intended.

References

Alexander, P. (1992). Domain knowledge: evolving issues and emerging concerns. *Educational Psychologist*, 27, 33–51.

Alexander, P. (1997). Mapping the multidimensional nature of domain learning: the interplay of cognitive, motivational, and strategic forces. In M. Maehr & P. Pintrich (Eds.), *Advances in motivation and achievement*, Vol. 10 (pp. 213–250). Greenwich, CT: JAI Press.

Alexander, P., Graham, S., & Harris, K. R. (1996). A perspective on strategy research: progress and prospects. *Educational Psychology Review*, 10, 129–154.

Association of Curriculum Development. (2002). *Teaching students with learning disabilities in the regular classroom: using learning strategies*. Alexandria, VA: ASCD.

Bandura, A. (1986). *Social foundations of thought and action: a social cognitive theory*. Englewood Cliffs, NJ: Prentice Hall.

Brown, A., & Campione, J. (1990). Interactive learning environments and the teaching of science and mathematics. In M. Garner, J. Green, F. Reif, A. Schoenfield, A. diSessa, & E. Stage (Eds.), *Towards a scientific practice of science education* (pp. 112–139). Hillsdale, NJ: Erlbaum.

Brown, A., Campione, J., & Day, J. (1981). Learning to learn: on training students to learn from tests. *Educational Researcher*, 10, 14–21.

Brownell, K., & Jeffery, R. (1987). Improving long-term weight loss: pushing the limits of treatment. *Behavior Therapy*, 18, 353–374.

Calkins, L. (1986). *The art of teaching writing*. Portsmouth, NH: Heinemann.

Cameron, C., Hunt, A., & Linton, M. (1996). Written expression as reconceptualization: children write in social time. *Educational Psychology Review*, 8, 125–150.

Danoff, B., Harris, K. R., & Graham, S. (1993). Incorporating strategy instruction within the writing process in the regular classroom: effects on the writing of students with and without learning disabilities. *Journal of Reading Behavior*, 25, 295–322.

De La Paz, S. (1999). Self-regulated strategy instruction in regular education settings: improving outcomes for students with and without learning disabilities. *Learning Disabilities Research and Practice*, 14, 92–106.

De La Paz, S., & Graham, S. (2002). Explicitly teaching strategies, skills, and knowledge: writing instruction in middle school classrooms. *Journal of Educational Psychology*, 94, 687–698.

Derry, S., Levin, J. R., Jones, M. S., Osana, H. P., & Peterson, M. (1998). *Fostering students' statistical and scientific thinking: lessons learned from an innovative college course*, unpublished manuscript. University of Wisconsin: Madison.

Deshler, D., & Schumaker, J. (1986). Learning strategies: an instructional alternative for low-achieving students. *Exceptional Children*, 52, 583–590.

Englert, C., Raphael, T., Anderson, L., Anthony, H., & Stevens, D. (1991). Making strategies and self-talk visible: writing instruction in regular and special education classrooms. *American Educational Research Journal*, 28, 337–372.

Gaskill, P., & Murphy, K. (in press). Effects of a memory strategy on second-graders' performance and self-efficacy. *Contemporary Educational Psychology*.

Gottfried, A. (1990). Academic intrinsic motivation in young elementary school children. *Journal of Educational Psychology*, 82, 525–538.

Gould, J. (1980). Experiments on composing letters: some facts, some myths, and some observations. In L. Gregg & E. Steinberg (Eds.), *Cognitive processes in writing* (pp. 97–127). Hillsdale, NJ: Erlbaum.

Graham, S. (1990). The role of text production factors in learning disabled students' compositions. *Journal of Educational Psychology*, 82, 781–791.

Graham, S., & Harris, K. R. (1989a). A component analysis of cognitive strategy instruction: effects on learning disabled students' compositions and self-efficacy. *Journal of Educational Psychology*, 81, 353–361.

Graham, S., & Harris, K. R. (1989b). Improving learning disabled students' skills at composing essays: self-instructional strategy training. *Exceptional Children*, 56, 201–214.

Graham, S., & Harris, K. R. (2000). The role of self-regulation and transcription skills in writing and writing development. *Educational Psychologist*, 35, 3–12.

Graham, S., Harris, K. R., & Fink, B. (2000). Is handwriting causally related to learning to write? Treatment of handwriting problems in beginning writers. *Journal of Educational Psychology*, 92, 620–633.

Graham, S., & Harris, K. R. (2002). Prevention and intervention for struggling writers. In M. Shinn, H. Walker, & G. Stone (Eds.), *Interventions for academic and behavior problems, II: preventive and remedial approaches*. Bethesda, MD: NASP.

Graham, S., & Harris, K. R. (2003). Students with learning disabilities and the process of writing: a meta-analysis of SRSD studies. In L. Swanson, K. Harris, & S. Graham (Eds.), *Handbook of learning disabilities* (pp. 323–344). New York: Guilford.

Graham, S., Harris, K. R., & Fink-Chorzempa, B. (2002). Contributions of spelling instruction to the spelling, writing, and reading of poor spellers. *Journal of Educational Psychology*, 94, 669–686.

Graham, S., Harris, K. R., Fink, B., & MacArthur, C. (2001). Teacher efficacy in writing: A construct validation with primary grade teachers. *Scientific Study of Reading*, 5, 177–202.

Graham, S., Harris, K. R., Fink, B., & MacArthur, C. (2002). Primary grade teachers' theoretical orientations concerning writing instruction: construct validation and a nationwide survey. *Contemporary Educational Psychology*, 27, 147–166.

Graham, S., Harris, K. R., MacArthur, C., & Fink-Chorzempa, B. (2003). Primary grade teachers' instructional adaptations for weaker writers: a national survey. *Journal of Educational Psychology*, 95, 279–293.

Graham, S., Harris, K. R., & Mason, L. (in press). Improving the writing performance, knowledge, and self-efficacy of struggling young writers: the effects of self-regulated strategy development. *Contemporary Educational Psychology*.

Graham, S., Harris, K. R., & Mason, L. (2004). *Powerful strategies for teaching writing in the classroom*, in preparation. Baltimore, MD: Brookes.

Graham, S., Harris, K. R., & Troia, G. (1998). Writing and self-regulation: cases from the Self-Regulated Strategy Development model. In D. Schunk & B. Zimmerman (Eds.), *Self-regulated learning: from teaching to self-reflective practice* (pp. 20–42). New York: Guilford.

Graves, D. (1983). *Writing: teachers and children at work*. Exeter, NH: Heinemann.

Hammill, D., & Larsen, S. (1996). *Test of written language*, 3. Austin, TX: Pro-Ed.

Harris, K. R., & Graham, S. (1996). *Making the writing process work: strategies for composition and self-regulation*. Cambridge, MA: Brookline Books.

Harris, K. R., Graham, S., & Adkins, M. (2004). *The effects of teacher-led* SRSD *instruction on the writing and motivation of young struggling writers*. Manuscript in preparation.

Harris, K. R., Graham, S., & Freeman, S. (1988). The effects of strategy training and study conditions on metamemory among LD students. *Exceptional Children*, 54, 332–338.

Harris, K. R., Graham, S., & Mason, L. (in press). Improving the writing performance, knowledge, and motivation of struggling young writers in second grade: the effects of self-regulated strategy development. *American Educational Research Journal*.

Harris, K. R., Graham. S., & Mason, L. (2003b). Self-regulated strategy development in the classroom: part of a balanced approach to writing instruction for students with disabilities. *Focus on Exceptional Children*, 35, 1–16.

Harris, K. R., Graham, S., & Mason, L. (2002). POW plus TREE equals powerful opinion essays. *Teaching Exceptional Children*, 34, 74–77.

Hayes, J., & Flower, L. (1980). Identifying the organization of writing processes. In L. Gregg & E. Steinberg (Eds.), *Cognitive processes in writing* (pp. 3–30). Hillsdale, NJ: Erlbaum.

Hayes, J., & Flower, L. (1986). Writing research and the writer. *American Psychologist*, 41, 1106–1113.

Jacobson, N. (1989). The maintenance of treatment gains following social learning-based marital therapy. *Behavior Therapy*, 20, 325–336.

Kellogg, R. (1986). Designing idea processors for document composition. *Behavior Research Methods, Instruments, and Computers*, 18, 118–128.

Kellogg, R. (1987). Effects of topic knowledge on the allocation of processing time and cognitive effort to writing processes. *Memory and Cognition*, 15, 256–266.

Kratochwill, T., & Levin, J. (1992). *Single-case research design and analysis: new directions for psychology and education*. Hillsdale, NJ: Erlbaum.

Levin, J., & O'Donnell, A. (1999). What to do about educational research's credibility gaps? *Issues in Education: Contributions from Educational Psychology*, 5, 177–229.

MacArthur, C., & Graham, S. (1987). Learning disabled students' composing with three methods: handwriting, dictation, and word processing. *Journal of Special Education*, 21, 22–42.

MacIver, D., Stipek, D., & Daniels, D. (1991). Explaining within-semester changes in student effort in junior high school and senior high school courses. *Journal of Educational Psychology*, 83, 201–211.

McCutchen, D. (1988). "Functional automaticity" in children's writing: a problem of metacognitive control. *Written Communication*, 5, 306–324.

Meichenbaum, D. (1977). *Cognitive behavior modification: an integrative approach*. NY: Plenum Press.

National Commission on Writing (2003). *The neglected "R:" The need for a writing revolution*. New York: College Entrance Examination Board.

National Council of Teachers of English (1975). Composition: a position statement. *Elementary English*, 52, 194–196.

Persky, H., Daane, M., & Jin, Y. (2003). *The nation's report card: writing*. Washington, DC: US Department of Education.

Pintrich, P., & Schunk, D. (1996). *Motivation in education*. Englewood Cliffs, NJ: Prentice Hall.

Pritchard, R. (1987). Effects on student writing of teacher training in the National Writing Project Model. *Written Communication*, 4, 51–67.

Riley, R. (1996). Improving the reading and writing skills of America's students. *Learning Disability Quarterly*, 19, 67–69.

Saddler, B., Moran, S., Graham, S., & Harris, K. R. (2004). Preventing writing difficulties: the effects of planning strategy instruction on the writing performance of struggling writers. *Exceptionality*, 12, 3–18.

Salomon, G., & Globerson, T. (1987). Skill may not be enough: the role of mindfulness in learning and transfer. *International Journal of Educational Research*, 11, 623–637.

Sawyer, R., Graham, S., & Harris, K. R. (1992). Direct teaching, strategy instruction, and strategy instruction with explicit self-regulation: effects on learning disabled students' compositions and self-efficacy. *Journal of Educational Psychology*, 84, 340–352.

Scardamalia, M., & Bereiter, C. (1986). Written composition. In M. Wittrock (Ed.), *Handbook of research on teaching* (3rd ed., pp. 778–803). New York: MacMillan.

Scardamalia, M., Bereiter, C., & Goleman, H. (1982). The role of production factors in writing ability. In M. Nystrand (Ed.), *What writers know: the language, process, and structure of written discourse* (pp. 175–210). San Diego, CA: Academic Press.

Schunk, D., & Zimmerman, B. (1998). *Self-regulated learning: from teaching to self-reflective practices*. New York: Guilford.

Sexton, M., Harris, K. R., & Graham, S. (1998). Self-regulated strategy development and the writing process: effects on essay writing and attributions. *Exceptional Children*, 65, 235–252.

Slavin, R., Madden, N., & Karweit, N. (1989). Effective programs for students at risk: conclusions for practice and policy. In R. Slavin, N. Karweit, & N. Madden (Eds.), *Effective programs for students at risk*. Boston: Allyn and Bacon.

Stein, N., & Glenn, C. (1979). An analysis of story comprehension in elementary school children. In R. Freedle (Ed.), *Advances in discourse processes, 2: new directions in discourse processing*. Norwood, NJ: Ablex.

Stokes, T., & Osnes, P. (1989). An operant pursuit of generalization. *Behavior Therapy*, 20, 337–355.

Thomas, C., Englert, C., & Gregg, S. (1987). An analysis of errors and strategies in the expository writing of learning disabled students. *Remedial and Special Education*, 8, 21–30.

Wentzel, K., & Wigfield, A. (1998). Academic and social motivational influences on students' academic performance. *Educational Psychology Review*, 10, 155–176.

Wong, B. (1994). Instructional parameters promoting transfer of learned strategies in students with learning disabilities. *Learning Disability Quarterly*, 17, 100–119.

Wong, B. (1997). Research on genre-specific strategies for enhancing writing in adolescents with learning disabilities. *Learning Disability Quarterly*, 20, 140–159.

Zimmerman, B., & Riesemberg, R. (1997). Becoming a self-regulated writer: a social cognitive perspective. *Contemporary Educational Psychology*, 22, 73–101.

Index